Stolen 1

Also by Decima Wraxall
Black Stockings, White Veil
Letters From a Digger
Going Home
Bloom

Decima Wraxall

Stolen Fruit

Stolen Fruit
ISBN 978 1 76041 954 7
Copyright © text Decima Wraxall 2020
Cover photo: Melissa Wraxall

First published 2020 by
GINNINDERRA PRESS
PO Box 3461 Port Adelaide 5015
www.ginninderrapress.com.au

I dedicate this book to Aunt Aileen, Uncle Bill and Cousin Polly.
I'll be forever grateful for their support and encouragement
in my teenage years.

Let no one say the past is dead. The past is all around us and within.
— Oodgeroo Noonuccal

Prologue

In the 1930s, Hitler and his bully boys began the Nazi rampage in Europe. By 1940, Australia had joined the horrors of World War II. By late June, Britain was flying for survival in summer skies. My mother, heavily pregnant, awaited my birth at Newcastle, her second child. Far from the humble bark hut which she called home, in the Mount Royal Ranges of northern New South Wales, she felt lonely and disorientated.

This fictionalised saga portrays life of the pioneer generation who survived the Great Depression in Australia. My grandparents, father and mother, siblings, myself, uncles, aunts, friends and lovers, are shown in all their majesty and weakness.

Facts merge with fiction for literary reasons, becoming one with myths and legends. Some characters have been invented and certain time frames adapted to help capture the flavour of this vanished era.

Childhood flames before me. Magic dances with misunderstandings, joy abuts against frustration, all-powerful adults in control. Light and shadow combine, making me the woman I am today.

And now, let's enter the theatre of life. In the hush and expectation after the curtain rises, settle down and watch as friends and family assume their roles.

Part One

1

The mailbag ticked like a time bomb. Joly turned a key. The padlock clicked. Letters spilled over the solid timber table. He pushed them aside.

Neville Chamberlain had met with the German chancellor, Adolf Hitler on 30 September 1938.

Joly seized the paper. A headline leapt at them: 'Peace For Our Time'.

British Prime Minister, Neville Chamberlain, has just returned from Munich, waving an Anglo-German agreement. In a speech he made at Heston Aerodrome, Mr Chamberlain said, I believe it is peace for our time. We thank you from the bottom of our hearts.'

Joly raised his eyebrows. 'Peace? Pieces, more likely.'

Genn frowned. 'Don't be so darn negative. It's an agreement.'

'Hitler won't let a piece of paper block his ambitions. How long before Nazi thugs murder men, women and children?'

Sunlight danced on bark hut walls. It mottled her toddler's face.

She gathered Victor into her arms. 'Surely, troubles on the other side of the globe won't...'

'...affect us?' Joly weighed his stained felt hat. Flames leapt and consumed. 'Our blokes will be in the thick of it.'

She swallowed. 'World War I was meant...'

'...to end all wars? I never believed that.'

'Still, we can hope.' Genn gulped. 'Would my little man like a walk?'

Victor wriggled. She helped him on with his boots.

Joly drained sweet, black tea. Put down his enamel mug. Hugged them with work-roughened hands. 'Bye, you two. No rest for the wicked.'

In the Mount Royal Ranges of northern NSW, Genn breathed the aroma of mint and thyme. The creek sang on stones. Their cow lowed of white, creamy milk. Joly swung into the saddle of his big bay mare. Victor waved a chubby hand.

Joly cantered away.

The boy gurgled over a brilliantly coloured beetle. Giggled at a dart of lizards. Kookaburras chortled in a tall eucalypt.

'Boy tired, Mummy. Carry me.'

Back at the cabin, she settled Victor into bed. 'Time for a nap, little one.'

One month dragged into another. Drought and heat creased farmers' brows. They bought hay for winter. Distant troubles melted away.

She fed Victor cereal, spoonful by spoonful. Wiped his face with a bib. Sang him nursery rhymes. Sometimes she forgot that nasty little man with a silly moustache.

Joly returned from a visit to his sister, Aileen, at Newcastle. His grim face told her the worst. 'The SS are forcing Polish people from their homes, luv. Beating up young and old. Breaking shop windows. Painting anti-Jewish slogans.'

She gulped. 'How can you know that?'

'Met this refugee. Young bloke – Nazis took his father at gunpoint. He hasn't been seen since. The lad fled. And he reckons there are hundreds if not thousands of similar tales.'

Genn clutched Victor. She'd do anything to keep him safe.

At work, Joly shared worries with Genn's cousin, his mate, Walt Stephens. 'We've seen far from the worst of it.'

'I fear you're right. So much for the peace agreement.'

They built fences, bashed suckers from trees. Crutched sheep.

1939 dragged on. In Europe, war shone its jackboots.

Fossicking in Tomalla creek. Thoughts of conflict rippled from their minds. Prospecting dishes swirled. Joly's big hand scooped away sand.

Glittering specks of gold. He scraped larger ones into a small bottle of water. Screwed on the cap.

A small man with a crooked smile, Walt said, 'Can't wait to find that mother lode.'

Joly grinned. 'My hopes rest on a property at Kangaroo Tops. If it can be had at the right price.'

Walt frowned. 'Cleared?'

'No, it's scrubby and a bit away from the main road. No house – I hope to God that puts other buyers off.'

Joly's buggy jolted along the dirt road to Hunters Springs. The date was 3 September 1939. They expected an important announcement by Prime Minister Menzies.

Genn hugged her parents, Hilda and Rick and her brother, Geoff. 'Hello, everyone.'

Sombre faces. Adults gathered around the dining table, Victor on Genn's knee.

The His Master's Voice wireless crackled into life. A solemn voice, 'Fellow Australians. It is my melancholy duty to inform you…as a consequence of the persistence of Germany in her invasion of Poland, Great Britain has declared war on her… As a result, Australia is also at war.'

Hilda clutched the table. 'No – not another jolly war.'

Joly clenched his fists. 'That mongrel Hitler.'

Genn forgot to warn him about bad language.

'What the blazes is Hitler thinking?' Rick burst out. 'I'd have his guts for garters.'

Hilda's voice was sharp. 'Rick!'

Genn hated to hear her father rebuked. The recoil of a shotgun when he was a lad had seriously injured his upper right arm. Bruising persisted for months. Doctors sent him home to die. He had flourished – except for that wizened arm. He wore long sleeves, even on the hottest day.

Hilda poured boiling water into the teapot. Rose-patterned teacups passed from hand to hand.

'Milk? I made these biscuits fresh this morning.'

Joly stirred his tea as if to wind it up. 'God help us all.'

'Mummy, Mummy.' Victor wriggled. 'Drink? Boy drink?'

Genn held out his mug. 'Here's your milk, little one. Careful.'

Victor drained it. He looked around with an expectant smile. Everyone chuckled.

Genn beamed. 'Clever boy.' She thought of others like him, trapped in a dreadful war.

'Good lad!' Hilda, a Sydney girl, could now shoot a snake with the best of them. She drove a buggy with élan. Weeded a row of beans – even if she had mistaken Rick's sharpest timber-hewing adze for a hoe.

New recruits rushed to join the AIF. Youngsters of seventeen or eighteen couldn't wait to leave for overseas. Hell-bent on adventure. Lads put up their ages. Officials ignored smooth faces.

Walt said, 'I must do my bit.' He signed up in November.

Genn embraced him, heart heavy.

Joly said, 'I'll miss you, mate.'

Tears in Walt's eyes. 'Same here.'

Poppy had lost her smile. Usually she laughed over the worst situation.

Joly hugged her. 'We'll all miss that husband of yours. Anything you need, Pops, Just ask.'

She nodded, unable to speak.

Walt's farewell was the first of many.

Joly joined the Home Guard. Classed medically unfit for war service, due to painful and stiff knees, he trained every Sunday. About thirty locals, under the command of World War I diggers, learnt manoeuvres, defence and survival skills. On a bivouac in the bush, Joly met Shorty, Trevor Rose, from Stewarts Brook. Even taller than Joly, Shorty became a lifelong friend. They knew how to handle weapons, experienced in stock slaughter and control of feral animals. Veterans taught them to stalk and attack the enemy. They carried sticks in lieu of rifles.

Joly grinned. 'We'll get real ones soon enough.'

Genn worried about Joly's knees. No wonder they play up, she thought, the heavy loads he carries. She felt a guilty relief, at having him safe from battle.

Joly confessed to mixed emotions. 'I would've liked to serve overseas. But with all the young blokes gone, who'd protect Australian women and children? And a man worries about Jap invasion.'

'Invasion? Don't be so damned silly.' She put a hand on her stomach, anguished for her unborn child.

The Phoney War dragged on – declared, but without any battles. By November, the waiting had everyone on edge.

Genn shivered. 'I hate being trapped in this nightmare.'

Joly's glance lingered on Victor. 'Same here. I'd give anything to wake up.'

Life became one long goodbye. Each farewell seemed harder. Relatives, neighbours and friends shouldered kitbags. Some recruits were bound for Britain, others for the Middle East. Walt trained in Egypt.

In May 1940, Poppy's buggy stopped at the fence, frost crackling under the wheels.

Genn put down her knitting, a matinee jacket. They hugged.

'And how's my favourite boy?'

Victor giggled.

Genn brewed tea. 'It's good to see you, Pops. How's Walt?'

'His letters keep me sane. Though half the lines are blacked out.'

'We write to him each week.'

'That's wonderful. He loves to hear from home.' She glanced at her friend's bulge. 'Enough of me. How about you?'

'A month to go. Give or take. I'll be glad when it's over.' She put down her enamel mug. ' Victor's almost three. Feeds and dresses himself.' Victor hid his face.

'Good for you, lad. Easier for you, Genn, with a new baby – or so they tell me.' Poppy bit her lip. 'We'd hoped to begin our family.'

'I can guess how you must feel.'

Poppy squared her shoulders. 'Many are worse off.' She made to leave, her eyes moist. 'See you after the birth.'

Genn dreaded the thought of a month with her sister-in-law, Aileen. Both she and Jack smoked. And if it hadn't been for her... Genn shivered.

She put Victor into his warm coat for a ramble. 'Come along, pet.'

A butterfly, jewelled with bright colours, fluttered against golden buttercups.

'Mummy, look – a flutterby.'

She laughed. 'We call it a butterfly. But yours is a good name too.'

Back at the cabin, Victor fell asleep.

Beauty nickered outside.

Joly worked nearby, and often dropped by for afternoon tea. He noticed her frown. 'OK, sweetheart?'

She stood, heavily pregnant. 'What were we thinking?'

'Bringing a child into the world at such a time? There's always a war raging somewhere.' He buttered a slice of fresh damper, spread fig jam. 'Mmm! I love Hilda's treats.'

Genn glanced outside. Daisy chewed her cud, ribs sharply defined in the harsh light.

'You'll need to buy more hay.'

'Leave it to me, pet. You have enough to worry about.' A cheery wave, and he returned to work.

Genn reviewed her packing. A warm dressing gown snuggled next to slippers and toiletries. Pretty maternity dresses huddled near her layette. She added a flashlight, and an alarm clock. A final check. She snapped the locks shut. Oh, why hadn't she settled for the Brancaster Maternity Hospital at Scone? She liked Doctor Pye's ready smile, his quiet efficiency. 'You've chosen a city hospital for your confinement, I see. Leave early, dear, after last time.'

Joly harnessed the mare. In the long early morning shadows, he loaded Genn's battered port into the buggy. At Hunters Springs, Hilda and Rick embraced her. 'Do take care, darling. Let us know if there's anything you need.'

'I will.'

'Time to make tracks, folks.' Geoff took the driver's seat.

Genn wiped her eyes. 'Bye, Mum, Dad.'

Joly put Victor on his lap. The rutted road clung to steep hillsides, and plunged down steep inclines, valleys far below.

In the lowlands, the Bedford picked up speed. Dust spiralled behind them. Joly closed and opened over thirty gates. 'Can't wait for them to install cattle grids.'

Geoff accelerated. 'Not much likelihood of that with this war.'

A locomotive huffed into Scone station, spitting cinders. Enlisted men hugged mothers and sweethearts, and shook their fathers' hands. They shouldered kitbags and stepped aboard. Leant from windows. Wolf-whistled pretty girls.

'All aboard.'

A porter stashed Genn's case. Joly enfolded her in his arms. 'Take care, sweetheart.'

She swallowed. 'You too.' She should have warned Joly about his drinking but Geoff hovered nearby. Genn kissed away Victor's tears, biting back her own. 'There, there, it's all right. Mummy will be back soon.'

Joly swung the little boy onto his shoulders. 'Wave goodbye to Mummy.'

Genn picked her way past soldiers sprawled on the corridor floor.

A fresh-faced soldier leapt to his feet. 'Have my seat, missus.'

She flushed. He noticed my condition – how embarrassing. 'Thank you so much.'

He doffed his hat and left to join his mates.

'There's a gentleman, no mistake,' said an older woman. 'Mabel's the name. When's the nipper due?'

'Late June. By the way, I'm Genn.' She clutched her worn leather handbag. Glimpsing Victor's stricken face, she bit her lip.

The woman shot her a sympathetic glance. 'Saw you out the winder

– it's hard to leave little ones. Seems only yesterday my son was that age.' She swallowed. 'He's joined up. I run the property. Lost me hubby.'

'I'm sorry. You're so brave.' Genn blotted her eyes.

'I muddle through. Hubby would expect no less. Neighbours help.' Mabel blew her nose. 'What a pair we make.' She laughed through tears. 'This dreadful war. What's to become of us?'

The train jiggled and wobbled. Water sloshed about in a big bottle on the wall.

Genn twisted her handkerchief. 'My cousin Walt is in the Middle East.'

'Good for him. Every able-bodied chap must do their bit.'

Muswellbrook, Singleton and Maitland swarmed with enlisted men. Mabel said, 'Poor beggars. Goodness knows what they'll face.'

At Broadmeadow, the women exchanged best wishes.

A crowd milled about on the platform. People laughed and cried. Soldiers shouted farewells. Abandoned beside her suitcase, the hubbub made Genn worry. Suppose Aileen didn't turn up?

Her sister-in-law pushed her way through the jostling throng. Tall and gaunt, blue wool costume. The well-cut skirt and jacket hung off her. Not surprising, Genn thought, the way she pecks at her food.

Aileen wheezed, 'Good trip?' Glossy black hair with a widow's peak. 'Keeping well?'

'Yes, thank you.' Genn's head throbbed. 'H-how are Len and Pat?'

Aileen took the port and grimaced. 'Len's at high school and Pat's in primary, a real pet. Adores her father.' Aileen signalled the bus driver.

The ticket collector hefted Genn's heavy port. He groaned. 'Brought the family silver, love?'

Aileen winked. 'Don't tell anyone, will you?'

He laughed, pulling the bell. 'Secret's safe with me.'

Aileen said, 'Joly all right? And Victor? You must've hated leaving him. Still, the lad's in good hands.'

An old lady moved to make room. 'Not long to go now, luv. What do you want?'

She blushed. 'A healthy baby.'

'I'm with you there.'

Cottages gasped for air on either side of the street.

Aileen said, 'Jack reckons it won't be long before the Phoney War ends in bloodshed.'

Genn only half-listened. Eyes closed, she drifted to Hunter's Springs. A shiver of glacial air. Steamed-up windows. She pictured her mother lifting Victor from his bath and towelling him dry. Snuggled up in his warm pyjamas, her mother would read him one of his favourite books. If only I were there, to kiss him goodnight.

'You all right, dear?'

'Yes, yes. A bit tired.'

Bus brakes screeched.

'Warners Bay. Our stop.'

The conductor helped Aileen off with the port.

She abandoned her burden at the foot of the apartment stairs, wheezing, 'Jack will fetch it.'

He opened the door. Cigarette in one hand, beer bottle in the other. Moist, tobacco-laden kiss. Barely in his thirties, he'd lost most of his hair since last they met. The living room smelt of old ashtrays and liniment.

'Nipper ready ta drop, eh?'

Genn forced a smile. She surreptitiously wiped the damp patch from her cheek.

Aileen suffered a fit of coughing. 'I'll rustle up a cuppa.'

Jack carried her port it upstairs. Out of breath and sweating, he said, 'Ouch! Didn't know your old man had struck it rich.' He dumped it into the spare room.

Room? It felt more like a large cupboard. She slumped on the narrow bed, longing for home. Tree ferns and wild orchids. Droplets of moisture transformed to rainbows against the dark escarpment. The ripple of the creek. Another image rushed back, one from childhood. A magnificent team of Clydesdale horses, pulling an enormous load of wool. Huge animals with fluffy hooves and manes. Silhouetted against the flaming sunset sky. Red as blood...

At fifteen, Genn had begun to bleed. She feared some dread disease.

Her mother had flushed. 'You're a young woman now. This will happen every month.' She had thrust a home-made calico sanitary belt with safety pins, and some towelling pads, into her hands. 'I've meant to give you these.'

'Every month?' This pain and mess? Surely not?'

That had been the limit of Genn's sex education. Not that any country child could remain ignorant about the facts of life. Horses, cattle, cats, chooks... Every species of bird and animal lived the mystery of reproduction. She glimpsed coupling in the farmyard. Saw the birth of kittens, puppies and calves. Watched a bull nuzzle faces with a cow after copulation. It didn't take any great stretch of the imagination to realise humans must indulge in similar activities. Thin tarpaper walls in her parents' bedroom sighed with revelations.

Hilda had told Genn of her own teenage years. 'Nineteen. Just engaged. My fiancé, your father, pulled me onto his knee. Afraid of being pregnant, I rushed to tell Mother.'

The older woman's laughter had mingled with tears. 'Sat on young Rick's knee, did you? I'm sure you won't be in the family way.'

Hilda had chuckled. 'I guessed there was something I didn't know. But Mother offered no further enlightenment.'

2

Genn chuckled over her mother's innocence. Outside her window, she glimpsed one tiny scrap of blue, squeezed between buildings. Aching for the wide horizons of home, she hung up her dresses. Arranged underwear in a drawer. She thought, I'm stuck here, weeks before my baby is due. Well, I'll not pretend to enjoy myself to please them.

Aileen called, 'Supper's ready.'

They tucked into chops, creamed potatoes and honey carrots. Aileen sliced bread, passed the butter. Pat, nearly seven, chattered away. Len seemed lost in the self-conscious unease of adolescence. Jack shared tales of this or that family member. Genn began to relax. The kids finished their homework, cleaned their teeth.

'Goodnight, Auntie.'

She gave them a hug. They eased her sense of loss.

Jack tuned the wireless to the World Service: 'Hitler has invaded France and the Low Countries.'

Jack said, 'Mark my words, Blighty's next on his list.'

Genn gasped. 'Don't say such a thing.'

Aileen brought out an atlas. On 14 May 1940, Nazis had crossed the river Meuse.

Len raised hard questions. 'Will our soldiers stop them? Can the Allies win?

Pat's head was in a book.

Jack frowned. 'The buggers have broken through the French lines.'

Aileen plumped up cushions, tidied magazines. 'I forgot to tell you, Genn – a few of the lads will drop by tonight. Perhaps you'd like to freshen up?'

Genn had no idea what a 'few lads' might mean. But she put on lipstick and changed her frock.

The doorbell jangled.

Soldiers' duffel bags clinked with enough beer to serve the whole Australian army. They clustered around the wireless, some arm in arm with girlfriends.

'The Hun have forced the Netherlands and Belgium to surrender.'

Jack worked the opener. 'No stopping the buggers.'

Beer passed to eager hands. One cigarette lit another.

Genn gagged in the fug of smoke. I'll be like cured ham, by the time I leave.

Aileen rolled back the rug. She wound the gramophone. Danced to the rhythm of Glenn Miller's swing. Wheezing, she stood aside for Dizzy Gillespie numbers, and the 'Vienna Waltz'.

Aileen laughed at jokes no decent woman should understand. Genn felt like telling her a thing or two. She scowled over the soldiers' fake good cheer. Hated their tall stories and silly grins.

Jack filled glasses. 'To King and Country.'

Excitement glittered in young eyes. 'We'll show 'em the stuff Aussies are made of. 'What do ya reckon, Terry?'

Terry, all freckles and red hair, grinned. 'I could whip the Hun single-handed, no mistake.' He downed a beer. Poured another. Burped.

'On ya, Terry.'

Laughter. Glasses clinked. Bottle lids clunked.

His drinking reminded Genn of her husband. Oh, dear God, let Joly stay sober.

Terry gave a maudlin rendition of 'Kiss Me Goodnight, Sergeant Major'. Claps, cheers and whistles.

He swayed towards her, eyes struggling to focus. Foam slopped over the sides of a glass. 'For you, missus. On your lonesome.'

Her tone was frosty. 'No, thank you.'

'One won't hurt you.'

'I do not drink. And neither should you! Y-you're drunk... A disgrace...'

Terry flushed brick-red. Every eye turned in Genn's direction. Soldiers slammed drinks onto the table. They picked up kitbags. Recalled previous engagements.

Aileen shot Genn a furious glance. She escorted recruits to the door. Stormed back into the room. 'I've had enough of your holier-than-thou attitude. You've insulted my guests.'

Genn tossed her head. 'Terry acts as if war's a Sunday school picnic.'

'He's off to defend our country. Might die – or return home badly injured. And you dare to tell me they don't know the danger?'

'B-but I…'

'Listen to me. You'll ask for a small shandy or lemonade. Laugh even if you don't get the joke. And no more lectures.'

Genn stomped off to bed. She should pack her port. The baby kicked as if it wore hobnail boots. I'm stuck here until… She lay on one side, then the other. Anger faded into doubt.

Next afternoon, she mumbled, 'I'll try to be nicer.' It was the closest Genn ever came to an apology. 'It's just… Terry reminded me…'

'Of Joly when he drinks?' Aileen raised her eyebrows: 'A hard-working man like Joly deserves an ale or two.'

'Two? If only he'd stop at that. For God's sake, Aileen. Binges last days, a week.'

'Genn, he's a good provider. He deserves some fun.'

'Fun? Is that what you call it?' Genn knitted bitterness into the silence.

Her father had said, 'Drink's proved the downfall of greater men.'

Hilda added, 'Why tie yourself to a drunkard?'

Yet every other boy had paled into insignificance beside Joly. Her love would solve the problem.

After his latest fall from grace, Joly had begged her to monitor his drinks. 'Until I recover. No more booze for me.'

'When will you act like a real man?'

'I've said I'm sorry, Genn.'

Late in May 1940, a group of AIF lads clustered around the wireless at Warners Bay.

'German tanks have reached Amiens. British Expeditionary Force counter-attacks have failed to stop them. Panzer forces have driven them to the English Channel. Large numbers of retreating British, French and Belgian troops are trapped on the French coast at Dunkirk.'

Shocked glances. 'God help them.'

Genn shivered.

Jack crushed his bumper into an overflowing ashtray, lit another. 'Poor buggers. Won't stand a snowflake's chance in hell.'

Even Churchill would later call it 'a colossal military disaster...the whole root and core of the British army stranded at Dunkirk...men face death or capture.'

Aileen wheezed. 'Churchill can't leave them to die?'

Jack shrugged. 'Where would Winnie find enough ships?'

The question glanced from one young man to another. How many men must die in the fruitless effort to save them?

That night in dreams, Genn tried to run, pursued by Huns with guns.

A rescue mission, Operation Dynamo, began on 26 May. The British navy gathered a flotilla of unlikely craft. Skippers were signed into the navy for a month. Hundreds of tugboats and fishing vessels were pressed into service.

Jack's eyes shone. 'Cloud cover's reducing enemy air attacks.' He praised British ingenuity. 'Most of those boats were never designed for the open sea. They're bringing back our boys.' Jack looked up from the wireless. 'Sunshine on Dunkirk means added danger. Our troops are under fire from Nazi aircraft above, and enemy submarines below. God help 'em.'

Fear walked beside Genn and Aileen while they shopped, gossiped, and peeled the vegetables. Fear walked the streets. Fear knotted the guts of untried young men soon to face the hazards of warfare, smiling for their friends.

Operation Dynamo gathered speed. It ended on 4 June 1940. Over three hundred thousand British, Belgian and French troops had been saved from almost certain death.

Jack shouted, 'Three cheers for Winnie!'

Churchill called it 'a miracle of deliverance'. His famous 4 June speech was just the rallying cry the nation needed:

'We shall fight on beaches...we shall fight on the seas...we shall fight on the landing grounds...we shall fight in the fields and streets... we shall fight with growing confidence and strength in the air...we shall never surrender.'

The apartment laughed and sang.

Jack said, 'Dunkirk's an example of defeat turned into victory. You'll do it, lads.'

Cheers reverberated around the room. Men hugged sweethearts. Beer frothed and clinked into good wishes.

Genn raised her glass of lemonade. She looked lovely in her prettiest maternity dress. A blue glass bead necklace set off the colour. 'Innocent or foolish, the boys deserve our compassion.'

Aileen choked. 'You're right. They're great lads.'

Genn chuckled over their jokes, often missing the point. She ignored their drinking. Stories danced into the early hours. It was fun, after all.

Another evening. Jack put down his beer. 'Axis forces have invaded almost every country in Europe. Except England.'

Aileen whispered, 'Can that be far off?'

One boy clenched and unclenched his fists. 'We've got to stop them.'

Others shouted in assent.

Genn shuddered at the thought of England being invaded.

The boys brought her soft drinks and biscuits.

She found solace in telling them how she and her husband had met. 'I was a baby, Joly a curious two-year-old. He shoved a finger in my eye. A sure sign, some said, that we'd marry.'

Soldiers chuckled. 'Here's to the nipper.'

Aileen wound up the player. Boys and girls danced and sang along to 'Begin the Beguine' and other favourites. Aileen wheezed on the sidelines. Faces sombre, the boys made their farewells. Even the most optimistic among them knew invasion was only a heartbeat away.

Genn drifted to happier times. Her second meeting with Joly. Him eighteen, her sixteen. Sparks crackled between them, bright as his gold-red hair. He declared himself smitten by the feisty girl with blue eyes. He loved his sweetheart's flawless skin, luminous eyes, and retroussé nose.

Folk said, 'You're a lucky man.'

'He's nice enough.' Hilda frowned over her spectacles. 'But with limited education and prospects.'

'Joly reads everything he can lay his hands on. He takes a keen interest in world affairs.'

Rick touched her on the shoulder. 'But he does drink.'

'He's promised to give it up.' She felt amazed they couldn't see his potential. He enthralled everyone with his yarns. Had a flair for recitations. His voice resonated with emotion as he recited the Robert Service poem, 'The Shooting of Dan McGrew': 'A bunch of the boys were whooping it up in the Malamute saloon…'

Joly's dramatic gestures and resonant voice brought the tale of a gambler and his love called Lou to life. Applause greeted every performance.

Joly built fences for one landowner. A second had him trapping rabbits. He grew potatoes for farmers, learnt cattle or sheep work for graziers, gaining a reputation for hard work, reliability, and the ability to turn his hand to anything. 'Squatters may be short of money. But they enjoy butter, cream, meat, vegetables and fruit in abundance.'

Genn hated him being so far away. She untied the blue ribbon that held the fragile treasure of his letters. His poetry celebrated the miracle of their love. Sometimes he recited *The Rubaiyat of Omar Khayyam*. 'A Book of Verses underneath the Bough…' Oh, their bitter-sweet reunions.

On his return, they sometimes joined young people from local farms for rodeos, picnics and cricket matches. They thought nothing of a forty-mile ride, then danced all night, riding home the following morning.

One year slipped into three. Genn and Joly's meetings surged with the sweet agony of desire. At the last minute, she stilled his questing hands. 'We must wait.'

He groaned. 'It's almost more than a man can bear.'

Folk applauded men for sowing their wild strawberries. Joly was a virgin, unusual for men even in that era.

Hilda and Rick's opposition never faltered.

Genn voiced her frustration on a ride into the bush.

Joly said, 'Be patient, sweetheart. Soon you'll be twenty-one.'

One fine spring day, Joly tied up their horses. He found a few pennyworth of gold in a local stream. Blue wrens drank in their own reflection. They munched tomato and lettuce sandwiches, drinking mugs of dark, sweet tea.

Time for a siesta, on a rug. Drifting in the liquid harmony of a thrush, Joly held her tight. 'Oh, my darling.' Deep kisses. Lithe young bodies. Golden honey-blossom scent. His fingers caressed her pert breasts. Stroked her inner thigh. Sensations aflame. Yearning unstoppable.

Afterwards, Joly tenderly kissed her. 'Sweetheart! My dearest, sweetest one – that was the most wonderful, beautiful moment of my life.'

She buttoned up her jodhpurs. Delight edged with shame. 'Suppose I'm pregnant?'

He crossed his fingers. 'Sweetheart, you won't be.' Joly departed to his distant worksite.

Genn missed a period. It must be late. But she was always regular… Anxiety nibbled like a mouse. It couldn't be, not her. Two months. Not a drop of blood. She struggled to appear untroubled.

Hilda noticed her silence. 'Are you ill?'

She gulped. 'No, Mum, I'm fine.'

At last Joly returned.

'Oh, what am I going to do?'

He grasped her hands in his. 'What are we going to do? Marry of course.'

'Mum and Dad would never consent.'

'Dearest, we'll visit Mother and Father at Warners Bay. Get hitched. One small white lie, maybe two. My brother Bill and Aileen can be our witnesses.'

Amazingly, Rick and Hilda consented to the holiday. Chaperoned, of course, by Joly's parents.

Joly said, years later, 'Neither family could have afforded a grand wedding. Besides, things needed to be rushed a bit.'

Genn told the registrar she was twenty-one. Gave a city address. The ceremony was over almost before it had begun. Wonder in her eyes. Joy in his.

The newlyweds shared a long kiss. They didn't waste a penny of their precious savings. Not even on a celebratory cup of tea in a local café. Joly's wedding gift? A second-hand Singer sewing machine.

Joly said to Genn, 'Best you tell your parents.' He returned to a distant worksite.

Several times the truth trembled on Genn's lips. She let the moment slip by. Weeks passed.

Joly arrived at the farm to see his bride. He whispered, 'Have you told them?'

She flushed. 'Not yet.'

A constable rode through the farm gate. The pair exchanged a worried glance. The officer tied up his chestnut mare, striding into the house. He refused Hilda's offer of tea.

Grim-faced, he addressed the newly weds. 'You have taken part in an illegal wedding ceremony.'

Hilda slumped onto a chair. Rick turned ashen.

The officer went on, 'Joly faces a gaol sentence of up to six months for marriage to a minor.' He fixed the couple with a glare. 'Unless the wedding was sanctioned by one of the girl's parents.'

Joly pictured the clink of handcuffs.

He was stunned to hear Hilda say, 'Officer, I gave them permission.'

He shot her a grateful glance. Rick looked as if he'd swallowed barbed wire.

The constable put away his notebook. He grinned. 'Well, folks, seems I've had a wasted journey.' He winked at Joly and shook on it. 'Let me be the first to offer congratulations. I'll have that cuppa, after all.'

Rick took Joly's hand, voice gruff. 'Take good care of my little girl.'

The constable rode off. Joly gave his new mother-in-law a hug. 'I'll be forever grateful for that, Hilda. Sorry for the deception.'

'I couldn't have you starting married life that way.'

Joly grinned. 'And now for more good news.'

Genn flushed scarlet.

Hilda hadn't noticed her daughter's bump. She gulped. 'Oh, my goodness! A baby. I'm too young to be a grandmother.' Adding quickly, 'I don't mean – why, that's wonderful. He can call me Nan. Sounds younger than Granny.'

Rick joined in the excitement. Grandparents. It didn't seem possible.

Traffic rumbled at Warners Bay. Jolting her back to June 1940, she felt the silken touch of a hand, then a foot, inside her womb. Her heart lurched. Girl or boy? The Other One, the child who never was. Conceived too soon after Victor's birth. They'd planned a three-year break between children. But with Victor not yet one, she had found herself six weeks gone.

Joly's brow had furrowed. 'A second child – the last thing we need right now.'

Her eyes welled. 'So it's my fault?'

'Hush, sweetheart. Somehow, we'll find the dosh. We aren't the first couple in this pickle.'

Aileen arrived on a visit. Genn's story poured forth. She hadn't meant to tell.

Aileen looked thoughtful. 'Heard of pennyroyal? I believe it does the trick.'

An indrawn breath. 'Take something harmful – to my baby?'

'I thought you wanted to be rid of it?'

'Yes…no…yes ' Genn's head spun. Not so much as a flutter in her womb. 'It's horrible. My own flesh. Oh, Joly – what should I do?'

He shrugged. 'You women decide.'

She seethed. It's just like him. Leaving hard decisions up to me.

Aileen leant close. 'Right now, it's just a few multiplying cells.'

Nights proved the worst. Genn thrashed through horrible dreams. She adored everything about babies. Their helplessness, their smell…

On the third day, Aileen took her aside. 'It'll soon be too late.'

Aileen gathered the leaves. Genn couldn't bear to watch. The kettle bubbled. Leaves steeped.

Aileen strained the liquid. 'Ready?'

The mug ticked.

'Don't make it hard for yourself.'

'Oh, give me the damn thing.' Genn shuddered. Never had anything tasted so bitter.

'Your troubles will be over in twenty-four hours. Keep walking.'

Genn battled nausea and cramps. Towards evening, she began to bleed, gritting her teeth against the pain. How could I have… If it wasn't for Aileen…

Joly set his jaw. 'You need the doctor.'

'Suppose he guesses?'

'We'll face that bridge later.'

'And what about little Victor?'

Aileen took the boy in her arms. 'He'll be safe with me.'

Joly lit the lantern. Harnessed his borrowed horse, Beauty. He helped his wife up into the buggy. Covered in blankets against that raw night, she glimpsed a lopsided moon. Billions of stars wept into the velvet blackness. She clung to the narrow seat, biting back pain. Iron-clad wheels bumped over corrugations and potholes on the corduroy road.

Frozen water cracked like panes of glass. Ice crystals glittered, jewels in the lamplight.

At the farm, Rick greeted them in his pyjamas.

'Miscarriage?' He turned ashen.

Hilda rushed to make tea. Genn didn't touch a drop. Oh, what will happen to me? She heard the blessed thrum as Geoff warmed up his Bedford motor. Waves of pain.

Plovers screamed.

The moon kept vigil from one side of the utility, then the other. Jolts and bumps, fifty-eight miles of torture. Multiple stops to open and shut gates. Rattling across wooden bridges, she gritted her teeth. Protecting her abdomen. I must survive for Victor.

Scone Maternity Hospital. Hushed voices. Sister with a flashlight, cool sheets. A crescendo of pain. Her brow dripped. Blood and tissue between her legs. A dish of water, towel, pads.

'A sponge will soon have you comfortable.'

A warmed draw sheet stilled her shivers.

Nurse smiled. 'I've saved the specimen for Dr Pye.'

She felt relieved to see him.

Pyjamas peeped below his trouser legs. Face sombre. 'I'm afraid you've lost your baby, pet.'

Her eyes brimmed.

'These things happen. You're young and strong. Better luck next time.' He shook Joly's hand. Darkness swallowed him whole.

Genn forbade Joly to speak of it again. Fifty years later, Joly would confess their secret to his elder daughter, after his wife had died.

Evening at Warners Bay. Genn farewelled yet more soldiers. Glimpses of bravado and fear in their eyes. Did a happy evening lighten their burden?

Her bulk made it difficult to get comfortable in bed. Nocturnal toilet visits were a trial. Her baby kicked, massaging a tender spot in her abdomen. Surprisingly, it began to feel better.

Regular contractions began. Aileen rushed Genn to Doctor For-sythe, a trim fellow with silver hair. By then, the pangs had settled.

'Hmm! Given your history...' He admitted her to Merewether Ma-ternity Hospital.

Genn exulted at leaving the smoky flat. She chatted with nurse Kel-era and Sister Waide. 'It only seems yesterday when I took my son Victor home.' The train journey to Scone had seemed endless. 'You can imagine my pride, showing Joly our firstborn. 'Is he good enough for you?' She smiled. 'The way he clasped us both in his arms was answer enough.'

She made friends with another expectant mum. Frances wound her long hair into a chignon. It gleamed, black as a raven's wing. She hinted at a previous miscarriage. Genn daren't ask the circumstances.

They stood on the balcony, caressed by a Pacific breeze. Pallid winter sun peeked from behind the clouds. Translucent waves rose into great walls of green water. They hesitated, then crashed. Foaming and folding and swirling over the furrowed sand.

Frances shivered. 'I long to wake up.'

'And find the war's a bad dream? Don't we all? I've farewelled too many young lads these past weeks. Smiling, so I wouldn't weep. Relatives and friends have gone, too.'

The 'some never to return' hung between them.

Frances gulped. 'My hubby's in the Middle East.'

'So is my cousin Walt – wouldn't it be funny if they met? He's train-ing in Egypt. I can barely read his letters for the blacked-out bits.'

'So many of T-Tom's words are missing, too. And each one is precious.' She wiped her eyes. 'Folks say it'll be over by Christmas.'

'The war? I've lost hope of that.' Genn glimpsed a group nurses emerge from the waves. Kelera, her favourite. 'Oh, look – our hospital icebergs.'

Frances shivered. 'Better them than me.'

Kelera arrived on duty, bubbling with exhilaration. Her blonde curls peeked from under her cap, still damp.

Genn shivered. 'Must be freezing out there.'

'It's bliss! You girls should try it sometime.'

They laughed. 'Not in winter, thank you.'

Back in the ward, Frances winced, a hand on her stomach. 'It's started! I'll be first to the labour ward.'

'No way. My baby will arrive before yours.'

Her friend's contractions seemed the real thing. Then stopped. Frances groaned. 'Just when I thought…'

Their ongoing joke helped keep war worries away.

One evening Genn's contractions lingered, way past their usual cut-off point. 'This may be it.'

Frances gave her a hug. 'Good luck. I'll not be far behind you.'

Another contraction stilled Genn's laughter. Stronger. Lasting longer. She breathed in harmony with her body.

The rhythm paused. Sister Waide said, 'We'll move you into the labour room.'

Frances gave Genn the thumbs up.

A bearded wardsman sped his gurney along the corridor. Wheels squeaked on polished linoleum. A glitter of lights. Genn closed her eyes, breathing with the pain.

'One, two, three.'

A narrow theatre bunk. Sudden anxiety. Would she be punished for the other one?

Kelera palpated her abdomen. 'Excellent. Baby's head's engaged.' Her slim hands warmed a Pinard stethoscope. The metal bell pressed against Genn's abdomen. 'Strong heartbeat.'

Yet another contraction. Like a strong menstrual cramp, only much, much worse. Genn went to speak. The words tumbled over one another, shells caught in a wave.

Kelera patted her shoulder. 'Don't try to talk. You're well into labour.'

Genn breathed in and out through her mouth. Gripped by a contraction. Rapid, sighing breaths. Muscles stretched. Her pain peaked. Faded. She lay exhausted. A beach awaiting the next onslaught.

The room was dim. Strange shadows. A moment of panic.

Kelera patted her shoulder. 'You're doing well. It won't be long now.' Cool fingers probed for a pulse, anchoring her to the outside world.

Sister Waide's voice. 'Give her the injection, nurse.'

Light glinted from a stainless steel kidney dish.

'Sorry if this hurts.'

A needle stabbed into Genn's buttock. The fluid stung. Contractions ebbed and flowed. She struggled to maintain the rhythm of breathing. Sand and salt water boiled against the shore. An undertow rushed her towards the deep.

Dr Forsythe stood at the foot of her bunk, gloved hands ready. Little crinkles of a smile near his eye, above the mask. 'When the next contraction comes, dear, push hard.'

A strong, bearing-down sensation. It wrung at the very depths of her body.

'Push hard, dear,' he said, 'Well done. Just a little more. Good. Another push. Hold it.'

She drifted in a void. Blood pounded in her ears. Voices echoed. Panic. Was she awake or dreaming? The room flooded with brilliant, translucent light. A loud wail.

Doctor Forsyth said, 'It's a girl.'

A clock showed six a.m.

Genn heard the rasping cries of her newborn daughter. Apart, and yet still part of her. The umbilical cord attached. Kelera placed the infant on her chest.

Genn checked fingers and toes. 'What a wee mite. Half the size of Victor.'

Kelera cut the cord. Took Dessie to be weighed. Returned with a huge grin. 'Here she is. All six pounds of her.'

Genn cradled Dessie against her chest. Blissful. Relaxed. The other one floated before her. Missing a face. She squirmed. The child who never was. Tears edged between closed lids.

Doctor Forsythe smiled. 'You've done very well, dear. Could've had her under a tree. Nothing to cry about.'

Sister Gloria Waide patted her shoulder. 'We women sometimes weep for sheer joy.'

He chuckled. 'I've noticed.'

Genn shrank from the kindness in their eyes.

Back at the ward, Frances hugged her. 'I'm so glad for you. A pigeon pair.'

Genn donned her prettiest nightie. Visiting hours. Pat arrived in school uniform. Pigtails adorned with red ribbons.

Aileen grinned. 'She couldn't wait to see the new baby.'

The child edged forward. 'Flowers for you, Auntie.' Orange and yellow daisies.

'What a beautiful bouquet, Pat – you must know I like bright colours.'

'Gosh, Mummy! Look at the baby's tiny hands and feet.'

Aileen chuckled. 'Dessie's a real pet. You must feel proud.' She glanced around. 'Last time, you were the only woman without a husband.'

'You're right. Mothers, sisters and aunts now – and two chaps in uniform.'

'Waiting to go or on leave?' Aileen sighed. 'Jack sends his best. Len's not yet home from school.'

'Give them my love.'

3

Frances went into labour. The ward's predictions were confirmed. Women cheered her eight-pound son. Frances said, 'If only my Tom were here.'

'Get your mum to bring her Kodak.'

'Good idea. Snaps to show his mates.'

Genn's doctor arrived. 'You live far from medical care, I believe, Mrs Wright? Best to stay another week.'

She reluctantly accepted his verdict.

The Battle of Britain raged in distant summer skies. 'Young RAAF Pilots risk lives on every mission.'

Frances's eyes shone. 'Imagine their bravery!' She read of downed Messerschmitt aircraft. 'Every kill brings us closer to victory.'

Genn changed the subject. It felt wrong to talk of killing with Dessie in her arms. Like many mothers, she followed Dr Truby King's advice on infant care. His book *Feeding and Care of Our Babies* and his wife's follow-up, *Our Babies*, had been her saviours with Victor. Genn said, 'Infants may seem helpless and dependent. Truby says they must be shown who's boss.'

Someone said, 'Exactly. He's one of our leading Australian paediatricians – a New Zealander, actually. Says never let a child get away with bad behaviour. Even once could result in loss of control. Babies need a strict regime. Feed, sleep and regular bowel movements. And never pick up infant if it cries – or give a feed before it's due.'

Some mothers exchanged shocked glances. A lively debate followed.

An older woman said, 'Routine builds character. Best not to cuddle or pet them too often.'

Frances's eyes filled with tears. 'I mean to kiss and hug my baby. Whatever that man says.'

Genn frowned. 'Careful, Fran. A spoilt child is misery. Best to let babies cry themselves to sleep.'

Frances shivered. 'I couldn't do that.'

Genn shrugged. 'It's for their own good. At three, Victor's a real darling.' She picked up her knitting, pink wool, for a matinee jacket. Twisted yarn, a pearl row followed then plain, making up the pattern as she went along. She shared her views of toilet training. 'Dr King says every mother's goal should be to teach infants to be clean. I held Victor over the potty at six weeks.'

A voice added, 'You must support their wobbly head.'

Frances sighed. 'Sounds a lot of trouble to me.'

Genn changed needles. 'Clean nappies are your reward.'

A young mother raised the rumour that Dr King's Plunkett Society had started the Karitane Nurses movement. 'He did lower the infant mortality rate. But I hate some of his ideas. He says higher education for women would be detrimental to our maternal functions.'

There were hoots of laughter.

'Thankfully,' she went on, 'a brilliant woman called Elizabeth Lloyd Bennett – one of our earliest women doctors – proposed a more positive point of view.'

Frances said, 'Good for her.'

Genn sniffed. 'I only went to sixth class. It's served me well enough.'

Doctor Forsythe strolled in. 'I've decided to let you go home, Mrs Wright. Will tomorrow suit?'

Happiness shone. 'Wonderful – I'll telegram my husband.'

Frances shared her news. 'I'm leaving the same day.'

They spent a night made restless by excitement. About to pack her port, Genn heard the wail of an ambulance.

A nurse erupted into the ward, ashen-faced. 'It...it's Kelera. T-taken by a rip.'

A collective wail roiled around the ward. Women hugged, wept.

'Kelera? Oh, no.'

Frances burst into sobs.

Genn's eyes blurred. 'I can't believe – oh God, Why?'

Doctors ordered Genn and Frances to stay another night, writing up something to help them sleep. 'You need time to recover from the shock.'

Sister Waide brought sleeping draughts.

Genn drained the clear liquid. She felt emptier than the medicine glass. 'Oh, Sister – why do the nicest people go first?'

'There's no rhyme or reason to these things.'

Genn and Frances swapped addresses. Her mother carried the port. The little group waved and were lost to sight.

Aileen arrived to help Genn. At Broadmeadow station she told of soldiers they'd known. 'Remember young Billy? Tall, shock of black hair. He asked after you. And Michael's in France.'

'I – uh – enjoyed their visits.'

Aileen gave a mischievous smile. 'We're lucky to have chaps like them. Do visit us soon. Bring Joly next time.'

Genn put Dessie in the seat corner, cradled in a pink bunny rug. Aileen waved a lace handkerchief. The giant beast huffed away, spitting clouds of grit and smoke. Images of evening soirées at Aileen's apartment crept back. Genn's sense of loss came as a shock.

She eyed photos of the Three Sisters in the Blue Mountains. Clear water jiggled, sloshed and gurgled in a big bottle on the wall. Oh, for the sweet water of mountain streams.

The train swayed through Maitland, Singleton and Muswellbrook. Groups of soldiers and their loved ones had assembled at each station. Would this nightmare ever end?

Genn had been away six weeks. She feared Joly might seem like a stranger.

The baby's fists flailed the air, her cries urgent. In the privacy of the empty carriage, Genn suckled Dessie. Changed her nappy. The train motion lulled her back to sleep.

'You'll soon meet Daddy and your brother.'

She recalled how Joly groaned over forms. Jolyon Lenly Elmo. 'A man can't fit those names into a tiny space.' Gennevra Amy Victoria wasn't easy for her, either. Dessie would be the sole name for her daughter. Clearly, a son needed two. Victor Jolyon.

'Oh, the acres we'll buy,' Genn whispered to her sleeping baby, 'Kangaroo Creek is just the start. There'll be ample room for you and your children. Of course, Victor will play the most important role. Your daddy will build me a huge farmhouse kitchen, with large pantry.'

Everything hung on acceptance of Joly's offer.

The train hissed to a stop at Scone. A fire crackled and leapt in the waiting room.

The bus driver, Mr Turner, doffed his hat. 'G'day, missus.' He stashed her shabby port among mailbags and parcels.

Every turn of the road brought the scents of home. Rich fields of lucerne, horse studs and weeping willows met her joyful eyes. Herds of Aberdeen Angus cattle dotted the fields of Belltrees, the White property. The driver delivered boxes of groceries and mail all along the upper Hunter.

Mr Turner glanced at her in the rear-vision mirror, 'My son's a pilot. Battle of Britain. They've stopped the invasion. But for how long?'

Genn gripped the sleeping baby. 'Long enough, I hope.'

He drew to a stop at Moonan Flat general store, near the Victoria pub. He grinned. 'All the best to you and the little 'un.'

Geoff embraced her. 'Welcome home, sis.' She turned back the bunny rug. He whistled. 'My, word. Dessie's a real trimmer.'

In the Upper Hunter, he dropped off bread, parcels and locked bags of letters into mail boxes, some forty-four-gallon drums.

Genn said, 'I often think of you and poor old Dad riding all those miles delivering the mail.'

'I dreaded winter. Tough for both us and the horses.'

'Snow built up on their hooves until…'

'They walked on stilts. Ice would suddenly drop off. Crack. The horse would stumble. I narrowly missed many a fall.'

Genn said, 'Do you recall the time Dad fell ill? I took over, riding off under clear skies. In minutes, the clouds roiled and growled. I shivered in rain and sleet.'

'Not even a jumper.'

'My throat felt as if someone had ripped it with barbed wire. At home, Mum rushed me to bed. Brought water bottles, hot soup. It took me weeks to recover.'

'I took over.' He gave a wry smile. 'Often wonder how we managed.' Geoff patted the dashboard. 'Thank the Lord for my Bedford.'

The vehicle clawed up steep passes into the Mount Royal Ranges. Grass trees undulated on steep hillsides of the Black Cutting. Kangaroos bounded over rocks and logs. Valleys and farms hid under a haze of blue. A wedge-tailed eagle glided on thermals.

Genn breathed in the cool mountain air. 'Almost there, little one.'

At the home valley, Peggy leapt and wagged.

Genn patted her. 'I'd forgotten the splendour of country skies. Horizon to horizon, pink cumulus clouds – wow!'

Geoff hooted with laughter. 'The sky usually goes from one horizon to another, sis.'

'Not like this, silly. In the city it's squeezed between buildings.'

'Guess you're right.'

Her eyes drank in the lazy curl of smoke. Eucalypt bathed in orange light.

'We're home, Dessie.

Joly strode to greet them. He engulfed her and the baby in a great hug.

Victor clung to her skirt. 'Mummy! Mummy! Stay with boy?'

Everyone laughed. 'Yes, son. Mummy will stay.' She bent to show him the new arrival. 'This is your little sister.'

Victor sucked his thumb.

Geoff grinned. 'He's been expecting a playmate.'

Frosty air brought a glow to Genn's cheeks.

Joly kissed her, hunger in his glance. 'God, it's been a long time.'

Her blue dress was one of Joly's favourites. He breathed her scent of eau de cologne. Coral lipstick. Curves. Luminous eyes.

'Your daughter.'

He hesitated to take her in his big hands.

'She won't break, Joly.'

He awkwardly cradled Dessie in his arms.

Genn lifted Victor. 'Oh, my little man. How I've missed you.'

A buggy creaked to a stop inside the gate.

'Why, it's Poppy…and her nieces.'

Joly helped them down. Hugs all around.

Poppy chuckled, 'We've heard tell there's a new baby.'

Victor hid behind Genn's skirts.

Poppy took a peek. 'A real pet, and no mistake.' She turned towards Victor, 'You're a lucky big brother.'

The girls pestered her to have a nurse.

'When we're inside.'

Afternoon tea. '

And how is Walt?'

'He says to tell Joly he misses fossicking.'

Genn chuckled. 'That's hard to believe.'

Joly grinned. 'No doubt the old bugger's still looking for the mother lode. Out there in the desert.'

They all laughed. For once, Hilda ignored the swear word.

'From what I've seen, Walt will be searching for his El Dorado until the day he…' Geoff coughed. 'Er…forever.'

The girls took turns to nurse the baby.

Genn watched their every move. 'Mind Dessie's head.'

The adults chatted of Walt's days as Joly's mate. Days before war had stolen lives. Days during the Great Depression when gold was their saviour.

Hilda invited Poppy to stay for the evening meal.

'I'd like to get home before dark.' Embraces and pecks. She kissed Dessie, settled her nieces in the buggy. Laughter in her eyes and a quip on the lips, she flicked the reins. They trundled off into the sunset.

The table steamed with boiled mutton, carrots and pumpkin. Creamed potato melted on the tongue, aromatic with fresh parsley and home-made butter. Joly took seconds of meat. They lingered over cups of strong black tea. Talk drifted away from the war. Genn felt relieved.

Rick and Hilda eyed the new arrival. 'Do spend the night.'

Joly shook his head. 'I've an early start tomorrow.'

Genn's cheeks burnt at his glance.

Geoff rose. 'I'll drive you.'

Joly shook his head. 'No, no. I'll use the buggy. But I'll need to keep Beauty for a while, Rick.' His mare had recently died. 'Until I can find a horse to buy.'

'I'll ask around.'

Joly put on the collar on the black mare, fitted the surcingle and traces. He patted the cedar buggy, painted black. 'It has served us well. One day we might afford a motor car.' Chains jingled. He added the breastplate, folded the hairs of her tail to fit the crupper. Eased the mare between shafts. 'I never cease to marvel how the swingle bar keeps horses on a straight course.'

Light faded. Geoff helped stash their things into the buggy. They lit kerosene lanterns.

Hilda held the baby, warmly wrapped. 'She's such a pet. I can't bear to let her go.'

Genn kissed her mother. 'You'll see her again soon.'

Hilda hugged Genn for the sixth time. 'A shame you can't stay the night.'

'Next time. I promise.' She slipped into a coat, put one on Victor. 'Don't come outside into the cold.'

Joly tucked rugs and a tarpaulin around them. 'Gee up, girl.'

The mare trotted off, lanterns bobbing in the blackness. Peggy lolloped ahead. Ice cracked under the wheels. Millions of stars glittered in the frosty sky.

He squeezed Genn's hand. 'Almost there, sweetheart.'

An aroma of red eucalypts filled the cabin.

Joly gave her a kiss. 'For you, darling. Welcome home.'

Genn smiled at the bunch of red leaf tips. 'They're lovely.'

She recalled her first visit. Cobwebs had festooned walls to rafters. She had stamped her foot. 'I won't set foot in this place until you do something about those spiders.'

Joly had seemed astonished. 'Harmless. They keep down the flies.' He told her of having shared camps with centipedes. 'Even the occasional snake. Never had any problems.'

'That may be. Get rid of them.'

Joly had grinned. 'Yes, ma'am.' He swished around with a broom, and carried many outside on the bristles. 'There...happy now?'

Years later, unable to suppress a shudder, she would recount this story to her children. She told of tarantulas – huntsmen, actually, but that's what folk in the mountains called them. 'Centipedes and other insects scurried about in the timbers above. They fell down without warning. It was dreadful. I made your father add a calico ceiling.' Genn added, 'I enjoyed living there. Cool in summer, warm in winter.'

Victor leant against her, almost asleep. They tenderly placed him in bed.

Joly whistled. He crumpled newspaper. Added twigs and branches. Lit a match. Fire leapt and crackled. He put on a billy of water.

Dessie wailed. Genn put the infant to her breast, sitting on their massive bed. Joly had made it by driving saplings into the ground for legs. Bark covered a timber frame, the base. Genn had insisted on a kapok mattress.

She said, 'Gosh. Where will Dessie sleep?'

'I'll find something.' Joly disappeared into the darkness. He returned with a leather horse's collar, dusting it off with an old rag. 'This will do for now.'

'And where, might I ask, will she sleep when the horse is wearing it?'

Joly chuckled. 'This one's an extra. I'll borrow one of your father's spare drawers. Until Dessie's ready for a cot.'

Beauty munched oats.

Joly cut Peggy slices of cold mutton, stored in a green zinc meat safe. It hung from the branch of a eucalypt, rocked by every breeze. 'Get this into you, old girl.'

He attached a chain to her collar. She curled up in the kennel.

Flames danced with memories and dreams. They drank sweet cups of billy tea.

He reached out. 'Oh, sweetheart. You'll never know how much I've missed you.'

'I'm so happy to be home. Aileen means well…'

'It can't have been easy.' He cradled her body against his. 'Oh, my darling. Let's go to bed.' His big hands fumbled to undo the buttons of her dress. 'Sweetheart, will it be all right if we…it won't hurt you?'

'Silly! It's weeks since the baby.'

Joly's voice was a gasp. 'My own dear, sweet love.'

Their clothes fell to the floor.

Genn turned back the crazy-pattern quilt. She wanted him so much. Yet felt strangely nervous.

He sensed her hesitation. It excited him. She seemed like a young girl who had never been with a man. He guessed she needed time, aroused her with long caresses and deep kisses. In the flicker of firelight, he traced the silky smoothness of her naked body. Felt her movements quicken. Her sighs told him all he needed to know. They merged into one. A wave rose, green and translucent. It carried them to the summit. Ecstasy. Chuckles.

Exhilarated by everything about her, Joly cradled Genn in his arms. He blew a tendril of her brown hair from her brow. 'My precious darling. Finally mine again.'

She gave a languorous sigh. 'And so happy to be home.' Genn told of her loneliness in the city, the feeling it would never end. 'At hospital I watched the ocean. I saw every mood from sunrise to sunset.' She shivered. 'Just then, it felt as if a big wave claimed us both.'

He stared at her. 'You too? Exactly what I felt.'

Shadows danced on the wall. Somewhere a dingo howled. It wasn't the first time they had shared a vivid moment.

In the early hours, Dessie cried for a late supper. Genn's breasts tingled. She craved that moment of nurture and bonding.

Joly brought the baby. 'Here she is, love.'

Dessie latched onto her nipple. Genn cradled Dessie in her arms. She gave Joly a grateful smile. Marvelling at her good fortune. A husband who cared, and two healthy children.

4

Joly's head thumped. He and Victor suffered a debilitating fever, drenched by sweats. An itchy rash covered their bodies. Victor cried should Genn touch his legs.

Joly said, ' I feel as if mine are on the point of breaking.'

She cooked broth. 'Take a spoonful. Good boy! Another…'

Joly managed half a mug, and pushed it aside. At last he felt well enough to sit out of bed. 'A bit wobbly on my pins. Not quite ready for work.'

Dessie screamed, tensing her tiny legs.

Genn felt the child's brow. 'A fever.' Dreading the mystery illness. 'It could be fatal for a six-week-old baby.'

Joly saw exhaustion in every line of his wife's body. 'You're all in.' He lurched to the wicker armchair. 'Leave Dessie to me.'

She hesitated. 'Are you sure? Baby needs fluids…'

'A couple of bottles of boiled water should do. Sleep in the tent. It'll be quieter.'

Genn fell into bed. She heard nothing until morning.

Joly cradled the distressed baby. 'One day I'll be old, and it'll be your turn to care for me.' His big hand gently massaged her stomach. 'Maybe it's colic.' He told her of his life. 'Not that I expect you to understand, sweetie. But my voice might be soothing. A midwife called Mrs Mallory brought me into the world. A slab hut behind the Linga Longa Inn, at Gundy. Back then, it was a simple pub. I was mother's seventh child. We grew tomatoes, cucumbers, carrots, beans, potatoes… Swapped vegetables for oranges and figs.'

He chuckled. 'Wait until you're old enough to remember your grandmother, Florence. You'll love her wonderful stories. A twinkle is never far from her brown eyes. She bore eight lively kids. Laughed over our pranks. Our clothing may have been patched, but we Wrights were a close-knit mob.'

Flames leapt to his earliest memories. 'I asked Mother how old I was. Can still hear her amused voice, "Two." How long before Christmas?' Six weeks seemed an enormous amount of time. I decided not to think about it. Back then, redheads aroused suspicion. Our neighbour's wife had a daughter about six, me couple of years younger. I was in town with Mother. The lady extracted coins from her purse. "Buy ice creams for you and Joly." She wriggled with embarrassment. "I can't." Her mother looked annoyed. "Why ever not?" A sideways glance. "He's got red hair."'

Joly watched the flames dance. Red sparks shot up the chimney.

'On my first day at school, I was too shy to ask about the toilets. Squatted down behind a tree. That's what we did, out in the bush. Kids walked past. I made to stand. You've guessed it – my pants copped the lot. I bolted.'

Another memory rushed back. 'I rode a pony called Goldie to school, a lovely, gentle animal. I grew too big, and my father sold her.' He brushed his eyes. 'Bill, Sid, Aileen and I hiked four miles to the one-room schoolhouse at Ellerston. Father reckoned it was good for us. We went barefoot all year round. Father couldn't afford shoes. Summer heat scorched our soles. Frosts brought the misery of chilblains. Mother had the solution. We dipped our feet into alternate dishes of hot and cold water. It eased the itch, stopping ulcers.'

Joly adjusted the baby's position. She suckled on a bottle.

'One day, Aileen and Bill found a smooth knothole in a dead log. I was fascinated. "Why is the wood polished around the edges?" Sid grinned. "Poke in your finger and see."'

He chuckled. 'Let me tell you, Dessie, it's no fun having a wasp attached to your finger. I yelped with pain.'

Red and bluish flames curled around the crackling logs. Were the baby's cries less intense?

'Father took me out of school. He set up a tent in the bush. Showed me how to run a line of traps. "Catch all the rabbits you can, lad." He left me with a fortnight's rations. Strangely, I didn't feel afraid.' Joly shook his head. 'It horrifies me now. Fancy leaving a kid of eight unsupervised. My favourite toy a pocketknife. I whizzed through mental arithmetic. The teacher asked our class to do long division. I was away when it was taught, easily reaching the solutions in my head. The teacher went crazy. "Where's your working out? You've copied. I've marked your answers as wrong." I was devastated. It still rankles, after all these years. If only he'd had the initiative to test me with different numerals.'

He felt as if Dessie were listening to every word. 'My next teacher, Mr Lance, strode into the classroom with an enormous bundle of canes. We exchanged glances. What sort of monster… Funnily enough, he never caned a single student. I credit him with my love of the written word. My formal education all but finished in third class. Later, Mother enrolled us at the Junction School, Bar Beach. She still hoped we'd get an education. Five hundred boys, and me one of only two with red hair. They taunted us. "Get a load of the weird kids with red hair." Chanting a ditty: "What made the donkey buck? Ginger! Ginger!" I landed a punch. A bigger boy beat the hell out of me. My mate bleached his hair. "Now they call me Snowy. It's better than Ginger." I pretended my uncle was Ned Kelly. It didn't help. Every day Mother patched up my wounds. One kid threw a stone, leaving me unconscious. "I didn't bring you here to fight." Father took us out of school. "Time for you boys to become men."

'I turned twelve that March. We helped father build a netting fence at Kurricabark. It snakes for miles across the spine of a stony mountain. Took eighteen months to complete. People called it an amazing achievement. Packhorses carried swags, tents, camp ovens and food. Sid, Bill and I took turns to cook. We carried water from the valley far below. Slept on a bed of grass between two logs. A lantern flickered with stories. We read everything from Wild West yarns, to classics like *Oliver Twist* and *Tom Sawyer*. And I loved poetry.

'Squabbles erupted over bed space, or something else. Our brother Bill turned dispute into laughter. His twin, Sid, would find thorns in the most innocent remark. "What did he mean by that?"

'Can you believe we chased each other with centipedes?

'I shouldn't tell you of another game. We wriggled grass straws inside funnel web spiders' burrows. Coaxed them out. They reared up, fangs dripping venom. I'd grab them from behind, and the chase was on. We shrieked with laughter. They're among the worlds' deadliest spiders. Not even an antidote.

'I loved evenings when Father's mates happened by. Long white beards. Pipes glowing red in the darkness. Stars dripping points of light. The men recited bush poetry around the campfire. They told stories of bushrangers and gold. We couldn't keep sleep at bay. Father shooed us off to bed.

'Your uncle Arthur achieved his Qualifying Certificate for secondary school. Father said, "Further education is a waste of time." Arthur argued, but Father wanted help building roads. It proved hard yakka. We used picks, shovels, horse and a tip-cart. Ready to widen a road, Father drilled holes into a rock face. He inserted dynamite, warning seventeen-year-old Arthur, "Light the long fuses, not the short ones. I need time to get away." Arthur mixed up the two. The blast came almost immediately. It threw Father, rocks and debris into the river.

'Drenched to the bone, he waded ashore, murder in his eyes. Arthur ran, but not far enough. Father flogged him. The blood and bruises were horrible. Mother and Father had a terrible row. He didn't dare hit her. She cried, bathing my brother's wounds.

'There was an uneasy silence in the house. Thoughts unsaid, eyes failing to meet eyes. Whispers in the dark. We knew Arthur was brooding. None of us guessed what was on his mind. When his bruises faded, he packed a bag. "The old man will never beat me again." He fled to Victoria.

'We badly missed our big brother. Father never spoke his name for years. Mother was heartbroken. Arthur had some sort of breakdown.

Wrote to her after he recovered. He worked as a railway porter until join-ing the Victorian police force.' Joly shook his head. 'He's risen through the ranks. Wouldn't be surprised if he's commissioner one day.'

He stroked Dessie's brow. 'I've never forgotten the day my sister Florrie…empty saddle, broken bridle…' A long silence. 'My favourite playmate. Florence Dorothy. Her four, me a year older.' He shook his head. 'Florrie was too young for such a mad horse. Shouts, recrimina-tions. Sobs. I covered my ears. The following days are a blur. I ran and ran, not wanting to cry. She's interred in a valley at Omadale Brook. Mother could never bear to visit her grave.' Another silence. 'Maybe I'll take you there one day.'

The wind keened and wailed.

'At fourteen, I had curly red hair halfway down my back. Father said, "The lad looks like a girl." Mother hid her scissors. She couldn't bear to destroy such splendour. Your great-grandmother, Margaret Con-nolly – they called her Marion – tended to wander. Father had me mind her.'

Joly rearranged logs. Red sparks leapt.

'Sometimes, Granny's mind cleared. She told of life as a little girl in Ireland. Folk dancer. The teacher rapped her across the toes if she took a misstep. But I'm rambling. What was I telling you? Ah, yes: Father found the scissors and hacked off my hair. Granny would have nothing to do with me. "You're not Joly. He's got long hair." "Yes, Granny, I am." "Never seen you before in my life."

'The priest arrived. She refused to let him in. "You know me, Mar-garet. Look at my collar." She shouted, "It should be the bloody hang-man's collar."'

Dessie's wails had ceased. Joly placed his daughter in the large drawer, adjusting her covers. Stumbling into bed.

Genn woke at first light. Joly snored, deep in slumber.

She felt Dessie's brow. 'Cool, thank goodness. The fever's gone.'

The little girl whimpered, and nuzzled for the breast.

Joly planned a return to work. He suffered a relapse. No sooner had he recovered than Genn took ill. By some miracle, the baby remained well.

Joly became nurse, cook and housekeeper. It took ages before the three of them felt well.

Much later, a doctor solved the puzzle. Their illness had been dengue fever. 'Outbreak at the time. It's spread by insect bite, not person to person. Your daughter was protected by mosquito netting.'

Joly built a fence here, laid trap lines there. Riding home, he felt exhilarated. Nothing was sweeter than sharing the hours after work in Genn's company. He liked the pretty dresses she wore each evening, made on her Singer machine.

Outside the cabin, Joly sang. He poured warm water into an ablutions dish. He'd made the washstand from odd-shaped tree branches. His size eleven boots dropped to a hessian mat. He stripped to the waist. A glisten of foaming Lifebuoy soap, muscles rippled. He put a flannel to his face, snuffling, like some huge, exuberant dog. Topped and tailed, he grabbed a clean towel from a number eight wire hook. Changed into clean trousers and shirt.

Joly breathed in the aroma of baby powder and cooking. He tiptoed to see Dessie, asleep in her makeshift crib. Victor, in his pyjamas, clambered onto his father's knee for a story. He tucked his boy into bed, kissed him goodnight.

Stew simmered in the camp oven. Joly removed it from hot embers, brushing aside glowing coals. Ravenous from the aroma of parsley and spices. A slice of fresh damper dripped butter. Genn ladled the stew onto tin plates. They laughed and shared stories of their day. Tucking into vegetables and kangaroo meat.

He spooned up the rich sauce. 'This is delicious. I'm amazed at the variety of meals you make. A bit different to suppers before I married.' He told of working twelve or thirteen hour days with Walt. 'We left before sunrise and returned in darkness. Buggered when it came to cooking.'

'Didn't you prepare food in advance?'

'We rarely had time. Once a farmer gave us a box of apples. We stewed the lot, and hung the kerosene tin container under the shade of a eucalypt, covered with a clean corn bag. It caught every breeze. First thing evening, we downed a full pannikin. It gave us energy to light a fire and start cooking. One night, Walt took the first dip. He seemed alarmed. I asked, "What's up?" "A strange, hairy object." "Most likely the core of an apple." "I don't think so. Strike a match, Joly." We saw the corpse of a huntsman spider. And every type of bug from flies to ladybirds. We'd consumed this mixture for days.'

She chuckled. 'The extra nutrients probably did you good.'

Joly put down his spoon. 'We're so lucky being here with our little family. Think of people in London. That awful Blitz. Huge fires. Whole streets reduced to rubble.'

Genn shivered. 'Bombed day after day. How can they bear it? Huddled in musty air-raid shelters. Under beds or tables.'

Joly drained his tea. 'And it can't be easy for our Walt, under siege from the Afrika Corps. Tank attacks, artillery barrages. Probably the only thing that keeps him sane are dreams of gold.'

'Would he think of that?'

'It's as good a diversion as any.' He went on, 'Gold's in my blood too. It was my greatest thrill to watch Father on his haunches at Dry Creek. Metal prospecting dish. Fingers brushing aside rubbish. And with luck, a few pennyweight of gold.'

'I like to hear about your American grandfather.'

'Ah, yes, Joseph Ananias Wright. Mining engineer from New York. At the Ballarat fields, he survived the Eureka stockade. Married Granny, Marion Connelly, at Gulgong. That's where my father Sidney was born.' He glanced at the clock. 'Well, my love, time to stop magging. Better finish our garden fence. Wire netting will keep possums and kangaroos away.'

He removed boulders with a crow bar. Victor and Genn shifted smaller stones.

The plot dug, she added old manure. 'This improves the soil.'

They carried water from the creek.

Victor planted some seeds. 'When will they grow, Mummy?'

'Water them until they germinate. That's when they peep through the earth. Then we water them some more. In this heat, they'll soon dry out.'

Came the day when Victor shouted, 'Look, Mummy, leaves.' He daily inspected his climbing beans. Intrigued when they gripped timber stakes. Marvelling when flowers developed tiny beans.

Potatoes, sweetcorn, tomatoes, carrots and cucumbers went mad in the rich soil.

Joly grinned. 'A bumper crop.' He left for work on a property nearby.

A mutton stew simmered in the camp oven. Genn mused, Slow-cooking makes meat succulent and tender. I love the flavour. Ovens like hers had first arrived with settlers from England and Ireland. She wondered how long before they were produced in Australia. Her grandmother, Jane Victoria Stephens, née Vine, had used them. Genn imagined the effort it would have taken, feeding a family of eight adult children. Baking eighteen loaves of bread each week. Kneading the bread: once, twice, a third time. Her grandmother would have built up the heat with wood or bark, then let the fire burn down. With the bread risen in the oven, did Jane hang the oven on a low hook? Or let it stand on a bed of hot coals, with more heaped on top? How many batches did she make? She guessed there were multiple ovens.

Jane had cooked on an outside fire for years. In December 1911, her husband, James 1st, bought their first stove, probably a Christmas present. She pictured their excitement, the waiting for mortar to cure. Jane never got to use it. She died in her sleep, at only fifty-four. Genn wiped her eyes.

Two days later, her son Albert took ill. Nineteen, and in agony from appendicitis. The nearest doctor lived two days away. A neighbour took him the first twenty-five miles in a cart, over rutted road. Darkness forced them to stay overnight at Moonan Flat. The following day, Albert's cart jolted another thirty miles, bouncing through river crossings. At Scone, the neighbour stopped for a drink or three at the local pub, leaving Albert in the cart, semi-conscious. That afternoon, he reached hospital. The doctor postponed surgery. Perhaps he figured the boy was beyond help, The following morning, 13 December 1911, Albert died. His shocked father arrived too late. A sister miscarried her first child.

Genn's reverie erupted into clouds of smoke.

'Oh, no. No…'

Flames licked at bark near the fireplace, creeping around protective sheets of corrugated iron. A thrown dish of water sent acrid smoke around the cabin.

Genn lifted Dessie from her crib. 'Quick, Victor. Let's find Daddy.' She raced along the path. Her baby felt heavier by the second.

Victor whined, 'I'm tired. Carry me.'

'Just run, will you!'

He burst into tears. She'd never make it at this pace. An idea flashed into her mind. Risky, but she had no choice.

'Sit down, Victor.' She placed the sleeping baby beside him. 'Mind your sister. Mummy will be back.'

He whined, but sat, an arm around Dessie.

Genn ran as never before or since. Her lungs felt ready to burst. She screamed, 'Help!'

Joly dropped his mallet. 'What's…'

'Cabin. Fireplace on fire.'

He sprinted towards the hut. His mate Jack Rangers right at his heels.

Genn grimaced, a stitch in her side. Suppose the men arrived too late. She reached her children.

Victor lifted a tear-stained face. 'Mummy. You left me.'

She scooped up Dessie. 'Come along, Victor.' She raced off. He whimpered in her wake. 'Hurry, son.'

Plumes of smoke roiled above eucalypt. Her view was blocked. Suppose the fire had destroyed everything. She turned a corner. Shaking with relief. The walls were intact.

Jack and Joly stamped out flames on roof bark.

'Thank God you're all right. What can I do?'

'Keep the kids safe. We'll manage here.'

She soothed the wailing baby. Victor sat beside her on a log. The men rushed buckets of water from the creek. They poured it onto the smouldering bark.

Victor tugged at her sleeve. 'Mummy, let me join in the game?'

'Why not? Fetch your little bucket.'

The fire was finally extinguished. They coughed, faces, arms and clothing covered in soot.

In that awful moment of counting the cost, Joly shook his head. 'Roof's entirely gone. We'll rebuild the fireplace in corrugated iron. A spark must have lodged between the bark. And your lovely stew is charcoal. That's a major loss.'

They dissolved into gales of laughter. Remarkably, the calico ceiling had survived. Scorched here and there, it had prevented soot from covering everything in the cabin.

Her teeth jittered. 'Gosh, we're lucky. How'd you do it?'

'I'd secured the roof bark with twisted lengths of wire. It took seconds to slash through that.'

Jack nodded. 'We lifted the weights and poles. Whole thing came off.'

She said, 'We'll have to sleep in the tent for a while.'

Next day, they carefully removed screws, lifting down the calico. Genn insisted they tip the soot into containers. 'We can't let good potash go to waste. Perfect for the garden.'

Laughing, they washed the calico in a deep pool of the creek.

'We can't dry this over bushes, 'Joly said, 'Time for a wire clothesline.' He added strong props.

Genn patched the damaged calico on her Singer.

Joly replaced old rafters with new saplings. Humming, he stripped roof bark from nearby eucalypt. 'Aborigines used it to make gunyahs and canoes.'

Jack Rangers built the new fireplace. He cemented stones in place at the base. They replaced the calico ceiling.

At last, they could move back in.

Joly grinned. 'This calls for a celebration.'

He cooked huge flapjacks. Wide-eyed, Victor watched his father throw them up in the air. With a twist of the wrist, he flicked them over.

'Learnt that trick from an old Indian hawker. I was a boy not much older than you.'

Victor clapped his hands. 'Again, Daddy. Do it again.'

They spread the pancakes with honey. Joly was an expert at finding wild hives.

Geoff, Hilda and Richard came on a visit, shocked to hear of the family's near disaster. 'It's such good fortune Joly was nearby.'

Geoff said, 'Lucky you saved the castle.'

Genn laughed. 'Some folk might think living in a hut would be dreadful. But it's a quick sweep and whiz around with a duster. In ten minutes, the housework's done.'

Hilda nodded. 'And you get to spend time with the kids.'

They celebrated Dessie's first birthday at Hunters Springs on 20 June 1941. Nan brought out a sponge cake. Dessie buried her fist in the icing.

Nan laughed, 'After all my trouble. Wipe her hands and face, Genn. There's more cream on her cheeks than in her mouth.'

In October, Dessie wriggled from Genn's arms, toddling to her Nan. Hilda beamed delight. 'Well, I never. Walked right to me.'

Claps.

Joly grinned. 'She knows grannies are special.'

Hilda pulled a face at the 'grannies'. 'She took her time. Fourteen months.'

Rick said, 'Still, well done.'

Dessie's face was wreathed in smiles.

'I'm relieved she's finally taken off. They get heavy to carry.' Genn shot her son a proud glance. 'Of course, Victor walked at only nine months. He's so advanced. Aren't you, darling?'

Victor hid his face. Genn persuaded him to tell his Nan of anteaters, koalas and kangaroos, glimpsed on walks in the bush.

'My, oh my. You are a lucky boy.'

'We feasted on dewberries, gathered mushrooms. Plucked wild cress from Tomalla Creek. It's delicious on sandwiches, Mum.'

'We used to pick it when you were a kid.'

Victor tugged at her arm, 'Nan, we saw a big, big snake. It had a red belly. Kept shooting out its tongue.'

'Oh, dear. I hope you kept away.'

Genn shivered. 'It disappeared under rocks. To think how easily Victor might have been bitten.' He had clung to her, long after it had disappeared. Better not mention that. 'Reptiles have their use in nature, but not close to the house.'

Hilda nodded. 'Your father taught me how to handle a 0.22 rifle. Geoff was about two. He said, "Look, Mummy – honey." The movement of that brown snake did look liquid. But not for long.'

Genn laughed. 'Every woman in the bush must know how to handle a rifle.'

5

Joly closed his paper. 'For years, Curtin has wanted to strengthen defences. Australia has no modern aircraft, heavy bombers nor aircraft carriers. Just a few tanks. We'll be sitting ducks if the Japs invade.'

Genn bristled. 'That's not about to happen.'

'It's more likely every day.' Joly explained the Brisbane line. 'On invasion, north Queensland and the top half of Australia, would be ceded to the Japs. Only the southern half could be defended.'

'Saving half the population?' Genn spat out every words. 'It's unthinkable.'

'Better than losing the lot. In wartime, hard decisions have to be made. Women and kids have left already.'

The thought of foreign soldiers on their doorstep had her ready to scream. Thick glasses, swords. What sort of world would her children face?

On 7 December 1941, hundreds of Japanese fighters, bombers and torpedo planes attacked Pearl Harbour.

At Hunters Springs, Geoff looked shaken. 'The Yanks have declared war on Japan.'

Joly said, 'Imagine the buggers attacking, without provocation.'

'Let alone warning or declaration.' Rick set his jaw. 'They've sunk US battleships. Damaged cruisers and aircraft carriers. Hundreds of aircraft lost.'

Joly said, 'The death toll must be in the thousands. God knows how many are wounded.'

Hilda's eyes welled over. 'All those poor young men. Will this carnage ever end?'

Joly gave a helpless gesture. 'End? It's scarcely begun. But I fancy the Japs will get more than they bargained for from the Yanks.'

Talk of the sea and air war in the Pacific shivered around the table.

Rick drained his cup, 'Curtin's right. We want our boys home.'

Geoff bit hard on his slice of cake. 'I've admired Churchill...'

Joly frowned. 'But he's crazy to keep our 9th Division troops in the Middle East.'

'Leaving us unprotected.'

In January 1942, Joly learnt that Rabaul had been heavily bombed. 'We need a wireless, Genn. Reading about invasion would be too late.'

Geoff and Joly set a long aerial on a high pole, and made the connections. Oh, Victor's excitement.

Genn admired the veneered cabinet and fretwork over the speaker. 'My, look at that golden brown cloth.'

Power came from two car batteries. In foggy weather, voices edged between crackle and static.

Joly patted the cabinet. 'I'm glad we have it. But I'm guessing news is restricted to avoid panic.'

Soldiers on leave brought gossip. Civilians fled south, and carried truth as they saw it.

Afterwards, folk could never be sure about sources of information. Joly would recall something from the wireless, when it might have come from rumour, or the paper.

15 February 1942.

Joly said, 'Can you believe it? Singapore's fallen.'

Victor looked puzzled. 'How did it fall?'

Genn shook her head. 'Impregnable, they said.'

'Remember, my dear, the *Titanic* was also unsinkable.'

Curtin described the Singapore defeat as 'Australia's Dunkirk. It will be followed by the Battle of Australia.'

Genn gulped.

The sombre voice went on, 'Thousands of men have been taken prisoner in Malaya and Singapore.'

A voice said, 'One of the worst defeats of the British Army. Pearl

Harbour…Singapore…Malaya…Pacific Islands. New Guinea is under attack.'

Joly glanced up from the wireless. 'We'll be next.'

Her mouth lost every drop of moisture. 'Don't say such things. N-not in front of Victor.'

Dessie slept peacefully in her small cot. Genn felt like gathering them both in her arms, and growling, claws at the ready. An inner voice whispered, Worse is coming.

She shushed the intruder, saying aloud, 'It won't happen.'

Victor looked from one to the other. 'What's not going to happen, Mum?

'None of your business, young man. It's way past your bedtime.'

She thought, How do I sound so normal, with my nerves in tatters?

Joly held her close. 'Oh, sweetheart.'

On 19 February 1942, Darwin endured massive Japanese bombing raids. Authorities claimed minimal damage. Later, Broome and Wyndham were also bombed. Anxiety reached boiling point.

A headline screamed, 'A Blitz of the Worst Kind'.

Joly frowned. 'Contradicts what the government's saying. Mind you, the Darwin bombing is nothing compared to what London's endured.'

All Australian troop leave was cancelled.

'Bloody Japs are on their way. Doubtless the buggers have always had their eye on our country.'

Joly struggled to sort through rumours and half-truths. 'Some say the Jap attacks were carried out to reduce Allied air retaliation in their invasion of Timor. Others insist it's to do with Malaya.'

Curtin told Australians, 'No more looking away now. Fate has willed our position in this war.'

Joly clenched his fists. 'We've got to make plans. I'll get a pistol. We'll gather stocks of food.'

'And then?'

'We'll take the kids into the scrub. Hide in isolated ravines. Japs would never find us. There are oodles of rabbits. You're a whizz at cooking in the camp oven.'

Genn stamped her foot. 'Roughing it with our kids? You're mad. And who wants to eat rabbit every day?'

'We can't wait until the hordes arrive. We need an action plan.'

In March 1942, General Douglas MacArthur narrowly escaped from the Philippines. He arrived in Brisbane, setting up headquarters to manage the Pacific war.

Only a month later, Joly read that Roosevelt had made General Douglas MacArthur Commander of the Pacific.

Genn said, 'I'm glad he's organising our defences.'

Joly grinned. 'There's a lot of resentment in Queensland over the yanks. They're saying: Oversexed, over paid and over here.'

She giggled. 'That's terrible.'

'Our lads are envious of them. Tailored uniforms. Better pay. And they get the girls.' Joly grinned. 'Troops are making defensive roads and airfields up north. There are barbed-wire barricades around beaches. And they've planned demolition strategies to fend off invasion.'

Poppy spent the night. Small and cuddly, she laughed and teased the little ones. Dessie on her knee, she read the children stories. When they fell asleep Polly's fears shivered into the night.

'Isn't it odd? My Walt's off fighting on the other side of the globe. And here we sit, unprotected. Invasion expected any day.'

Joly sighed. 'Curtin's doing his best to bring the 9th Division home.'

'God bless him. And I can't wait to see Walt.'

At first light, the children crept into Poppy's tent. A wisp of moon hung low towards the horizon. The sky tried on peach, indigo and yellow. It settled on gold. The air resonated with song.

Poppy whispered, 'Listen to the dawn chorus. Birds have rehearsed all night.'

Dessie wriggled with excitement.

Victor played hide and seek. He hid in the smallest spots with shrieks of laughter at being found. 'Again, Auntie Poppy. Again.'

On a walk before breakfast, Dessie clung to Poppy's hand.

Genn smiled. 'You'll make a wonderful mother.'

'If I ever get a chance.'

Threat of invasion walked beside them on cool mornings. It hung on the hot midday air. Followed them to bed each night. Somewhere a dingo howled. In the light of a full moon, they glimpsed the big red predator.

Genn sighed. 'Nature knows nothing of our foolish human world.'

On rambles, Dessie toddled, leading Genn by her little finger. Victor collected everlasting daisies, bachelors' buttons, and red gum tips. The whisper of leaves and the fluting notes of a thrush took them far from threats and war.

Victor arranged the flowers.

Joly looked dreamy. 'Your gran, Florence, could never resist a bunch of gum tips. All they had in the bush.'

The little boy asked about Florence. Where did she live? When would he see her again?

Warners Bay seemed so far away. Keeping him amused, Genn almost forgot the danger their country was facing.

Joly turned on the wireless in May 1942. 'Battle of the Coral Sea. The Yanks have stopped the Japs taking Port Moresby, thank God.'

Genn shivered. 'The AIF troops are winning?'

'It looks like the Pacific war has turned our way.'

They hadn't long to celebrate. Mini subs invaded Sydney Harbour.

Joly gulped. 'Homes shelled. Right here in Australia. Not much damage. And only one unarmed merchant ship was sunk.'

'So there's nothing to stop…' Genn's teeth began to chitter. She rushed to check her sleeping children.

Joly took her in his arms, 'Oh, my darling.' There seemed nothing left to say. He unrolled an oiled cloth. Ensured his pistol was in working order.

Genn dreamt a Japanese soldier crept into the hut. She stabbed him with a pair of scissors. Blood covered her hands, dress… Torn between elation and despair, she shuddered at the prostrate body. *They've made me a killer.* For several seconds, in that twilight land between sleep and waking, horror clung to her. Images broke into fragments. Drifted away. Overwhelming relief.

Mother submarines shelled Sydney and Newcastle ports. In later years, it sounded unbelievable. But they heard the dull thud of explosions, right up in the Mount Royal Ranges.

Joly said, 'I'm told the Japanese have sank merchant ships. A lot of sailors are dead. The military have brought in convoys.'

'To protect them? Didn't they have them earlier?'

'It's easy, luv, to be wise after the event.'

Sailors fought the Battle of Midway in June 1942. Six months after Pearl Harbour and one month after the Battle of the Coral Sea.

Joly was exultant. 'The Jap navy has lost four aircraft carriers. Most of their fleet.'

General Macarthur said, 'The security of Australia is now assured, though the battle is far from over.'

The PM advised caution.

Joly said, 'Curtin's right. Our future isn't secure. Not until the Japs concede defeat.'

On 20 June 1942, Dessie turned two. A brief moment of elation fluttered like a ragged butterfly.

Stilled by Curtin's call: 'Australians must sacrifice peacetime things. Invasion is a menace capable hourly of becoming an actuality.'

Joly and Genn shared an anguished glance. A soldier told them of Japanese invasion currency, adding fuel to their fears. She sorted clothes to carry into the wilderness. The children's needs took priority. 'They grow so fast.'

He checked food stores and ammunition. 'We'll need enough for hunting and guerrilla warfare.' They were about to visit her parents. 'Let's wait to tell them.'

Dessie sat on Grandfather Stephen's lap. She stroked and kissed his shiny pate.

Hilda chuckled. 'Rick never left the house without a hat. Always self-conscious about his hair loss. Until this little one came along.'

Dessie stood on tiptoe. She peeped over the top of the kitchen table. Everyone clapped. 'What a big girl.'

When the children were older, they would wonder over Uncle Geoff's thin, weak voice. Joly told them, 'He suffered diphtheria as a child. Unkind people called him Squeaker.'

Churchill and Roosevelt were still finding excuses to keep the 9th Division in the Middle East.

By October 1942, Joly seethed. 'It's been twelve months. Australia needs battle-hardened troops now.'

Geoff read out Curtin's leaked cable. 'We look forward to the fulfilment of the understanding that the 9th Division shall be returned as soon as possible in the New Year.'

Poppy joined the family at Hunters Springs. They gathered around the Stephens's wireless. Poppy tickled Victor under the chin and tousled Dessie's straight blonde hair. They giggled.

Victor grabbed Dessie's rag doll. 'Nah, nah, nah…'

She burst into tears.

Genn said, 'Behave, you two.'

Rick turned up the volume. 'Japanese forces approach Singapore… Prime Minister Curtin has judged the threat to Australia grave. In a New Year message, he alerted Australians to the danger. Australia now looks to America, free of any pangs to our traditional links of kinship with the United Kingdom.'

Hilda paled. 'America? Britain's our mother country.'

'That may be,' Joly's face was grim. 'But I fancy Churchill has enough on his plate, defending England.'

Poppy looked sombre. 'He doesn't care about us.'

Joly looked up from the wireless. 'It's been weeks. Now Churchill's badgering Curtin to divert the 9th Division to Burma.'

'Burma?' Genn blinked. 'Curtin mustn't let us down.'

Nan brought her grandchildren home-made biscuits. Offered slices of cake. It was considered gross neglect of housewifely duties to serve bought ones. The youngsters loved being fussed over.

She showed them her paintings. Victor liked the one of highland cattle, with lots of purple and pink along the path.

Dessie's favourite was of dicky birds, chests puffed up, seated on branches. 'Nan, are they feather trousers?'

Hilda laughed. 'I do believe you're right.'

She gave the children paper and coloured pencils. Victor drew an image of a plane crashing in flames,

Dessie beamed over her scribbles. 'Look at mine.'

Nan smiled. 'I love your drawings.'

Later, Genn said to Joly, 'If…if invasion does happen…we'll pretend to the kids it's a big adventure.'

He hugged her. 'Good girl. Victor would love that. And, you know, rabbits wouldn't be our only fare. Though the humble bunny did save many lives during the Depression.'

Genn imagined life on the run. The water aglow with sunset, golden insects on the rise. A big freshly caught rainbow trout. Grilled over a slow fire, in Joly's contraption made from number eight fencing wire. The delicious aroma. With luck, she might serve it with wild mushrooms, cooked on a hot stone. And maybe a few boiled new potatoes? Life on the run mightn't be so bad.

A large part of their diet already came from the bush. Kangaroo tails made delectable soup, and the steaks were delicious. Baked wood pigeons were a real treat. And local streams abounded with native perch and eels.

'We'd forego luxuries like bread. But I could make damper,' said Genn. The ingredients were simple enough to carry on horseback. Flour, baking powder and a sprinkle of salt. 'Cooked in the coals, it's scrumptious.'

Yes, indeed, they'd do very well in the bush. But she mustn't worry her mother. Not yet.

Soldiers returned from New Guinea. Gaunt spectres of their former selves, veterans wore tattered uniforms and gaping boots, some wrapped in wire. Tales of near starvation brought tears to Genn's eyes.

'Bullets are far from their only risk up there. Tropical diseases like malaria and dysentery wreak havoc. And scrub typhus is said to be a death sentence. Not to mention tropical ulcers. Destroy flesh right to bone and sinew. Doctors use maggots to eat the rotting flesh.'

She blinked, 'Surely not?'

'Sounds horrible, but they work. I pity the poor beggars in the quagmire of Kokoda track. Fungal diseases, pulpy, bleeding feet.'

Pictures in the paper of Fuzzy Wuzzy Angels brought a glow to Genn's eyes. 'Those stretcher bearers show our men wonderful kindness. Goodness knows the number of lives they've saved.'

Victor wanted to know all about the tribesmen.

'They're heroes to our men on the battlefield.' Joly turned to Genn, 'Nurses put plaster on soldier's foreheads, with the date and time of morphine injections. Prevents the risk of overdose.'

'Sounds a wise precaution.'

On Saturday nights, Joly hummed as he filled a large round tub with hot water. He placed it beside the fire. The children were first to be dunked.

Genn briskly applied a washer to ears and necks. She towelled Victor dry. Did the same for Dessie. 'Time for bed, kids.'

Joly went last. By then, the bathwater was rather on the grey side.

In summer, a pool between ferny banks of the creek made a perfect spot to bathe. The family splashed and soaped each other. Their little ones squealed with delight and laughter, naked bodies slippery as young seals. Flakes of golden light fell all around. The adults emerged full of laughter and chatter.

Joly and Geoff's debates on communism leapt and flamed. But Joly and his brothers followed the faith of dialectical materialism.

Geoff asked, 'What the devil's dialectical materialism?'

'Buggered if I know. But Marx and Engels reckon it's to do with the rights of the working man. We're lucky to have Stalin on our side. He'll bring the proletariat a brighter future.'

'Hang on there, Joly. Stalin's into mass murder.'

'Don't believe that, mate. Capitalist propaganda.'

On one matter, the men did agree: Russian victories had changed the fortunes of war.

Geoff said, 'The Battle of Stalingrad turned the European campaign the Allies' way.'

'Indeed. The Ruskies lured Nazis towards the Caspian Sea. Encircled them. Hitler insisted that the Wehrmacht remain in the city to break the deadlock. The Red Army held out for over five months.'

'Yes – says here, from 23 August 1942 to 2 February 1943. They exhausted Axis ammunition, food and men. The few remaining troops of the 6th Army surrendered. It's the Nazis' most catastrophic defeat since 1918.'

Genn knitted a jumper, bored with political discussions. She was relieved when Geoff went on his way and Joly returned to work. Delighted to see Poppy.

They shared tips on cooking, sewing and gardening. Punctuated with Poppy's hoots of laughter.

'From the moment I gave birth to Victor, I guessed it would be impossible to love another baby as much.'

Poppy glanced towards the little blonde girl. It beggared belief that her friend seemed proud of the remark.

Genn went on, 'The games kids play. Victor put Dessie's hand on a rock. Hit it with a hammer.'

Poppy looked incredulous. 'I'd have tanned his jolly hide.'

'Her screams brought me running. Victor stood there, every inch the culprit, saying, "Dessie hit her hand real hard." The front of her white dress dripped red. I was terrified Joly would arrive home early. He'd think Dessie had a major injury.'

'Whatever was Victor thinking? Is there much damage?'

Genn looked defensive. ' Victor is only five. Boys experiment. He hadn't meant to hurt her. I explained it's wicked to hit anyone. Let alone with a hammer.' Dessie toddled over. 'Here, luv, show Poppy your finger. Joint's a bit iffy. It works, though.'

'No thanks to Victor, eh?'

Dessie's second and index fingers were off-centre towards their tips. Poppy doubted they'd ever be straight again.

'The other day, Victor caught Dessie's hand in a rabbit trap.'

'Little beggar must be jealous.'

'Oh, no. Not Victor. Too many bright ideas. Dessie wasn't hurt. I gave him a smack. Hated doing it.'

'And not before time, I'd say.'

'Have I told you about Dessie's exotic tastes? Wood beetles. Such a pungent odour. Imagine the flavour.'

'You'll put me off having kids.'

'Everything goes in her mouth. Black ones with wattles are my worry. They're toxic.'

'What makes you say that?'

'Mum's cat died after eating one. And one old tom was paralysed for hours.'

'It's a wonder any kid survives. I don't know whether to thank you or thump you for telling me all that. When's Joly expected home?'

'About six. He's having a drink with Jack Rangers, after work.'

'Good for him. Well, I'd best be off.'

Genn waved. The buggy lurched from sight.

6

Genn fed the children. Read them a bedtime story. She imagined Joly swapping tales with Jack. Eight o'clock. She frowned. One drink, he'd said. Why does he do this to me? Alone with the kids. Her food went down in lumps.

Beauty would lurch along the rough track, missing trees by inches. Genn wrung her hands. A moonlit night, thank goodness. Nine o'clock came and went. At ten, she heard the creak of leather. Joly swung to the ground. Slipped the saddle and bridle off the snorting horse. Trod an unsteady path to the door.

'You reek of beer. And your tea's ruined.'

He swayed. 'Jack filled my glass when I wasn't looking.'

'When is it ever your fault? I'm off to bed.' She slipped on a hand-embroidered calico nightdress. Tears crept under her closed lids.

One boot fell, another. The sound of splashing.

Joly bumped into the cabin. 'Whoa, there!' He slipped off his trousers, put on pyjama bottoms. Slumped into bed. Reached out. 'Sorry, Genn.'

'Oh, go to sleep.' She turned her back.

Joly snored beside her. Normal folk could leave it at one or two drinks. Why couldn't he?

Next morning, Joly brought her a mug of tea, hands shaking. 'Won't happen again, luv.'

She raised her eyebrows. 'How often have I heard that one?'

'Sweetheart, I've said I'm sorry.'

Poppy's buggy stopped outside. A beaming smile. 'My little rat's finally coming home.'

Joly said, 'Marvellous. We've waited ages for this.'

Victor tugged at Poppy's skirt. 'I don't like rats. In Grandfather's shed, one bit my finger. Is it a real rat, Auntie Poppy?'

'Afraid, not, sweetie. A bad man called Rommel tried to insult Uncle Walt and his mates. Called them rats.'

Joly told Victor the troops had adopted the title. 'It's a badge of honour to be called a Rat of Tobruk. Uncle Walt and the boys spent their days holed up in desert trenches, and tunnels. They held out against Rommel's Afrika Corps. Longest siege in British history. Uncle Walt is a very brave man.' His face blazed with admiration. 'Men like him keep our country safe.'

Poppy pulled a creased photograph from her handbag, for the children. They glimpsed a soldier in uniform. Crooked teeth, wide grin.

Poppy's face glowed. 'My Walt.'

Victor scampered off to play, Dessie at his heels.

Joly laughed. 'Who would have thought? My mate Walt famous. You must feel very proud.

'Oh, I am – not that I'd tell him. I wouldn't want a husband with a swelled head.'

Genn laughed. 'Hardly. How long before he's home?'

'It's all hush-hush. But the 9th Division is expected soon.'

'I can't wait.' Joly lapsed into a moment's silence. 'The Lord only knows what the poor bugger's endured.'

Victor asked about the war. Dessie seemed oblivious to it all.

Victor told her, 'Japs are on the way. They'll slash your neck. All your blood will come out.' He made a choking noise, clutching his throat.

Dessie burst into tears.

Genn glowered. 'Stop your silly stories.'

He shot Dessie a sly glance. 'She's a baby. Cries over anything.'

'That's quite enough.'

Midnight. Sobs from the tent. Genn's torch flashed a path to

Dessie's side. A halting, tear-splotched tale of sword-brandishing soldiers.

'Hush, darling. You've had a nasty dream.'

Oh, for Joly to build their home. Have the kids sleep indoors. She straightened the covers, patting Dessie until her eyes closed.

Walt arrived on leave. He and Poppy dropped by. Joly was shocked by his pallor and weight loss. Genn felt every rib when they embraced.

Walt coughed. 'Began to think I'd never see you again.'

Joly shared a man-hug, concerned when talk of gold didn't even raise a smile.

Poppy whispered to Genn, 'He's absolutely depleted. Severe arthritis gives him gyp.'

Walt told of a swim in the Red Sea. 'We were bitten by crabs, but the water was good. You should have seen the magnificent sunsets. The water went from light green to pink, a glow reflected from the desert. Then came purple. In the moonlight, it turned to blue and silver. Never saw anything so grand before. Ships at anchor looked like toys.' For a few moments, the sparkle returned to his eyes.

They made their farewells.

Joly shook his hand. 'You'll be right, mate. You need a good rest.'

Walt nodded. Poppy flicked the reins and the buggy swayed away.

They met almost every week.

Walt's leave ended. He had gained weight, but looked weary.

Poppy sighed. 'He's not well – but it's not up to me. The doctor gave him clearance.'

'Shush, woman. There's a job to finish.' Walt squeezed her hand, a glimpse of his old self in his grin. 'It's north Queensland for jungle training. Then, off to New Guinea to mop up the Japs.'

Joly said, 'Look, old man, you've done more than your fair share. If you aren't fit...'

A wild look rushed into Walt's eyes, 'Must join me mates. Can't let them down.' And so it was that Walt left for the Atherton Tablelands.

Some of the 9th Division went on to Borneo. Walt joined those in New Guinea. He fought at Milne Bay.

Poppy wrote to Walt's new address. 'I miss him terribly. Laughter keeps him going. It's the same for me. By the way, I'm told congratulations are in order.'

'Thanks, Poppy. Yes, I've nabbed the place at Kangaroo Tops. We couldn't be happier.'

Joly pitched their tents. Grinning, he paced out the dimensions of their slab home. Gave her a smacking kiss. 'A place of our own.'

'It's perfect.'

They named it Wallaby Farm. Joly gazed toward scrub and eucalypts. 'A lot of clearing to be done. We'll plant lucerne and clover.'

'Our Herefords will win prizes one day.'

Joly said, 'Let's celebrate, attend the next dance. What do you think?'

'Wonderful. We haven't been out for ages.'

Joly whistled. He selected a tree. 'Timber for our home.' The light of dreams shone from his face.

Genn watched, mesmerised. Stripped to the waist, his muscles rippled with each blow of his axe. Those calloused hands rarely suffered blisters. His glance brought that old wobble to her tummy. 'Stand back.'

She took the children's hands. The huge eucalypts groaned as they thudded to earth. In the cloud of dust and broken branches, a host of bush creatures fled.

Dessie clung to her. Victor had eyes only for his father's best axe.

'You're not to touch it, son.' By and by seemed far away.

He assembled Genn's Singer machine, carried there on a packhorse. In her box of remnants, she found a lovely blue fabric, perfect for a blouse. Genn sang as she cut out fronts, back, sleeves and pieces for the collar. Sang as she pedalled away at the machine. Sang as she made buttonholes by hand, and sewed on buttons.

On dance night, she slipped on her new blouse. Yet to button it, Genn made to pin a plait around her head, dropping the bobby pins. In bending to retrieve them, the plait slipped between her breasts.

Joly eyed her cleavage. 'My…you really look something.'

The dance hall loomed out of darkness. Victor and Dessie giggled as they slid back and forth on the polished floor. Youngsters squatted on their haunches, eager hands pulling them along.

Dessie squealed. 'It's my turn.'

A pianist, two fiddlers and a bones man launched into the music. Joly and Genn enjoyed a waltz. The number finished. Their young ones grizzled on the sidelines.

'Come along, kids. You're tired.'

In an annexe, Victor's eyes kept shutting. 'I'm not sleepy.'

Dessie yawned. 'Neither am I.'

'Nevertheless, lie down.' Genn tucked in the blankets, settling them among other children lying on the floor.

She returned to the hall. Where was Joly? A tightness gripped her throat. Surely he wasn't outside, drinking?

She noticed Stella, a young neighbour. The lass sat alone, wilting like a tired rosebud. Had her boyfriend stood her up? Memory flashed back to another girl, another dance.

Genn had been seventeen. After the quickstep, Joly had disappeared. Other beaux clustered around fiancées and sweethearts. She bit back tears. Joly's brother, Bill, asked her for a waltz. He confided, 'One drink and Joly can't stop.' He proved evasive about Joly's whereabouts. Joly had staggered up for the last dance. Barely able to stand, let alone dance. Profound regrets. Begging for a second chance…

And now, the 'Pride of Erin' was in full swing. Oh, the laughter and carefree chatter, the flirting and fun. Stella looked forlorn. Genn imagined the sting behind her eyes, that pain in her chest. As for me…is history about to repeat itself?

She frowned. Joly ignored me when I was a girl. It's not about to happen now. I'm his wife.

A touch on her shoulder. Joly grinned. 'I've been chatting with Jack. Dance?'

She snuggled into his arms, longing to run her hands through his red hair. The moon slipped from behind clouds. Her evening was saved.

Genn saw Stella checking the time.

'You're the prettiest girl in the room.' Joly's eyes lingered on the thrust of her bosoms, under the thin fabric of her blouse.

She blushed. 'Joly. Behave.'

'I'm the luckiest man alive.'

They shared half a dozen dances. Strains of the 'Vienna Waltz' drifted across the paddocks. It mingled with calls of night birds. In the crowded hall, whistles, calls for an encore.

Genn said, 'Stella has boyfriend troubles tonight. Ask her for a dance.'

He glanced her way. 'Are you sure?'

'Of course.'

Stella flushed. 'But what about you? I couldn't...'

'Nonsense. I feel a wee bit tired. Let me sit this one out.'

The pair whirled away. She felt pleased to see a smile return to Stella's lips. *Tired* every second dance for the rest of the evening.

Stella sparkled. Cheeks pink with exertion. 'Thank you both so much. It's been lovely.'

Genn shrugged. 'You've done me a favour.'

Joly collected the sleepy children. Draped the rugs around them. Lit the lanterns. And untied the horse. They set off in the frosty darkness. Every star tinkled like bells. The moon guided them on their way.

They put the children into their beds.

Genn's eyes sparkled. 'My best evening for ages.'

Joly clasped her, his face aglow. 'That was kind of you tonight. Even if the gossips do say I've romanced a younger woman.'

She laughed. 'Let them talk. Who cares?'

Lips crushed hers. His hand slid inside her nightie, his voice was husky. 'I adore you.'

She trembled. His hands caressed her bare skin. Cupped her buttocks, her inside thigh... Genn felt sudden, overwhelming desire. Tossed aside her nightdress. Underwear followed. The rhythm of their bodies became one. Transcendence. The very hair follicles on her head tingled.

Joly let out a great, sigh. 'Oh, my darling. My dearest, sweetest wife.'
They fell into deep slumber.

Joly juggled construction of their slab house with paid jobs. The Hardy brothers occupied a large shed on their property, Greenfield.

Slowly, slowly the Wright dwelling took shape.

Genn smiled. 'What I've always wanted, a big kitchen and pantry.' Two bedrooms. 'The kids will sleep indoors at last.' She greeted Joly with pencil and paper. 'I've extension plans.'

He looked startled. 'Extensions? Steady on, luv. Give a man time to draw breath.'

Wallaby Farm had drawbacks. They relied on neighbours for emergency medical help. Luckily, Genn thought nothing of a fourteen-mile ride to the main road, and back. A packhorse carried home mail and groceries.

The Hardy brothers offered Joly more work. Progress slowed on their house.

Genn stamped her foot. 'Ours isn't even half-finished. And you run off to help others.'

'It's an income, luv.' The brothers assessed his woodworking skills. 'Their builder took apart a weatherboard cottage in the lowlands. He refuses to work here. They've offered me a contract to rebuild.'

'You won't take it?'

He avoided her eyes. 'This is our chance to save. Not a fortune, but more than I could make at Wallaby Farm.'

'You might damn well have asked me first.'

She missed her period, barely a month after the dance. Was it punishment for the child who never was? She burnt with shame.

Joly looked perplexed. 'Why are you upset, sweetheart? We both love kids. We'll need labour for Wallaby Farm. We can afford...'

'It's not about the money, Joly. I'm just...not ready to be pregnant.'

'You won't...do anything silly?'

Tears welled in her eyes. 'Don't.'

During her fifth month, Genn shopped in Scone. Conversations were abruptly terminated.

One woman smirked. 'I hear your husband was very taken with Stella at the dance.'

She seethed.

'People say things. They think you had an affair.'

'While they're gossiping about us, luv, some other poor bugger is being left alone.'

Genn brushed Dessie's hair until it shone. She kept the children immaculate. Poor they might be, but nobody could criticise her for neglect.

Joly completed the Hardy cottage. Genn hadn't long to feel pleased.

The Hardy brothers made another offer. 'Work on our place for three pounds per week. Your wife can help with housekeeping and cooking.'

'Care for them – with a new baby? I thought we were settled here.'

'So did I, sweetheart. So did I.' He rested his big hands on her shoulders. 'This income will put us on our feet.'

'A shared house? Conflict, misunderstandings…'

'It won't be as bad as you think, sweetheart.'

In old age, Joly told Dessie, 'No extra wages were offered for your mother. It stuck in my craw. And I'd realised my dreams of Wallaby Farm were just that. A man must have been mad to think anyone could make a go of that scrubby place. Using nothing but an axe, saw, mattock, and brute strength.'

He packed their belongings into Geoff's Bedford.

Genn took a last, nostalgic walk around the slab house. Gazed towards the valley and creek, the tree ferns and wildlife. 'We…we won't need to leave our little home for good?'

'What could I say?' Joly sighed. 'I saw heartbreak in every line of your mother's body.'

At Greenfield, Geoff exclaimed, 'Splendid job, Joly. From slab house to weatherboard cottage. You could set up as a carpenter.'

He laughed. 'It's easy when you have all the pieces cut and marked.'

Victor and Dessie ran into the future, the wind at their backs. They made aircraft noises, spinning their arms like propellers. Shrieking delight, they rolled over and over down a grassy knoll. Climbed back up and did it again. Peered into the shed, aromatic with hay, leather and horses. Checked the hen house.

Genn lumbered around on an inspection. Wide front veranda, big yard. Four bedrooms and two sleepouts. A large living-dining area, and a washroom-cum-laundry. She thought, Linoleum's easily mopped. But a lot more housework.

She told Hilda, 'You should see my kitchen and fuel stove. I can cook anything. And loads of eggs for baking cakes and puddings.'

In her sixth month of pregnancy, Genn tired easily. 'I never stop. No time for walks with the kids. I miss my independence.'

Joly hugged her. 'Let's stay until we get our heads above water.'

Part Two

Dessie's Story

7

I felt excited by our lovely, big house.

Mum said, 'Don't be silly, Dessie. This house isn't ours.'

The Hardy brothers were different as lard and trees. Jim was polite and serious. Always Mr Hardy, even to Mum. Hunter, the younger, told us to use his nickname. Pinkie.

I asked, 'Why Pinkie?'

'When I was a tiny baby, mother called my toes pinkies. I've been Pinkie ever since.' He grinned, 'Call me anything you like. So long as it's not late for dinner. Now you know my secret, Blondie. Don't tell anyone, will you?'

'My name's Dessie.'

'Blondie's my nickname for you.

I liked his plump cheeks and merry eyes.

'When you grow up, Blondie, I'll marry you.'

His words made me embarrassed. I didn't know why.

Still, as Mum told Poppy, 'It's wonderful the way Pinkie plays with the kids. Keeps them amused for ages.'

I enjoyed his game of Two Little Dickie Birds Sitting on the Wall. Victor, almost seven, loved it just as much.

Pinkie's shoulders were the wall. He made the birds from paper, sticking them on with spit.

'One called Peter, the other called Paul. Fly away Peter, fly Away Paul.'

It took ages for me to guess his secret. His left, and then his right index finger, hid them somewhere behind his shoulders. We joined in the chorus, Two little dickie birds…

He showed me the bare tips of his fingers.

I puzzled over how the paper Dickie Birds had flown away.

'Do you want them to fly back?'

We screamed, 'Yes.'

'Well, call them.'

I shouted for Peter, and the bird fluttered back.

Victor called back Paul, and there he was.

Daddy glazed cottage windows. Globs of putty fell to the ground. The rooster gobbled them.

'Shoo, you stupid bird.' He threw pebbles. 'Off with you. Chase him away, kids.'

The rooster ran off, squawking.

Daddy groaned. 'Silly bugger. It'll harden inside him. I must finish the garden fence. Keep the chooks out.'

Mum called us for lunch. We left the rooster scratching for worms.

Our meal finished, I slipped outside. The rooster lay on his back, eyes half-closed. He feebly flapped his wings, emitting terrible squawks.

'Quick, Mum. Kill the rooster before he dies.'

The adults laughed. 'There goes our Christmas dinner.'

Poppy drove up in her buggy. Walt was off fighting the Japs in New Guinea. She looped the bridle over a gatepost, and introduced two young cousins. 'John and Helen.'

We rarely saw other children. Victor hung back. I examined the ground.

Poppy chuckled, 'Don't be shy, kids. They won't bite.'

Mum rode up on Dolly, her favourite horse.

Poppy narrowed her eyes. 'I'm surprised to see your mum in the saddle.'

Victor looked puzzled. 'Why, Auntie Poppy?'

She tousled his hair.

Mum dismounted with difficulty.

On the veranda, Poppy helped remove her riding boots.

'Here's a box of plums for you, Genn.'

Poppy handed around lamingtons and slices of sponge cake. Poured cordial. Asked, 'And how are your imaginary friends?'

I told her of Oliver, Jemima, Lamp Spider and the others. 'Lamp Spider is horrid. But he always hangs around.'

'Ah, yes. He's a bully. But Jemima will know how to deal with his sort. Now your mum and I want to chat. I'm sure you have a lot to show John and Helen.'

Mum grinned. 'It's a lovely day outside.'

Imaginary playmates were fun. But how could we amuse real ones?

Victor scuffed his foot in the dust. 'Want to see our ant lions, John?'

'Ant lions? Does your father keep them in a cage or something? What do you feed them?'

Helen hung back. 'Are they big?'

Victor laughed. 'You'll see.'

We crawled under the house, at the edge of the veranda.

Victor pointed to cone-shaped holes. 'Soil's riddled with 'em. The ant lions use these traps catch to catch ants.' He unearthed one of the tiny insects.

John's face fell. 'That's all they are?'

'Wait. It's fun. You'll see.'

Victor picked up an ant. He placed it at the edge of a cone. It hurtled down the slippery slope. Brutal jaws battled to the death.

John shouted for a go.

Shrieks of laughter.

Mum yelled, 'You kids aren't playing under the house again? I've had enough of washing filthy clothes.'

Helen counted to ten. Victor hid among wattles on the hill. She found him, hidden by tall grass. Squeals and giggles. I squeezed into a small space under a bush. Scratchy twigs. I hardly dared breathe. Found! Screams of excitement.

Victor asked, 'Who's for an egg hunt?'

Helen pushed aside a large tussock. Her eyes widened. 'Oh, look! Six eggs. Mum buys hers from shop.'

I giggled. 'Hens love secret nests.'

Victor found one young hen, among stiff tussocks. 'She won't use Daddy's boxes.' Loud clucks of anger. 'She's hatching chicks.'

I said, 'Mum says chooks make fine meals for foxes. We lock them up at night.'

Victor stood very tall. 'I'll bring her back to the pen.'

He slid a hand underneath the broody hen, grabbing her legs. She flapped, and squawked.

Helen hung back, afraid she might be pecked.

Victor laughed. 'She won't hurt you. Boy! She's hot from sitting on her eggs.'

John felt her body. 'Golly. She's almost on fire.'

Victor shoved the hen inside a chook pen. 'A few days, and she'll forget about being broody.'

I laughed. He sounded exactly like Mum.

We raced inside for snacks. Helen wriggled excitement. 'I saw an ant lion. We played hide-and-seek. And...and Victor showed us a broody hen. That's when the mother hatches her chicks. And guess what, Auntie Poppy? I found six eggs! Under a tussock!'

'Never! How wonderful.'

Victor said, 'I'm dying of thirst.'

Mum went to get up.

Poppy put a hand on her shoulder. 'No, no, Genn. Let me.'

We drained glasses of cordial.

She turned to Victor, 'Guess you're excited about the new baby?'

He looked puzzled.

Mum frantically signalled for silence.

Shadows gathered. Paddocks bathed in golden light.

'I best make tracks.' Poppy gathered up her things.

Daddy strode into the kitchen. 'Poppy, great to see you. Helen and John, too.'

Mum packed her six eggs.

Daddy laughed. 'Make it a dozen, luv. We have plenty. And soon we'll have tomatoes and cucumbers for you, Pops.'

Poppy winked at Mum. 'Keep well, dear. Won't be long now.'

They embraced. John and Helen hesitated, hand in hand.

'Come on, kids. Hop in the buggy.'

John frowned. 'Ahh, must we go?'

Poppy chuckled. 'Come right away, or you'll get a flogging. Isn't that right, Uncle Joly?'

'I reckon.'

Poppy stashed their offerings in the vehicle. She flicked the reins. Her laughter mingled with the jingle of harness.

At last Mum broke her news.

I made no connection between her blossoming figure and the coming infant. Telling Pinkie, 'Mum's buying a new brother or sister.'

'Really? What do you think of that, Blondie?'

I shrugged.

'They cry a lot, I'm told.'

Crying babies sounded about as much fun as lavatory visits on dark nights.

It stood a long way from the house. A torch flickered me past the expanse of shadows and queer shapes. Unknown to me, Victor had hidden behind a tree.

He jumped out. 'Waahhhh!'

I leapt into the air, bolting for the house. My skin and clothes raced to catch up. 'V-Victor sc-scared me.'

'That's not funny, Victor. Never do that again.'

Another image. Galloping hooves, shadowy horses. Me cowering in the darkness. Was it a dream, or an overactive imagination? One thing I was sure about: Mum's concept of discipline.

She grabbed a leather belt. My misdeed was long forgotten.

'Don't hit me, Mum. I'll strap myself.' I couldn't bear inflicting physical pain. The strap barely touched my legs. 'Oh, what's the use of that? Put some sting into it.'

She brought the weapon down hard. Once, twice, thrice. My legs throbbed. The horror of the moment lurked in my subconscious.

Decades later, I would awake, sobbing, suspended by barbed wire. Vicious hounds bit at heels. Mum's voice, 'Hand me that strap.'

I woke, overjoyed to find myself safe in bed. Realising I was an adult, and in hospital, following the arrival of my first child.

Greenfield cottage erupted into turmoil, and over another birth.

In March 1944, Daddy telephoned Uncle Geoff. Mum's new baby was ready to be picked up. She caught her breath. My excitement was tinged with fear.

'What's up, Mum?'

I fancy she gritted her teeth.

'I'm fine.'

Mum told Dad, 'Don't forget my dressing gown. And bathroom things.' She reminded me, 'Use your toothbrush. And Victor, be good for Nana.' A hug and she was gone, along with Victor.

Uncle Geoff drove Mum to Scone. I guessed doctors kept babies at the hospital.

Aunt Lydia Rangers minded me. She proved to be kind, but I missed my mum. If I cried, she read me a story. Her nephew, Tony happened to be staying. He played Dominoes, Fiddlesticks or Snakes and Ladders.

Big Jack Rangers had brown skin and frizzy hair. 'It's all right, sweetie. You'll soon be home.'

It seemed ages. Later, I learnt it had only been two weeks.

Daddy told them us we had a little sister. I jiggled excitement.

We found Mum at Brancaster Private Hospital. Her beaming smile reminded me of a mother cat with kittens.

The sister handed Vivi to Mum. 'You have a lovely baby. Fat as butter.' She unwrapped the shawl.

I stared in wonderment.

'Eight pounds. What a whopper.' Dad gave Mum a hug.

A lifetime later, Mum would confide, 'I never had any problem raising two children. Three made a huge difference.' Cooking meals and baking bread for four adults and three children, while keeping a large house and minding a new baby couldn't have been easy.

In retrospect, I wondered, did she find time to bond with Vivi?

Mum told Poppy, 'Fortunately, Vivi's a good baby. Hardly cries at all.'

My sister's toothless gums were cute. I worried to see her at the breast.

'It doesn't hurt at all. In fact, I like it. You did this once.'

I looked askance. 'Me? Surely not?'

Oldies listened to the sombre tones of Big Ben on the wireless.

On 6 June 1944, A serious voice, 'This is the British World Service. Allies invade northern France.'

The Hardy brothers and Daddy huddled and worried. He glanced at the newspaper. 'A lot's censored. You have to read between the lines.'

Reading between the lines sounded very clever. I squinted hard, but only saw rows of print. One day soon I'd read like adults.

Victor looked anxious. 'Is there always a war?'

'It should end soon.'

'But what do the papers write about when there isn't one?'

Adults laughed.

A memory stirs. Daddy silhouetted in the lantern light at a cabin door. One of the few times we kids were up early. For two weeks every winter at Greenfield, Daddy took his annual holidays: trapping rabbits on a nearby property. Before dawn, he'd take a quick breakfast. Saddle Beauty. Kiss Mum, Victor and me. Vivi was usually asleep. Man and horse were gulped by the gloom.

Years later I asked Daddy about it.

'Lots of blokes went rabbiting for fun and extra income in those days. Few tackled terrain like mine. My mare and I picked our way down a vertiginous mountainside. It was almost too steep for man or beast. Pack bags bulged with traps.' By the third day, Beauty would be exhausted. 'I walked, leading her. Needed a stronger animal.'

He shook his head. 'Where did a man find the strength? Weighed down with heavy bags of traps.' His size eleven hobnailed boots slipped and slid down the tortuous trails worn by animals. 'On the valley floor, it took me most of the day to set out the traps. I ran three trails consecutively. Each about fifty yards apart. Traps were placed at the entrance to about twenty burrows, hidden under a sprinkle of earth.'

When activity ceased in one warren, he dug the entrances closed. 'Made it easy to catch ones I'd missed. Began new trails. Cleared whole paddocks. Afternoon, I ate mutton sandwiches. Drank a cup of strong, sweet tea. Quickly retraced my steps, to reduce the animals' suffering.' He collected four or five bodies, in hessian bags, a heavy load. 'Skinned them, and discarded the carcasses.'

He sighed. 'A terrible business. Terrible. Gentle creatures. The thought of it keeps me awake at night. But I had no time to dwell – the things a man does to survive. A last flashlight inspection of the traps. Struggling up the mountain after dark, I carried up to a hundred skins on my back – I'd given Beauty a break. Made fifty or sixty pounds for the fortnight. A fortune compared to my usual pay.'

Mum would take us exploring. She held my hand, Vivi in a sling on her back. Victor skipped along beside us. A nest squawked with wattlebird chicks, hungry beaks wide open. 'See, the mummy and daddy birds feed their young. Stay very quiet and still. Mustn't frighten them.'

The chicks gobbled a meal of insects. Their parents flew off to gather further supplies. We moved on. Leaves crackled underfoot. A dart of lizards.

Vivi cut her first tooth at five months. Mum rubbed lemon juice on her gums to ease pain. At six months, Vivi mouthed her first word, 'Mum'. 'The rest of you started with Dad.'

A problem of my own started about then. Was it insecurity at my changed place in the family? Or fear of visits to the outside loo at night? I wet the bed. Shame and embarrassment. Everyone knew how to solve my problem except me.

Mum frowned. 'If it doesn't stop, you'll have to wear nappies.'

The problem ceased as suddenly as it began. By October, adults had other matters on their minds.

News shivered around the cottage in November 1944. I vaguely heard of the American raid. Long-range B29 aircraft dropped strategic bombs on Japan.

Snatches of conversation. Daddy said, 'The Japs have fled Allied forces in the Pacific.'

Victor asked what 'strategic' meant.

Daddy said, 'With a bit of luck the end might be sight.'

Mum saying it was about time. 'War's been going on since before Dessie was born. I can't wait to see relatives and friends arrive home.'

8

Mum supervised Victor's lessons. Buff-coloured packets arrived weekly from the Blackfriars Correspondence School in Sydney. I longed for it to be my turn.

'Can't Victor come out to play?' I tapped my fingers on the table.

'Will you stop that noise? Get your colouring book. Draw some pictures. Play with Vivi.'

Mum washed nappies, baby clothes and linen. Ironed tablecloths, cooked and cleaned. I watched her sew or patch Daddy's work clothes, make curtains and dresses. She weeded the vegetable garden, too.

Wiping wisps of hair from her moist brow, she said, 'I'm worn out.'

'I can see that, sweetheart. Soon we'll move on.'

'It can't be soon enough for me.' She spoke of Pinkie's kindness. 'He's first on his feet after meals. "Don't worry about the washing up, missus. I'll do it."'

Daddy lent a hand with the tea towel. Victor and I stacked clean dishes. And Pinkie wasn't above grabbing a broom to sweep floors.

Vivi took her first, tentative steps. Everyone shouted, 'Hurrah!' She did it again, holding out her arms for balance. Oh, my excitement.

Daddy grinned. 'Only nine months and she's ready to take on the world.'

He looked thoughtful. 'There's a horse for sale in the paper. Ten pounds. Half-draught, broken for harness. Useful for both riding and the buggy.'

'What if he's no good?'

'I'll find out.' Daddy was gone a couple of days, a journey of over fifty miles. He camped in each direction.

Mum eyed the big bay gelding. His features were neither classic nor attractive.

90

Daddy rubbed his hands. 'See how quietly he stands? Gentle nature. Everything we wanted.' He told of the owner extolling the horse's virtues. '"Never flinches or shows anxiety when patted or saddled. See that calm expression and those intelligent eyes?" he said. I didn't show too much enthusiasm…'

'Lest the owner upped the price?'

'Exactly. "Only two years old," he said. "And sturdy enough to carry packs or rabbit traps while ridden. You could even use him for ploughing."'

Daddy made to pay. The owner suddenly realised the value of his horse. 'Sorry, mate. I can't bear to part with him.'

'How about a fiver above the asking price?' Daddy laughed. 'Those crisp notes clinched the deal.'

Mum stroked the horse's nose. 'What's his name?'

'I've called him Hungry. He always whinnies for more hay.'

One flaw emerged in Hungry's character: rages at meal times. Other horses avoided his feed box. He snorted and pawed the earth, eyes dilated, hindquarters positioned for attack.

Daddy chuckled. 'They know better than to get within six feet of his flailing hooves.'

He delivered a stern lecture. 'Never, ever go near Hungry when he's feeding. Even his front hooves would turn you into mincemeat.' He chuckled. 'As Walt would say, "He'd kick the Christ out of you."'

'Joly! Not in front of the kids.'

Years later, Daddy told of the first six months of 1945. 'The AIF and American troops fought the last conflicts of the Pacific. At Okinawa, the largest battle took place, with thousands of casualties. In the Philippines alone, seventeen thousand Americans lay buried.'

We kids didn't know the significance of 30 April 1945. Years afterwards, I learnt Hitler had shot himself in his bunker. Underlings set his body alight with petrol.

Daddy said, 'We weren't meant to celebrate anybody's death but…'

'In his case, you made an exception?'

'Thank God we'd seen the end of the Nazi regime. Pure evil.'

Allied leaders in Europe sealed the surrender and capitulation.

Mum understood one woman's words 'It seems more like a funeral than a great victory. So many died. Thank goodness I have the wireless to cheer me up.'

Adults seemed shaken. Parents' conversations stopped in mid-flight. By stealth, we discovered the reason for their shocked faces. Atomic bombs, dropped on Hiroshima and Nagasaki on 6 and 9 August 1945. Devastating damage and death. Daddy explained it all much later. Adults took opposing sides. Mr Hardy was for, Pinkie against.

Victor and I fitted scraps of conversation together like a jigsaw.

Daddy's low, worried voice. 'Horrendous… Just when a man thinks he's heard the worst…'

Pinkie, 'They're our enemies but…old, women, children…'

Daddy, 'Blinding light…radiation…everything destroyed…will this madness ever…'

Mr Hardy, 'Japs had to be stopped…'

Mum, 'Blast felt ten miles away… Ten miles! Suppose it gets into the hands of a madman?'

Despairing voices rose and fell.

I didn't want to hear any more. 'Let's go.'

The empire of Japan surrendered.

We heard a tremor in Daddy's voice. 'This is a momentous moment for everyone. Remember 14 and 15 August 1945, Victor. The war is over.' He added, 'Kids like you can play without fear of invasion.'

I shared the news with my invisible friends. Oliver could be male or female, according to my whim.

Jim, a family friend, shed a tear or two. He hugged my rag doll, Jemima. 'I told you we'd win.'

Baby seemed too young to understand.

And Lamp Spider shouted, 'Bring back the bombs… I want the bombs.'

Poppy called him a nasty piece of work.

Mum only half-listened to my games.

'Don't sit there, Mum. You'll squash Oliver,' or, 'Could Oliver have more cake?'

She called me for lunch.

'I can't come yet, Mum. I'm playing with Oliver.'

'Would you stop talking about that silly Oliver?'

'But Mum…'

'No buts. Wash your hands and come to the table. Now.'

Next time I mentioned my phantom playmates, Mum gave a slow shake of her head. 'Haven't you heard? They've been killed. Car crash.'

'Oliver says…'

'He's dead, I'm afraid.'

'She, not he…'

'I don't care whether it's he or she. Oliver is dead. They all are. Jim, Baby, Jemima, and that dreadful Lamp Spider. I don't want to hear about them again.'

I tried to talk with my friends in secret. But their magic life had gone.

A carriage trundled around raging skies. Lightning leapt and zigzagged, brilliant as day. Water poured from gutters. Wind rattled my windows. At last I fell asleep.

Night cracked open like an egg. The golden yolk of another day glittered from a huge pool of water, in a grassy hollow.

Victor made waves. He glanced around. 'Sneak inside the laundry. Fetch some soap powder.'

We splashed soapsuds into an enormous mound of foam. Shrieking over a sea battle, pieces of wood our gunboats.

Victor shouted, 'Take that, and that. Bang, crash, boom. My German guns blasted your British boat to smithereens.'

'Pow, crash, wham. My torpedoes sank yours.'

Mum called us to tea. 'It's wicked playing in puddles. Change those drenched clothes at once.'

Next day, Mum glanced around the laundry. 'That's funny. I thought there were three packets of soap powder.'

The phone jangled.

Mum told Dad, 'Walt's back. I've asked him and Poppy to dinner.'

The house rocked to laughter. Memories floated and criss-crossed the table.

Poppy held Walt's hand. 'It's just like old times. Walt's a bit thin, but I'll soon fix that.'

We chuckled over her jokes and riddles.

Men in uniform came and went. Some soldiers seemed jumpy, even angry.

Mum said it was called war neurosis. 'Many returned men suffer from it. Use it as an excuse to drink.'

Daddy frowned. 'Don't be like that, luv. The terrible things they've seen.'

One blazing day, a friend of Mr Hardy's took a nap in his shorts. We eyed his huge, bare stomach. Victor crept up, fascinated by the deep well of his belly button. He filled it with red plasticine. Our visitor roared awake. Mum made us apologise; he stayed grumpy.

Our next arrival brought smiles.

Mum called Uncle Bill kindness itself. I guessed that was a nickname. He took ill, shivering, sweating, and mumbling. It made me scared.

Daddy said, 'There's nothing to fear, Dessie. His sickness is malaria. Caused by mosquito bites. Affects a lot of diggers back from New Guinea.'

Uncle recovered. He told of working as a medical assistant in the army. 'Nursed many men through their rigors. In the grip of fever, they became delirious, saying foolish things. Doubtless I did the same.'

Mr Hardy put on his glasses to read. Uncle removed his, eyes flickering back and forth, inches from the newspaper. Mum called it astigmatism.

It fascinated me. Astigmatism. Another word for wobbly eyes.

Mum's cousin Bert received his army discharge. She was shocked by his appearance. 'To think that strong young men have been reduced to this.' One of the few soldiers from his battalion to have survived. Mum said, 'He's little more than skin and bone. Physically and mentally exhausted, poor man. Heaven knows how long it will take his ulcers to heal.'

I longed to ask about ulcers. But kept quiet. That way, we often heard things they didn't plan to tell us.

Dad told Mum of barbed wire, starvation, and floggings. 'Awful things on the Burma–Thailand railway. And the prison camp.'

In the middle of the story, they sometimes exchanged glances, shushing each other.

Another day, crouched behind a sofa, we heard Dad talk of the Sandakan death march. 'Starving men, forced to march hundreds of miles.'

Uncle Bill added, 'Struggling through jungle and swamps. Crammed into filthy huts. Dysentery. Fever. Killed by guards.'

'It's a miracle any of them made it home.'

We didn't know what dysentery meant. But killed was clear enough.

Victor and I slipped away. In the paddock, we found pink salt blocks, put out for cattle. Kneeling on hands and knees, we licked hollows and ridges worn by their rough tongues. I adored the strong saline flavour. Perhaps salt killed the germs. We never told Mum.

Victor led the way into the old shed. We ran to the top of hay, stacked almost to the rafters, whooping. Did it again. The aroma of hay mingled with the sweat of horses and leather odours. Our buggy rested against one wall. Spare saddles, bridles and harness hung on hooks. Fishing rods promised sun-drenched excursions to the river. Yum, rainbow trout.

Lumpy bags of potatoes chatted to Queensland blue pumpkins. Ringlets of wood shavings, fragrant with pine resin, reminded me of Daddy's woodworking projects. When I asked what he was making, he'd grin.

'A wigwam for a goose's bridle.'

I'd giggle, guessing he was being silly.

Shelves held planes and chisels. Jagged cross-cuts and handsaws hung beside axes, used for chopping firewood. Jars attached underneath shelves held nails and screws.

Victor eyed Dad's most prized possession. His best axe, of the finest steel, it sliced through timber with ease.

'I could cut your hair with this blade. Never touch it.'

'But Dad…'

'No buts, son. It's far too dangerous. And I don't want the blade damaged.'

Even on tiptoe, the forbidden axe remained beyond his reach.

Months passed. Despite Dad's warnings, Victor didn't stop trying. One morning, the smooth hickory handle rested in his hands. An expression of triumph suffused his face.

'You're not allowed to touch…'

'Says who? There's only you and me. Who'll tell?'

I bit my lip.

Victor ran a finger along the finely honed blade.

'Please, Victor. Put it back.'

'Ah, shaddup.' Eight-year-old defiance. He slung it over his shoulder.

'Daddy says…'

'I'm not going to hurt it, stupid.'

I whined at his heels. Where was our Mum?

We reached the wattle grove.

Victor spat on his palms, just like Dad. 'Stand back.'

A mighty swing. The blade grazed the trunk. It slipped, landing on the Victor's big toe, right foot. My brother dropped the axe. He yelped like a wounded puppy. Blood dripped onto the grass. I felt sick.

'Ouch, ouch. My toe. Oh my toe.' Face ashen. 'Say nothing, do you hear?' He limped to the shed and hung up Dad's axe.

I whimpered, 'What about your toe?'

'Stop snivelling. I know where Mum keeps the bandages.' He limped towards the house.

Mum stood, pegging out the washing. 'Why are you crying?'

'Because.'

'That's no answer. Where's Victor?'

'In the house. He cut his foot.'

'What?'

'Dad's good axe slipped…'

'His axe?'

Pegs bounced in all directions. A trail of blood led us to Victor. He frantically wound yards of cotton bandage around his foot. Glimpsing Mum, he burst into tears.

'That's enough. This wound needs stitches. I'll fetch your father.'

Dad rushed home, face grim. 'Now you know why I warned you not to touch my axe.'

Victor hung his head.

A telephone call brought Uncle Geoff and his green Bedford. He sped Mum, Dad, Curley and Victor to town. Twilight settled over the landscape. Pinkie served our meal and sent me to bed.

At breakfast I couldn't wait to hear all about it.

Victor wouldn't talk of doctors, or stitches. And he had lost interest in axes.

By 1945, horses had become his passion.

Mum's pony, Dolly, was quiet and calm. 'She's the perfect mare for a beginner.'

Victor managed short rides. 'I'll attend rodeos. Become a buck-jumper. Win prizes.'

One day, Dolly broke into a trot. She made a sudden turn. Victor tumbled towards earth in slow motion. A dull thud. Someone screamed. It took seconds to realise it was me.

Dad's boss took the veranda steps two at a time. He ran to Victor's slumped figure. Mum reached him at the same time. Blood ran from a small cut above his left eye.

Mr Hardy probed for damage. 'Move your legs. Good. Now your arms.' He looked at Mum. 'Boy's fine, missus. Nothing broken.'

'Thank goodness. Dolly's such a dependable mare.'

Mr Hardy shrugged. 'The best of them shy at times.'

Victor moaned.

Mr Hardy winked at Mum. 'Seven falls and you'll be a rider. Get back in the saddle, lad. Ride around the paddock.

Mum wrung her hands. 'Poor kid. Must he?'

I peeked between my fingers.

Dolly stood quietly. Mr Hardy gave Victor a leg up. My brother clung to the reins with his right hand, gripping the pommel with his left.

Mr Hardy walked beside the pony, holding the outer rein. 'See, young 'un, you've done it.'

Victor sagged from the saddle.

Mr Hardy caught him in his arms. 'Brandy, Missus.'

Victor coughed and spluttered. Mum allowed him to have his evening meal in bed.

Next morning he displayed a tiny bruise. 'When you're a rider like me, you'll get plenty of these.'

9

Christmas decorations hid in boxes all year. Magically, they reappeared every December. Mum transformed flat, honeycombed tissue paper into bells of red, green, purple and blue. Victor draped red and green paper chains around the living room. Daddy's wild pine tree sparkled with silver and gold. Multicoloured glass balls and angels hung from branches. Being the tallest, he fixed the gold star on top.

Christmas Eve. The house thrilled to the crackle of wrapping paper. Whispers and chuckles came from behind closed doors.

Daddy said, 'Santa's on his way, kids.'

Victor and I didn't mind going to bed early. Curley was already asleep.

I floated into Christmas morning. My eyes widened at Pinkie's pink glass necklace. A new colouring book from Mum and Dad, quickly put to use with a box of crayons and coloured pencils from Mr Hardy.

Victor wore his cowboy suit and revved a big blue truck.

Thanks to Mr Hardy, we enjoyed goose for Christmas dinner. The delicious, golden aroma of baking made my mouth water. Crisp potatoes and pumpkin. Minted peas, freshly picked from the garden.

Mum and Dad smiled. 'A toast to Mr Hardy. Very generous indeed.'

We clinked glasses of ale and lemonade.

A slice of breast melted in my mouth. I pushed aside a slimy morsel of fat.

Mum frowned. 'Fat's good for you.'

I wriggled in dismay.

Mr Hardy said, 'Gracious, we can't waste food. Think of starving children in Africa.'

Daddy nodded.

Victor piped up. 'Every scrap on your plate must be eaten, sis.'

Mum beamed. 'Good boy.'

I felt glad Curley was too young to join in. And Pinkie gave me a wink. He had chosen my sister's nickname, sparked by her blonde mop of hair.

I took a breath. The fat slid down my throat. I shuddered and kept shuddering. It almost took away my appetite for Christmas pudding and sauce. Victor found sixpence in his.

Lazy summer holidays stretched into weeks.

One morning, Mum packed us tomato sandwiches. Curley wanted to join us.

Victor brushed her aside. 'Nah! You can't keep up.'

'You kids are selfish. Why not take her?'

Daddy chuckled. 'It's probably not a good idea, luv. They'd forget her in some paddock.'

A laugh of kookaburras drifted on eucalypt-scented air. Stones in a creek slipped under bare feet. We trapped pollywogs in cupped hands, watching shiny black bodies wriggle free. I gathered native cress.

On a flat expanse of rock, we dried our legs. Munched tomato and cress sandwiches. I made plans for a cubby house. Suddenly a loud hiss. My heart stopped, then raced. Coils of black and red unwound from a prime position in the sun. Pouring into some dark cavern under the rocks. Pursued by a thousand imaginary serpents, we ran. Darting between trees, dappled by light and shadow. Leaves and twigs crackled underfoot. Startled kangaroos took flight.

Mum swept the veranda floorboards. Curley ran down the steps. She took my hand.

Before we could tell about our scare, her broom made contact with a soft, brown shape. It undulated under a bed. She motioned us to stay back. Slid a bullet into the chamber of the 0.22 rifle. Waited. Took aim. Crack!

Curley and I clung to each other. The head was missing. A five-foot brown.

Mum carried her kill outside. 'It's among the most dangerous snakes.'

Autumn rains promised nature's harvest. We selected containers and knives. A hint of white, near tussocks. I ran, thrusting a large mushroom with soft pink underside into my basket.

Victor whined. 'I saw it first.'

'Liar. It's mine.'

Mum stamped her foot. 'Stop fighting, you two. And, for heaven's sake, slow down.'

I hated her staid pace. We gathered mushrooms as large as side plates, others small and delicate, ready for butter and nutmeg.

Mum tutted at my can of battered specimens. 'When will you kids be more careful?'

The phone trilled.

Poppy said, 'I'm a mum. A daughter, Georgina. Walt and I call her Georgie. She sleeps right through the night…'

Mum asked how much she weighed.

'Seven pounds.'

Mum finally put down the receiver, writing the date on her calendar: 8 February 1946. 'All Poppy's dreams have come true.'

Daddy grinned. 'And Walt's, too, I suspect. Couldn't have happened to a nicer couple.'

They visited, faces wreathed in smiles. Poppy unwrapped a lacy, hand-knitted shawl. Georgie's tiny size amazed me.

'Please, Auntie Poppy, a nurse.'

Poppy showed me how to support Georgie's head.' Uncle Walt and Poppy wore beatific expressions. Not that I knew the word.

'Wonderful news, mate.' Daddy pumped Walt's hand. 'Congratulations. A fine girl and no mistake. You'll need a shotgun to keep the boys away.'

They roared with laughter.

Dad grinned. 'It must be something in the air. Lydia Rangers is expecting, too.'

I asked, 'What's she expecting?'

General laughter.

'Never you mind.'

Victor told me later, 'Expecting means a lady's getting a baby. It's already in her tummy.'

'In her tummy?' It seemed the silliest thing I'd ever heard. 'How could a baby get inside? Or come out?'

He was vague on the details. 'But I know it's true.' A bigger boy had told him.

Not long afterwards, Jack Rangers rode up on his roan horse. The animal's nose felt softer than velvet.

Jack said, 'Mind if I borrow your buggy, Joly? I'll need to take Lydia to town.' He winked at Daddy. 'To pick up our new baby.'

Lydia had minded me when Mum went to town for Curley. 'Is it the hospital where Mum found Vivi?'

He and Daddy chuckled. 'Something like that.'

Jack put the horse in harness and blinkers, added the collar. 'It's not for a month yet.'

'It's wise to be prepared, mate.'

Jack slapped the reins against the horse's neck. A cheery wave.

The following morning, Dad was amazed to see Jack Rangers emerge from our buggy. He later told Mum, 'Shaking and haggard, poor bugger.'

Victor and me, crouched under the veranda, heard every word.

'You look all in, Jack. Thought you wanted the buggy for the baby.'

'Lydia's pains came on sudden an' real bad. Late last night.'

'That's the way it happens, mate.'

'Never want to go through that again.'

They had set off for town. Lydia's nephew carried the lantern.

'My horse was spooked by the dark. Buggy almost tipped over.'

Dad whistled.

'I calmed the horse, edging the buggy back on the road. The pains were comin' real fast. The wife shouts for me to hurry.'

'But…you can't have gone all the way to Scone?'

'We never made it past the post office. I seen a light, and rushed inside. Lydia makes it to the veranda couch. Old woman helps remove her undies. A couple of grunts, an' the kid slides out. Big boy. I caught him.'

I gaped. Victor put a finger to his lips.

'A son? Congratulations, Jack. That calls for a drink.'

'Better not, mate. The wife's alone at home with the nephew an' our baby. She's goin' for a check-up next week.'

Victor and I slipped away.

'What did I tell you? Babies grow in the tummy, just like foals and calves.'

I couldn't quite believe it.

Mrs Taylor gushed, 'Goodness, you're a big girl now, Dessie. Only yesterday, you were a babe in arms. And my, this isn't Curley? And Victor. My word. What a lovely little family.'

Mr Felton took up his fiddle at the neighbours' party. People clapped. I liked his white, curling moustache and merry eyes. Daddy drained his glass. He and Mum joined other dancers, swaying to the rhythm of 'Moonlight on the Danube', 'Loch Lomond', 'Irish Eyes'… Tunes that made me sad, yet happy at the same time. I'd heard them when I was little.

Mr Felton's bowing arm raced back and forth. Dancers whirled around the room. They stopped, breathless, laughing. Called for an encore.

Mr Felton patted his dripping brow, with a white handkerchief. 'Time for my break.' He winked at me.

Daddy clinked his glass, making a toast.

Victor whispered, 'Reckon Dad's put away a few. Look at the queer way he's dancing.'

Mum led us to a shadowed annexe. Curley slept between cousins and neighbours' children.

She tucked us under blankets on the floor. 'Take a little rest.'

The rhythm of music welcomed my dreams.

Bright morning light. Victor danced with elongated shadows. Dew glittered on blades of grass beside the path. Curley toddled, holding on to my little finger. Dad and Pinkie stumbled along, complaining about the glare.

Mum strode ahead. 'I'll never know why men drink to excess.' Mum raged at us for days.

One day she yelled, 'I've told you kids a thousand times. Shut the gate. Those darn chooks will ruin my garden.'

We shooed them away.

Daddy glanced around. 'Where's Curley?'

Mum paled. She ran from room to room. Shook her head.

Victor and I scouted the yard. 'Not there.'

Mum gulped. 'She must have toddled out the gate.'

Daddy glanced towards the horse-yard. His face turned ashen. 'Oh, God, no. Not there.'

A mass of blonde curls. Grey woollen jacket and trousers. My little sister. In the worse spot possible: under Hungry's feed box.

Mum choked. 'Oh, no! Not there.'

Daddy put a finger across his lips. A voice might encourage Curley to move or startle Hungry. In the heavy silence, he padded towards the big bay. Placing his size eleven boots with the caution of a dingo.

I could barely breathe.

He edged forward. Inch by agonising inch. The muffle of footfalls.

Time had never passed so slowly. Every second throbbed with danger. My tongue clove to my mouth. Would Daddy reach her in time?

Closer, ever closer.

The end arrived with startling speed. In one, swift movement,

Daddy bent, scooping Curley into his arms. He soothed Hungry with pats on his neck. Edging back, little by little.

Daddy reached us, his eyes brimming. 'Here she is, sweetheart.' He embraced them both.

Curley giggled. 'Horsey, Mumma.' She pointed a chubby hand towards Hungry.

Mum coughed to hide her tears. I clung to Daddy's legs, letting mine flow. Victor was pale and tremulous.

Dad shook his head. 'Of all the places to find her.'

Mum blew her nose. 'Now, Curley, I know you love to stroke Hungry's nose. But promise us never, ever to go near him again. Unless Daddy or I take you.'

Curley nodded.

Daddy brewed tea. 'Hungry has more stamina than any horse I've owned. He loves human company.' He told of sitting around a campfire one night. 'Old fellow loped up out of the darkness. He loves me stroking or scratching his chin. Only trouble, it puts him to sleep. And if you'd ever had his great head resting on your shoulder... It's heavier than a log. I hated moving him on.'

Uncle Bill arrived.

Mum told him how autumn skies had brought one willy-willy after another. 'They whirled leaves in circles, ripping clothes from the line. I've never seen anything like it. Months afterwards, I spied two of Curley's dresses caught on the limbs of a giant gum, hundreds of feet in the air. And I picked up one of Victor's shirts in a far paddock.'

'Incredible.'

I said, 'I've lost my pink dress with bunnies.'

Mum sighed. 'It was her favourite.'

'What a shame, pet.' His eyes struggled to focus behind thick spectacles. He told us, 'Haven't been well. Raging thirsts, weight loss...'

'Does your doctor know what's wrong?'

'Diabetes. Special diet. Insulin daily. Now I'm fine.'

Dad watched Uncle use the syringe. 'It's incredible how you draw up the correct dose, given your eyesight.'

'I've practised.' Uncle tapped the cylinder, expelled air bubbles.

I watched him inject it into his arm, shuddering. 'You do that every morning?'

He grinned. 'There's nothing to it. Never felt better in my life.' He showed us a block of chocolate. 'I eat a few squares for hypos. That's when my blood sugar falls too low.' His eyes sparkled. 'I'm liable to pass out – or on. Unless it's treated pronto.'

Mum looked startled.

He laughed. 'It's nothing to worry about, Genn. Everything's under control.'

We loved Uncle Bill's jokes. Best of all, he chuckled over ours. I guess he was only in his thirties back then. To us kids he seemed old. We seldom saw Uncle Sid, his twin brother.

In later years, Auntie Aileen told us about the twins' birth. 'Sid arrived first. The midwife took a celebration drink or three with father. She didn't know a second baby was on the way. Bill lay unattended for some time, the cord around his neck. I often wonder if the shortage of oxygen affected his sight.'

Our parents left Uncle Bill in charge. Victor and I fought non-stop. Uncle humphed, rustling up the newspaper.

Victor stirred dirt into a thick porridge on Mum's kitchen floor. His blue truck and my cars bogged on the wet road. We revved and roared them out of trouble.

'That one's mine.' Victor shouted.

I grabbed the car back. 'Tis not.'

Uncle folded the newspaper. Put on his glasses. 'Clean up this mess. Immediately. I know a perfect way to use up excess energy.'

We threw away the mud. I washed Mum's saucepan. 'What does he want us to do?'

Victor mopped the floor. 'Dunno.'

Uncle Bill's stern voice took us by surprise. 'Scrub up, and into clean clothes. You have five minutes. Report to me.' He rubbed his hands, grinning. 'Fetch me some firewood.'

Heavy wood. Hot sun. Our bodies dripped. A couple of armfuls proved more than enough.

Victor threw a third on the ground. 'It's not fair.'

We hid behind a log.

A shout echoed across the valley. 'Out of there, you two. Get on with it.'

We staggered back and forth. The shed smiled on a huge pile of wood. Finally, he relented. We had lost every ounce of energy and mischief.

Uncle shared the miracle with our parents. They laughed until tears ran down the cheeks.

Daddy grinned. 'We'll leave you in charge more often.'

At breakfast, Uncle Bill joked and chuckled as usual. We'd forgiven him. He selected a slice of toast, kept warm on the hob. Eyes flickering, his knife cut into butter.

I glanced across at his side-plate, yelling, 'Stop!'

Daddy looked ready to explode. Then spied the cause of my alarm: a hairy huntsman spider, spreadeagled across Uncle's toast. Chuckling, he released it into the garden.

Our parents faced a hard decision.

'We need to sell Wallaby Farm,' Dad told Mum, 'It'll never be a goer.'

'But I…I'd hoped we'd be there forever.'

He sighed. 'When a place sells dirt cheap…'

Mum couldn't bear to farewell her dream.

Our buggy creaked to a stop at Wallaby Farm.

Daddy swung me to the ground. Victor leapt out unaided. Merino wool clouds drifted in a luminous sky. Stands of eucalypts watched from every hilltop. Daddy eyed our half-finished slab cottage. Dandelions and rough grass grew in Mum's kitchen garden. Dusty cobwebs fetooned the interior. A rat leapt over my foot. Outside, I heard the mournful cry of a curlew.

Daddy stashed the last of their things in the buggy. He gazed across the valley. 'Your gran, Florence, visited us here once, with Cousin Joy. You saw their photographs?'

I nodded, recalling Joy, a pretty girl of eighteen. Gran in a black costume, or suit.

'I put a tarpaulin around the front veranda, a perfect sleep-out. Late one afternoon, they set off, a bush ramble. I told them to be back by four. By five, a thick fog had rolled in.'

'They were lost?'

'Yes, Victor. I feared for Gran with the damp and cold, but knew a search would be hopeless.'

I shivered at the thought of them trapped in fog. 'Did you call?'

'They couldn't hear me. Grabbing my mallet, I thumped on a hollow log. The sound drummed through the forest. My arm screamed for mercy, but I kept right on drumming.'

Victor looked up. 'Then came the crackle of leaves.'

Daddy chuckled. 'Who's telling this story? I could have wept with joy to see those bedraggled figures. Gran fell into my arms, still clutching a bunch of wildflowers. Yellow bachelors' buttons, gum red-tips… They were cold and scratched from wait-a-while vines. Nothing dry clothing, disinfectant and a bowl of hot soup couldn't fix.'

Much later, Daddy told me of selling Wallaby Farm. 'It wasn't worth much. But we needed every penny. Your Uncle Geoff had suffered a disappointment in love. He was seeking a new start. He ached for the golden prospects of an orange orchard. Grandfather Rick dreaded leaving Hunters Springs. He'd lived thereabouts his whole life. He said, "You and Genn buying the place will make it bearable."'

'And Nan?'

'Hilda still missed city life. Your grandfather had planted a splendid orchard. Cox, Golden Delicious and Five Crown apples, all fine trees. He farewelled Williams, Packham and Beurre Bosc pears and eyed nectarine, plum, peach and delicious cherries. The meat house he'd built was shaded by a sizeable apple tree. A nameless seedling, with succulent yellow fruit, perfect for pies. Should have been registered.'

I recalled Grandfather in hat and veil. A smoker calmed his bees, ready to remove honey trays. Bees swarmed all around him. He never showed a hint of fear. Grandfather sold his hives to a local apiarist, another wrench.

Victor crept too close. 'Ouch, ouch!' His hand swelled to twice its size.

Nan rubbed it with an onion, but to no avail.

'The asking price for Hunters Springs was five hundred pounds. With three hundred as deposit, I thought getting a loan would be a cinch. But almost had to get down on my knees and beg for it.'

I felt sad to be leaving Greenfield.

Daddy said, 'Let's repay friends and neighbours for their hospitality.' They invited friends and neighbours to a supper dance.

Mum baked cinnamon-spiced apple pies, cakes and biscuits. The fragrance of baked lamb, potatoes and pumpkin made me ravenous. Beans and carrots lingered, ready for cooking.

Daddy removed weatherboards between two bedrooms. We decorated our splendid ballroom with paper chains and balloons. Daddy waxed the floor. We slid back and forth. It shone in the lamplight.

'What do you reckon, kids?'

'It's the best ever.'

Mum scrubbed Curley and me with Pears soap. The amber tablet reminded me of wattle tree sap.

I stepped from the tub, and towelled my dripping body. 'How long before…'

'Soon. Hurry and dress.'

Victor was next. Our parents took a turn.

Daddy gazed into the drizzly darkness. 'I'm glad it's not a downpour.'

Green glass beads glittered at Mum's throat, matching her dress, her hair swept up. She had never looked prettier.

Dad grinned. 'Belle of the ball.'

She giggled.

Pink rosebuds adorned my cotton dress. Curley's had pink and white spots. Each boasted a white Peter Pan collar, long sashes at the waist.

Mum helped me on with my black button boots, fastened with a special hook. Mum sighed. 'They're almost worn out.'

Dad checked his watch. 'What can be keeping them?'

Mum swallowed. 'It's a pity Walt and Poppy are away.'

'They'd have been here long ago, no mistake.'

We waited. And waited.

Victor said, 'It's nine o'clock, Mum.'

'I can tell the time.' The sparkle had left her eyes. 'They can't… couldn't have forgotten?'

Dad eyed work-roughened hands. 'I dunno.'

The squeak of metal wheels on gravel. A trot of hooves. Our dogs barked.

Dad grinned. 'Someone's here.'

I sucked the ends of my sash.

Mum slapped my hand. 'Stop that, Dessie. You're such a baby.' She retied the bow.

A shadowed buggy. Mr Spencer helped his wife alight. 'Sorry we're late.'

Dad pumped his hand. 'Glad you could make it, Reg.'

Dad held up a hurricane lamp. Water dripped from oilskin coats.

Auntie Vera pecked Mum on the cheek, kissed us. I loved her lavender perfume. 'Oh! We're the first. You have gone to a lot of trouble. It's a wonderful room.'

Daddy waved them into chairs. 'What's your poison?'

The ladies settled for a shandy, the men took beer. We children drank lemonade.

Victor wound up the His Master's Voice gramophone. Old-time waltzes like 'After the Ball' and 'If You Were the Only Girl in the World' quavered from the machine. Adults circled the floor.

Mr Spencer winked. 'C'mon, Blondie. Have this one with me.'

I blushed. Mr Spencer topped my Daddy, hair the same golden red. I felt giddy after he whirled me around the room. But liked his smile.

Dogs yapped. Mr Spencer's horse stamped and snorted. A chilling thought: there won't be anyone else.

A flush came to Mum's cheeks. 'Do have more to eat. Apple pie perhaps?'

Everyone had eaten their fill. Midnight came and went. I could barely keep my eyes open. Curley was long asleep. The Spencers left, bearing cakes, slices, pies.

Mum eyed the leftover food. 'Enough to feed an army. Why do people promise?'

'If the weather hadn't been miserable…'

'A drizzle? That doesn't excuse them.' She wiped her eyes. 'It's damn bad manners, accepting our invite then not turning up.'

And so ended their first, and last, attempt at formal entertaining.

10

Greenfield creeks gurgled goodbye. Hills sighed. Paddocks undulated grassy farewells. Daddy put our things in the buggy. Uncle Geoff had moved most of our stuff. I sat beside Mum and Curley.

'Gee up, girl,' Dad flicked the reins.

Victor rode Dolly, tied by a long rein. She trotted behind us. I waved to Pinkie, already missing his games. Mr Hardy was away. Hungry set off at a trot. On inclines, Dad glanced back to make sure Dolly was keeping up. A stiff breeze whipped our faces. Peggy and other dogs scampered ahead. Dust spiralled in our wake.

Dad gave a bitter laugh. 'So Jim Hardy gave you ten pounds?'

Mum nodded.

'After all your work? No doubt he rubbed his hands at such a bargain.'

'You expected generosity?'

Hunter Springs embraces one of the three heads of the river. Clear water bubbles from springs around hillsides of our small valley. Masses of sphagnum moss grow near rainforest trees.

Victor and I rolled around the orchard, puppies in clover. Apple trees hung low to the ground with red, green and yellow fruit. Peaches and pears lent their delicious aromas. Victor climbed high in a cherry tree, daring me to follow.

Mum shouted. 'Down from there, you two. Those branches aren't safe.'

Dolly grazed in the yard. I begged for a ride. Even after so many years, Daddy's loss of his little sister, Florence, made him wary of kids riding horses.

Mum said, 'We can't wrap them in cotton wool.'

She helped me mount the pony. I gathered the reins, feigning confidence. Dolly trotted down the road. She shied, catapulting me from the saddle. I landed with a splendid view of sky.

Dolly neatly placed one hoof between my spreadeagled legs. It prevented injury, but ripped my favourite cotton skirt, a rainbow check. I walked home, howling. The pony munched clover.

Mum said, 'Nothing broken, thank goodness.'

Victor puffed out his chest. 'Seven falls and you'll...'

Mum shushed him.

I wiped my eyes. 'I won't...'

'Nonsense. A short ride is what you need.' Mum stroked Dolly's neck. She gave me a leg up.

I clung to the pommel, sniffling. A turn of the yard.

'That wasn't so bad, was it?'

'Can you fix my skirt?'

'We'll see.'

We never had enough horses to hone our riding skills. And what I craved was a bicycle.

Nan's cottage seemed luxurious. 'Is this house ours, Mum?'

'Ours...and the bank's.' Mum asked Daddy, 'Are you taking that job with Walt at Tomalla station?'

'Three pounds a week's not enough. We need equipment and seed. I'll approach one of the lowland landowners. Get a rabbit eradication contract.'

She spluttered. 'You'll what? Leave Hunters Springs?'

'Only for a year. Two at the most. There's millions of rabbits. A man would make a fortune from skins.'

'Huh! There must be dozens of locals after work.'

Daddy was rejected by one owner after another.

Mum gloated. 'What did I tell you?'

He grinned. 'I've learnt one thing, luv. Most trappers only work long enough to buy booze and cigarettes. Property owners want total eradication. That's where I come in.'

He approached another station owner. 'I'll do such a good job, you'll be rabbit-free in a couple of years.'

The old man looked sceptical. 'Me son catches a few bunnies every so often. We do OK.'

His adult son sniggered, ready to show Daddy the door.

'Hang on.' Daddy said, 'I'll pay you twenty-five quid if you give me one paddock. Show you what I can do.'

The grazier exchanged an incredulous glance with his son. 'You'd pay us? What's the catch?'

'There isn't one, mate,' Daddy grinned. 'You blokes get on with your sheep work. I'll solve the rabbit problem. But I keep everything from skin sales.'

The grazier said, 'Fair enough.'

Daddy made to waltz Mum around the kitchen.

She giggled. 'Have you lost your senses?'

'When the old grazier saw my crisp pound notes, we shook on the deal.'

Her eyes bulged. 'You're giving him money?'

'Twenty-five quid? I'll earn twice that in a week. After he sees me in action, he'll beg me to continue.'

'And give you a contract, too, I suppose?'

'Probably. But that would only be about one shilling and sixpence an acre. Skins bring the real money.'

Mum sighed. 'What choice do I have? But the kids and I will go with you. I may even be able to help.'

'I hoped you'd say that. Between us, sweetheart, we'll make an excellent team. I'll trap or poison the blighters. Repair poorly constructed and maintained rabbit-proof fences.'

Within the fortnight, Mum had packed. 'I hate doing this.'

'Don't you think I'd prefer to be clearing paddocks and planting crops? We'll be back in no time.'

A slab cottage cowered at the foot of craggy peaks at Ben More. Steep gullies had spewed dirt, debris and gravel on land behind it. For decades, it had housed shearers or other workmen.

Inside the kitchen, open cans with sharp lids lay on the floor. Dust and cobwebs covered everything. The stove was grimy and stained with fat and rodent droppings. The pine table bore witness to dozens of hasty meals. And even hastier washing-up.

Mum stood, dumbfounded.

A mouse skittered over my foot. I screamed. 'Mum, I'm not sleeping here tonight.'

'None of us will. That's obvious.'

'The grazier said we could move straight in.'

'Did he indeed?'

Daddy gazed at old coats, broken boots and clothing. Cracked saddles, bridles and equine equipment were scattered throughout. 'Dry and comfortable, he said.'

'Dry, yes. Comfortable? Well! Rats and mice carry disease. Even the kids know that. It'll take at least a week to clean everything properly. Maybe two.'

Daddy pitched tents. Mum lit the stove. Victor put buckets of water on to boil.

She said, 'OK, kids. Grab your oldest things.'

Victor frowned. 'Aw, Mum…'

'Wanted to explore, I suppose?' She stamped her foot. 'All hands on deck, I'm afraid. Nobody can live in this mess.'

Aged seven, I helped sweep, dust and scour. We took to the kitchen with a stiff broom and soap suds. Cleaned a thick layer of dirt from the floor. Scrubbed cupboards, shelves and the table. Doused everything with disinfectant. The stove gleamed, our kitchen was ready to prepare food.

Mum put wildflowers in a jar. 'These make it seem like a home.'

Daddy dug a hole for rubbish. He and Victor demolished rats' nests, despatching occupants to the next world. Others left in a hurry.

One week became two. Windows sparkled. Horsey equipment went to a tack room. We still slept in tents. Rodents seemed convinced they were the rightful tenants.

Daddy nailed tin over holes, preventing entry. Set traps and laid poison. He gave strict instructions., 'Keep out of the house mornings, until I give the all clear.'

The invaders kept arriving. Mum's hands wrinkled from being too long in soapy water. 'I'm about at my wit's end. Will these pests ever leave?'

We heard a loud miaow. A large black tom with only three legs rubbed against mine. He purred like an engine.

'Friendly,' said Mum. 'He must've been caught in a trap, poor thing. Seems healthy enough.'

'Where are you from, Tom?' Daddy stroked his soft fur. 'Old feller's looking for a new home.'

'Can we keep him?' I asked.

'Maybe he belongs to one of our neighbours.'

Nobody enquired about a black cat.

I was delighted. 'You're here to stay, Tom.'

He may have only had three and a half legs but he ran as fast as any animal with four, leaping about with the assurance of a young lion.

Daddy stopped the poison. 'I don't want Tom eating a dead rodent.'

Each morning, Tom proudly displayed the bodies of rat or mice victims.

Daddy chuckled. 'He craves approval.'

Mum added, 'The moment Tom arrived, he licked his paws and set to work.'

Our invaders guessed the game was up. By the fourth day, they had vanished. We never saw another rodent. Tom had earned his board and keep. He settled back to enjoy the benefits of family life. A place on someone's knee. Pats. Strokes along his back. Delighted to eat the odd lamb chop or piece of sausage.

We moved indoors. Three family bedrooms, another for guests or workmen.

Daddy stored filthy old mattresses in the tack room. 'Thank goodness we've brought our own.'

At last we could explore.

Mum warned us. 'Keep away from rough gullies and steep cliffs behind the cottage.'

That was where our adventures began. Victor and I slid into a dry gully on our backsides. Scrambled up the steep bank to repeat the fun. We avoided jagged rocks and prickly bushes. In the shade of a kurrajong tree, we bit into sweet, crisp apples. Paddling in a clear pool. An image of the brooding mountain rippled into fragments.

Hills wandered towards lucerne-rich fields of the White property. Aberdeen Angus cattle's black bodies reminded me of fat fleas. On sunny days, the tranquil Hunter River drew us close. Water dipped under a steep bank. Weeping willows trailed languid leaves in greenish water. Dappled by shadow. A lacework of fine pink roots undulated in the current.

Bleached logs and litter hinted at the river's angry moods. A native oak trailed dry grass and debris.

Daddy said, 'See how the stream has changed course? Sometimes it hacks away the fields. Others, it glides past near the road.'

Victor filled his pockets with flat stones. He skipped them across pools. 'You'll never match me.'

I felt frustrated by my futile attempts. But in no way gender inferior. Wagtails hopped from rock to rock, calling, 'Sweet pretty creature.' I envied their soaring and diving in flight.

Mum brought Curley to swim. Little sister tried to scoop up spangles of light. They vanished from her chubby hands. She frowned with disappointment. We paddled in the translucent water. Delighted in the green, brown and gold pebbles.

Wild cotton grew in abundance on the flats. Hairy pods, soft beneath our fingers, split open to reveal cotton wool. Tiger-striped caterpillars underwent what Mum called a metamorphosis. They emerged from pale green chrysalis. Black and brown butterflies dried by sun and air took flight.

Brilliant flashes of lightning turned the shadowy landscape into day. Dark clouds hubbled and bubbled. We rushed indoors. Rain thundered on the tin roof. Dogs took refuge on the dry veranda. Claps of thunder shook the building. I shared my bed with Tom.

Next morning, dry gullies raged and overflowed. Waterfalls leapt. Frothy liquid raced to join the river's turbulent expanse of brown water. The Hunter lapped at the road. Trees, dead cattle, sheep, fence posts, tyres and forty-four gallon drums bobbed by. I clung to Daddy, sensing the danger.

Daddy trapped rabbits. He mixed strychnine with chopped carrots, lemon skin and thistle roots. The mixture smelt delicious.

Dad told Mum, 'Thistle can be boiled like any other root vegetable. A lovely flavour when not too old and stringy.'

We were never tempted to try them.

Soon the landowner noticed a marked reduction in rabbit numbers. He asked, 'Do you have any mates?'

Dad engaged Cecil Scamps.

Cecil and his bride, Linda, occupied the spare room. Like Uncle Bill, he suffered from attacks of malaria.

The pace of rabbit eradication increased. Cecil's bitzer died from a poisoned rabbit.

Daddy reminded him to burn strychnine-laced carcasses. 'One dose of poison kills most dogs. Others survive three or four fits, given a timely emetic.'

Peggy whined at the door. Our black kelpie suffered tremors in her limbs. She could scarcely keep her balance.

Daddy said, 'Quick, luv. She's taken a bait.' He administered a salt and water emetic. Grabbing her by her hind legs, he spun her around. She vomited. He kept a close watch. 'Your luck's in this time, old girl.'

Daddy prepared breakfast. In the shadowy kitchen, he hummed 'Lily of the Lamplight'. A piteous miaow rent the chilly winter air. 'What's the matter, Tom? Where are you, boy?'

Our cat's wail was edged with panic. Daddy scratched his head.

Where could that darn animal be? Then he recalled closing the oven door, before lighting the stove fire. Sometimes, Tom crept into the oven at night, soaking up the last warmth. Black coat. Half-light…

Daddy wrenched open the oven door. A cloud of smoke, followed by Tom. Wild-eyed, he fled to parts unknown.

Daddy felt dreadful. 'Almost burnt alive. How could I have been so careless?'

A week passed. Two. Long after we had given up hope, Tom ventured home. Thinner from living off the land, hair slightly singed. He berated Daddy. It was quite a while before Tom purred on his lap again.

The family took a taxi to town. Linda and Cecil minded Victor and me. Their behaviour was faultless – in front of our parents. That morning, Cecil chased his bride around the kitchen table, erect phallus on display. We watched in astonishment. Giggling, they raced away, slamming their door.

Groans, moans and giggles drifted into the tack room. It shared a wall with their bedroom. Victor spied a knothole. Peered through.

I wriggled. 'Let me see…'

He reluctantly stepped aside.

Their copulation seemed just another piece in the jigsaw of life. Some things parents didn't need to know.

A telegram brought sad news. Linda's father had died, a heart attack. Adult grief surprised me. We rarely glimpsed a tear in Mum's eyes.

She whispered, 'Linda's upset. Go and play.'

Victor and I pondered another insight into adult behaviour.

One chill night. Mum asked me to fetch her sweater.

'Come with me, Curley.' Her hand in mine, I cautiously opened the bedroom door. The dark held monsters, even with a flashlight. If anyone was going to get eaten, it wasn't me. I shoved Curley into the gloom. Screams.

Mum gathered the sobbing child in her arms. 'You naughty girl. Stop being such a baby.'

Mum called me skinny. In 1947 it was fashionable to be plump. Adverts assured Mum sugar was good for you. It guaranteed weight gain. Why not give me condensed milk, a favourite? My parents bought a whole carton. 'Eat as much as you like.' I spooned and drooled and licked my way through five cans. By then, I couldn't bear it.

Fred Scamps's brother arrived on holiday. He confided top secret information about Santa Claus.

Christmas approached. We kept our parents in ignorance of our new-found knowledge, wondering aloud what Santa might bring. Discretion proved worth it. My Christmas stocking yielded a brand-new skipping rope, plasticine, and a letters of the alphabet colouring book. Coloured pencils and a pencil case – perfect for when I started school in the New Year.

Mum had suspended Victor's correspondence lessons. 'After the holidays, you'll both attend Belltrees School.'

Every morning I asked, 'Mum, does school start today?'

She looked cross. 'Oh, go and play, will you? I'm busy.'

I skipped away frustration. Mastered jump rope.

Words leapt at me from can labels, magazines, and boxes. Mum helped me sound them out. I understood small sentences. Exciting news took my mind off this quest.

'We're off to visit your grandparents at Warners Bay.'

11

I'd been sad to toss out my old button-boots. And shabby sandals would never do. Not to visit Gran. At Campbell's shoe department in Scone, I was fascinated by the X-ray machine. Peering into the green screen, I saw the bones of my foot.

A shop assistant smiled. 'It ensures a perfect fit.'

Daddy told of the excitement brought by the discovery of X-rays. 'People paid sixpence to see their whole skeleton.' In the late fifties, machines would be withdrawn for safety reasons.

I fell for black patent leather shoes. The girl offered plainer pairs, cheaper ones. I shook my head.

Mum frowned. 'But these are so dear.'

Dad grinned. 'Ah, let her have them, luv. We can afford it.'

I lingered in the hat department. Tiny pink roses, white lily of the valley and pale pink ribbon, decorated a white straw bonnet. Mine was home-made, starched, and austere. 'Mum…'

She blanched at the price tag. 'You'll have to be satisfied with shoes.'

I carried the box into the house. 'Can I wear them?'

'When we leave for Gran's place.'

Every day I crept into Mum's room. Parted the tissue. Gazed at their perfection. 'Oh, how much longer?'

'Stroll around the house to break them in.'

Victor sniggered. 'Think you're somebody, don't you?'

'Behave, kids, or I'll bang your heads together.'

Her back turned, he poked out his tongue. I followed suit.

'Dessie. Stop that immediately.'

I hated removing the shoes.

Mum chose my new dress design from an *Australian Home Journal.* She smoothed out the bright floral fabric. Kept the pattern in place with one hand. Grabbed scissors.

Linda said, 'I'll loan you some pins.'

'Never use them.' Mum added a couple of inches for growth. She pedalled her old Singer, gripping a fold between her fingers for darts. Hummed 'When Irish Eyes Are Smiling' in an off-key soprano. The whole garment was finished, unironed, puckers ignored.

Mum had me try on my new dress. 'Stand still. There...what do you think, Linda? Only took me an hour.'

Linda gulped. 'It's a lovely material.'

Even I could see it hung like a sack. A bulky, double-thickness hem... 'Thanks, Mum.' I hesitated. 'May I wear my new shoes?'

'All you can think of are those jolly shoes.'

Linda called dresses 'frocks', buying most of them ready-made. When she made her own, I noticed she ironed one piece before joining it to the next.

Mum smiled at the novice. 'You'll soon get quicker,'

Linda raised her eyebrows.

Our holiday seemed no closer.

Mum despaired of my straight hair. 'It's so fine. And not much of it.'

Linda said, 'Crop it short. Makes hair thicker.'

'Good idea. 'Mum grabbed the clippers. She had always shorn Dad and Victor. 'There! all done.'

A stranger stared back from my mirror.

Linda frowned. 'It'll soon grow.'

Dad grinned. 'We leave for Gran's tomorrow, kids.'

Mum finished packing. She dunked Curley in our old tin tub beside the fire. My body shone, wet in the glow. In the fresh aroma of pink Lifebuoy, I stepped out and grabbed my towel.

Victor eyed the grey water. 'I'll take my bath in the morning.'

'Clothes off and hop in, thank you.'

Victor finished. He turned his back. 'I'll dry myself.'

Silky pyjamas. I brushed my teeth with peppermint paste. Gobbled some. Delicious.

Mum eyed the almost-empty tube. 'You kids must eat it.'

Bedtime loomed.

The next moment, Dad rattled my door. 'Rise and shine, kids.'

In the chill dark before dawn, I yawned. Shivering into my dress and cardigan. The stiff newness of patent leather. The toes were so-o-o shiny. A cereal breakfast.

A loud toot.

'Taxi's here. Give me those ports.' Dad helped the cabbie stow them in the boot.

Mum blew out the lamps. 'Hurry along, kids.'

We squeezed in, surrounded by bags and parcels. Curley sat on Dad's lap. Drizzle trickled down the windows. Windscreen wipers whirred.

It felt strange, speeding through darkness. Our rooster was yet to crow.

I stepped around puddles, blue and gold on the drenched footpaths. Mindful of my new shoes.

A couple of locals greeted Dad.

'Good day for it.'

'The rain's gone.'

A locomotive puffed into Scone station, spitting cinders. Victor and I raced for window seats. An elderly man took out a handkerchief, mopped his brow. Coins cascaded to the floor. We picked up pennies, halfpennies and sixpences.

'Thank you so much, children.'

A piercing whistle. I covered my ears. Town houses bathed in a mellow glow. Mum placed her folded cardigan under Curley's head. Her eyes closed. Victor poked Curley with a foot.

'Mum, Victor kicked me.'

'Liar...'

'Quiet, both of you. Let a person enjoy the scenery.'

We swayed past Newcastle suburbs.

I gaped. 'So many houses. How would I find my way home?'

Mum just laughed.

At Broadmeadow, Victor watched the train steam away. 'Gosh! Look at that.'

I plucked at Mum's sleeve. 'Please, lift me.' The brick railway bridge wall obscured my view.

'Quiet. I'm talking to your father.'

My hands gripped the top bricks. Shoes against the wall. The train shimmied from sight.

Mum jerked at my arm. 'Get down. Your hands are filthy. Oh, you naughty girl. You've ruined your shoes.'

I hadn't known the effect of rough bricks on shiny patent.

'You wicked child.' Mum slapped my legs.' You don't deserve new shoes.'

Mortification danced with heartbreak.

'What am I going to do with her, Joly?'

'Oh, dear. What a shame.'

'I correct the kids. You never back me up.'

'Here's the taxi.' Dad stowed our luggage. He tucked in his long legs, slamming the door.

The driver scowled. 'That's a car door, mate. Not a bloody barn door.'

Warner's Bay glittered in afternoon light. A rainbow of sails billowed in a stiff breeze. At Albert Street, Granny's hug made me feel safe and treasured. I delighted in her lavender aroma.

Her garden sang with orange calendula red sweet peas. Green and purple grapes trembled from a laden pergola.

Grandfather Wright, even taller than my daddy, plucked me a bunch. 'You'll like the green ones.'

The fruit melted in my mouth.

Uncle Charles glanced at my long pale legs. 'You'll soon get a tan.' In photos, he wore a smart uniform. Wavy blond hair, grin. Charles had served in the air force during the war.

I suspect Mum had looked forward to a quiet chat with her in-laws. I wanted a swim. Seagulls dived and soared in the briny tang. Wavelets crumpled into foam lace over my toes. A shriek of golden-brown children scornfully eyed my pale skin.

A freckled youth jingled coins in a pouch. Yellow trunks, multicoloured cap. 'Get your boats here, folks. Two bob for half an hour.'

Gleeful shouts, friends paddling in red and yellow craft.

'Please, Mum.'

'A boat?' She sat in the shade, one eye on Curley. 'I don't think so.'

'Shallow water, missus. She can't get into trouble,' said a bearded man 'Great fun for kids.'

'Victor, do you want a boat?'

He scuffed toes in the sand. 'Nah. Not me.

'Good lad. Such sense.'

Coins exchanged hands. The freckled boy handed over the oars. Other boats skimmed effortlessly over the bay. Mine spun in circles. Wavelets carried me further and further out. I fought tears. Freckles swam to my side. Taking the prow in a suntanned hand, he towed me to shore. Oh, the glorious sensation of dry sand between my toes.

Victor smirked. 'Serves you right.'

I feared being the butt of family jokes.

Grandfather starred that evening. We enjoyed his funny tales. And a repertoire of music hall ditties, sung in his fine tenor voice. In 'The Billiard Ball', our hero put it in his mouth, 'It was a fix, fix, fix, it was a fixture'. Songs by Harry Lauder like 'Stop your Ticklin' Jock' had the men laughing.

Grandfather told of his half-brother. 'Wild Billy. Always drunk. Loved fights.'

Dad grinned. 'I worshipped him as a kid. Everything I wanted to be.'

Mum glared.

'Cops used to put him in a cell overnight to sober up. After one riotous spree, the constabulary came to arrest him. "Righto, Jones,' says the sergeant, 'Arrest him.'" "No…last time he broke me jaw." The sergeant turned to Smith. "You take him in." "If Jones won't take him, neither will I." The sergeant hesitated. "Well…maybe we'll leave him this time."'

Everybody roared. Charles asked, 'Didn't Wild Billy strike gold?'

'Yes – and a good deal of it. Could have bought a place. Set himself up for life. Our Billy gambled or gave away the lot. Sometimes his pockets bulged with sovereigns and pennies. He galloped through town, scattering showers of coins. Kids scrabbled to retrieve them.'

Daddy's face shone. 'I couldn't wait to grow up, and be like him. Enjoying the greatest fun in the world.'

Mum sniffed. 'A drunk showing off? Some example.'

Dad told of his time as a young boy with his aunt Amy. 'I was about fourteen. She and Grandfather ran a wine shanty, secretly selling rum on the side. Amy ran card games for drovers and boarders. The loser shouted drinks for the bar. Casks of red wine were stored in a shadowed room. Auntie struck matches, then turned on the tap. The wine ran very slowly. The match would sputter out, a glass not quite full. In the time it took her to strike another, I downed the wine. Putting the empty one back under the tap. Auntie looked at me suspiciously.'

Mum glowered. 'Someone should have tanned your jolly hide.'

Grandfather went on, 'Wine at the bottom of the cask was thick and almost black. Some chaps waited for the dark stuff to start their spree. Made them drunk faster. But terrible hangovers.'

He sang everything from 'If You Were the Only Girl in the World' to operatic numbers. 'I took singing lessons with Dame Nellie Melba's teacher at Gulgong. She reckoned I'd have a career in opera, if I worked hard. My parents couldn't afford the tuition. Anyway, I'd lost interest by then.'

I yawned, eyes half-closed.

Mum took my hand. 'Come along, kids. It's way past your bedtime.'

Our family gathered at a park. A reunion and picnic with relatives from Victoria. Grandfather's absence was noted.

Uncle Bill chuckled. 'Never expect Father to join us on a Saturday. He's slipped away for a flutter on the dawgs with Mrs Littlewood.'

Grandma shot Uncle a dark glance. Was there some unspoken mystery about the lady?

Auntie told me years later that Gran had hated Grandfather taking an interest in Mrs Littlewood. Uncle Bill also squired her around town. 'Her husband became jealous.' Auntie told him, 'You don't need to worry about Bill. He has sugar diabetes.' She giggled. 'I explained it curtailed certain – er, activities. Uncle Bill had no further problems.'

Dad recalled the day his mother was away. 'We washed the floor with caustic soda. The cat lost all the hair on her tail!'

Uncle Arthur mused, 'I often think of the time Sid Bill sewed up a cut in the sole of Sid's foot. Blood everywhere. Sid gritted his teeth. Bill took Mother's curved needle and thread, peering through your thick glasses. You should have been a doctor, mate.'

'I would've liked to be one. Had my chance after the war. My eyesight scuttled that.'

Sid recalled Aileen's suitor, one nobody liked. 'We boys invited him to lunch. Mother wasn't home. We made him a special dessert. Aileen was too busy making cow eyes to notice.'

Dad chuckled. 'The poor bugger dived his spoon through a thick layer of cream, expecting a prune. His tongue detected something odd. He removed the item from his mouth…'

Sid chortled. 'Turkey droppings. I came up with the idea.'

Victor and I looked at each other. 'Poo? Yuk!'

Mum glowered. 'I'd have thrashed the lot of you.'

Aileen's eyes glinted, 'You boys ruined my romance. I never saw him again.'

Dad recalled pranks in tents. 'Apple pie beds… Bits of string pulled through dry grass to simulate the sound of a snake. I terrified more than one mate with that – especially new chums. Ah, the misdeeds of youth.'

We tucked into sandwiches, roast chicken, salads, corned beef, apple pies, and cakes.

Daddy put tea leaves in a billycan. 'Take this to one of those houses opposite, Victor. Ask the lady for boiling water.'

We heard Daddy saying, 'Nothing like a nice cuppa to finish a meal.'

Gran handed over an empty cup.

'Won't be long, Mother.'

Two boys opened the door.

The elder lad stared at my close-cropped hair. 'What's your brother wearin' a dress fur?'

The other lad giggled.

'Not my brother. She's my sister.'

'That ain't no girl.'

'I am a girl.'

'Course she is.'

The big lad sniggered. 'Let's take him to the toilet and find out.'

'No! I won't go.'

Their mother appeared at the door. 'What is going on?'

The boys feigned innocence. 'Nothing.'

Victor stammered his request.

'Hot water? Of course.' She smiled, taking the billy.

Dad glowered. 'We were about to send out a search party. What the devil kept you?'

Mum stamped her foot. 'A simple errand. Trust you kids to get into some silly argument.'

Daddy stirred sugar into his tea as if to wind it up.

Uncle Bill chuckled.

Daddy stopped at the Warners Bay corner shop for treats. Outside stood a young lady. Her long platinum-blonde hair captured my admiration. Nobody could mistake that glorious creature for a boy. We shared half-smiles. My ice cream dripped. I didn't even notice, or care.

Daddy said, 'You aren't going to waste that?' He gobbled the lot.

Mum shot my Goddess a scornful glance. 'Colours like that only come from a bottle.'

My cheeks flamed.

Grandfather told of his father, the first Joseph. 'A huge man. Strong and versatile. Bushman, mining engineer… Years older than his wife, Marion Connolly. Her mother realised the way the wind was blowing and locked up Marion's clothes. At seventeen, she defied the ban on nuptials. Dressed in black, she wed my father. Married by an out-of-town minister.'

Grandfather went on, 'I'll never forget Father's wonderful tales. He fought the Blackfoot Indians. Took part in the Mexican uprisings. Fossicked in the Californian gold rush. Played a leading role in the Eureka Stockade. I believed every word.'

Dad asked, 'Do you reckon all those things happened?'

Grandfather chuckled. 'Who am I to question a good yarn? Truth is elastic when it comes to campfire tales. Take away a scrap here, add a bit there.'

Decades later, my cousin John would research family history. 'The real Joseph Ananias Wright remains a mystery, more elusive than gold. Was his family ever in the US? Was he a convict? Given the dates, it's impossible for all those adventures to have happened to one man. He reminds me of James Thurber's character Walter Mitty.'

We left Gran's house in Albert Street. My regrets tingled with excitement.

The time had come to make friends, explore books.

12

I began school in brilliant sunshine, cool for January. Back then, children in small country schools started kindergarten at six or seven. Teachers taught classes from primary to secondary. Doubtless, five-year-old pupils would have made a difficult post impossible.

Mum took out her Box Brownie. My brother's face was solemn. Smart trilby, brown and fawn striped jumper, shorts. A fat puppy was pinioned between Victor's heels. It wouldn't stop licking and jumping.

My sister Curley smiled. She looked cute in her blue, crocheted lace dress. I loved her mop of blonde curls.

My face was partially shadowed. Arms rigid at my sides. Hair straight as a pin, long enough for a red bow. Mum had knitted my green cardigan. The short skirt emphasised my long legs.

The bus delivered mail and parcels.

Mum told the driver, 'Put the kids off at Belltrees School.'

Mum's final kiss. 'Wait until the bus stops before you get off. Make sure Dessie is with you.'

Victor looked embarrassed.

I glanced around. We were the sole passengers. I guessed other children lived near the school.

Mum held Curley's hand. They waved. Lost to sight.

Victor rigid in his seat. Afraid of missing our stop? Or worried over Dad's stories of teachers who caned for fun?

Victor whistled like Dad, to keep his spirits up. Cream weatherboard school. A group of students gave us the once-over.

Pert blonde with neat plaits, smart uniform, shiny shoes. 'What a funny cardigan.'

'And look at her skirt, Jenny.' Giggles. 'Home-made, poor thing.'

Only then did I notice the skew-whiff red, blue and green checks across the front of my skirt. As for my cardigan… Aunt Linda had muttered, 'Good wool spoilt.'

Inside the classroom, Mr Kurt handed around brightly illustrated ABC and reading books.

'May I help, sir?'

'Why, thank you, Jenny.'

She took over and placed a reading book in front of each child. I pictured one of them in my hands. The silky cover. New aroma. At the desk before mine, the supply ran out. Tears pricked my eyes.

Mr Kurt shrugged. 'You'll get yours when the stationery order arrives.'

I made to share. My neighbour snatched her book away.

At recess, girls chattered and shrieked. A question I daren't ask trembled on my lips. Where was the toilet? Mum said it wasn't nice to talk about such things. And Victor pretended he didn't know me.

I held out through the morning classes.

Mr Kurt loomed over me. 'Little girl…the new one. What's your name?

'Dessie Wright.'

'Didn't you hear me ask you a question?'

'No.'

'No, what?'

The class giggled. What had I said?

'You must respond, Yes, sir, or No, sir, to me. I asked about your religion. Victor, can you tell me?'

My brother shifted uneasily. 'Please, sir. What was the question?'

Mr Kurt rolled his eyes. 'Are you deaf, boy?'

Victor flushed. 'No, sir.'

'Jenny, perhaps you might enlighten this…'

'Idiot?' said someone. Chuckles.

'Certainly, sir.' Her glance was triumphant. 'Which church do you attend?'

Victor's face flamed scarlet. 'We don't go to church, sir.'

Glances of astonishment. Giggles.

'Where were you christened?'

'We weren't.'

Eyes swivelled in our direction. Daddy had said we were fortunate to be freed from the fetters of religion. Whatever that meant.

I had the feeling Victor's words confirmed we were odd.

Lunch recess. Two girls spun a rope, feet skipped. Apple sauce, mustard, spider. One, two, three, four…

Boys played cricket, thwacked balls against bats. Victor didn't glance my way.

Nauseated, I tossed my sandwiches into a bin. He didn't notice.

I knelt, in agony. Without warning, the floodgates opened. Yellow rivulets dispersed over the dry earth. Horror juggled with relief.

A damp and uncomfortable afternoon. Whispers and giggles. I tried not to mind.

Relieved to leave early for the bus.

Victor glared. 'You stink. That was dumb.'

'I couldn't find the toilet.'

'Didn't you see those two buildings on the hill?'

Mum met us at the door.

Victor dropped his case on the floor. 'Dessie wet her pants. And I couldn't do my sums.'

Her brow creased. 'For goodness sake. Didn't Mr Kurt show you the toilets?'

'No! And I'm the only one in first class without a reader.'

She turned to Victor. 'The teacher didn't explain your arithmetic?'

'Kids learnt long division last term.'

'Did they indeed?' She poured hot water into a dish, brought a towel, washer, soap. 'Change into fresh clothes, Dessie. Eat your Sao biscuits, kids. Then we'll sort this out.' She said to me, 'Doubtless, your reading book will arrive next week. I'll help you until then.' She talked Victor through his sums. 'Thanks, Mum. They aren't hard, after all.'

My second day of school. I wouldn't make the same mistake again. I entered a small building on the hill. Puzzled by a metal trough.

Children fell about with mirth. 'She goes to the boys' toilet.'

In class Mr Kurt rapped a ruler across my knuckles. 'I said to take out your reading book.'

I trembled. 'Please, sir… I don't have one.'

The class tittered.

Mr Kurt brushed back strands of grey hair. 'Oh! You'll get it later.'

We returned from school.

Mum asked, 'What did you learn today?'

'Nothing.'

'Did Mr Kurt give you a reader?'

'No.'

'Right.' She helped me with reading. Set Victor a few sums.

Mum and Curley were alone. A stranger barged into the house. He asked the whereabouts of a neighbour.

Mum said, 'Sorry. I don't know anybody of that name.'

He eyed her bosom.

She stepped back. 'Please, go.'

He sniggered. 'What's the hurry, missus?'

Peggy appeared – usually, she went to work with Daddy. The gentlest of animals, she stood in front of Mum and snarled, baring her teeth. The man took off in a screech of tyres.

Mum gave a shaky laugh. 'You fooled him, Peggy.'

A house was robbed further along the river.

Mr Kurt played his 'Take out your reader' game every week for six months. Perhaps he imagined education was wasted on a rabbit-trapper's daughter? My parents felt angry, yet ill-equipped to deal with the situation. I'll be forever grateful to Mum for filling the gap.

Daddy shared his encounter with birdlife. 'I was about to set a trap. A flock of happy families squabbled in a box tree above. The noise drove me batty. I shouted, "Will you shut up?" and threw the digger at them. Luckily, it missed. I'd hate to have hurt the poor things. Afterwards, they lowered their voices, whispering to each other. God knows what they called me.'

Daddy's paddocks were rabbit-free. The landowner called it paradise. His wife declared it was like winning the lottery every year.

New acres awaited. Cabans had no road access. We loaded tents and belongings into Hungry's pack-saddles, travelling on foot. In crisp, morning air, blades of grass dripped diamonds. Each of us carried something; mine was a golden syrup tin. It rattled wonderfully. I shook it once too often. The lid flew off, nails scattering in all directions. Daddy helped me retrieve them. Ants, sticks and stones bit my bare legs.

He set up the adult tent. Ours followed. A large one served as living room cum kitchen. The corrugated-iron fireplace stood at one end. Linda was expecting, so she and Cecil enjoyed a nearby cabin.

Whooping cough struck. Diarrhoea had kids rushing to the toilet, half a paddock away. Coughing left us exhausted. Mum nursed us through it.

Correspondence school brought my very own reading book. I caressed the smooth, woven cover. Greedily consumed the feast of stories. Begged for more. Traced the organic shape of cup hooks and pot holders with a sharp pencil. Cursive writing lay within reach.

Mum said, 'You kids learn more in one morning than weeks with that useless Kurt.'

No set hour marked the end of studies. Lessons finished, we explored. Chuckling at an echidna, rolled into a mass of spikes. We turned over and over down grassy slopes, squealing with laughter. Slid down bare earth embankments – great fun. But not for Mum.

She hand-washed our filthy trousers and knickers. 'Stop or I'll murder you both.'

Snakes were easy to spot. Small critters brought grief. I picked up a unique piece of wood, failing to notice a bull-ant. My right hand ballooned. I couldn't write for days.

We sniffed tiny orchids with brownish petals. The aroma brought to mind chocolate milkshakes.

In a dry creek, we found an area of flat rock, smoothed by countless floods. It seemed huge. Serving as cubby-house, picnic site and stage. On the hottest days we lazed in the shade, dappled by casuarina trees.

Morning drizzled in with stormy skies.

Dad said, 'It poured overnight. Drought's broken.'

Rivulets kissed parched pebbles, foaming into lace. Cecil's black and white kittens had never seen water. They batted it with their paws. Their mother wailed from the bank.

Mum laughed. She took their picture. 'Don't they know cats hate water?'

Tom had passed away from old age. Cecil found homes for the other kittens, giving Trixie, the prettiest of the litter, to me.

Victor started a scary version of hide-and-seek. 'Careful! They'll shoot us.'

I glanced around a deserted paddock. 'Who?'

'Japs. Didn't you see him? Oops, another.'

Old fears rushed back. 'You're kidding...aren't you?'

Victor told of evil faces, smirking as they passed. He dropped behind a bush. 'Surely you saw the shining on the barrel of that gun?'

I fell beside him. My tears were flowing fast. Legs scratched and bleeding, my cotton dress was torn. And ants bit me on the bum, among the blackened grass.

Victor seemed quite cheery. 'Ugly brutes. They'll slit your neck.'

'I haven't seen one.'

'Huh! They're here by the dozen. Swords dripping bright red blood. They've got Curley and our mum.'

My steps faltered in the dying sun. 'Let's run away. Hide.'

'You'd let the Japs kill them?'

My footsteps dragged. We reached our big tent.

Victor edged around the chimney. 'I'd make a dash for it...'

Voices. Calm women's voices. Linda, a teacup in her hand. Curley with her dolls.

Mum dropped her knitting. 'What are you up to, Victor?'

'Nothing.'

'Why the tears, Dessie?'

Fury engulfed me. ' Victor said Japs had you prisoner.'

'That's a silly game, Victor.' Then she laughed at me for saying the Japs were at the door, 'Don't you know the war's over? Three years or more?'

I felt foolish for not remembering.

'Dry your tears. I've made us a picnic lunch.'

We munched cheese sandwiches and bananas. Pine trees soughed. Clouds formed evil faces. A dog sat on its haunches. Dissolved.

Mum embroidered the bodice of a baby dress. The other day she'd hidden a tiny jacket.

I sat up. 'Mum, are you having a baby?'

She flushed. Pushed needlework into a bag. 'What makes you think that?'

'The baby stuff.'

'Er…it's…for a friend.'

'Which friend?'

'You wouldn't know her. Let's get rid of these picnic things. Come along, Curley.'

Victor watched her leave. 'Mum used to take her apron off for visitors. Now she puts it on. And she's getting fat, like Linda.'

Daddy considered buying a ute. 'If only a man could drive.'

Cecil grinned. 'I'll teach you. And my uncle could help with a reliable vehicle.'

'Good-oh. Let's make a road to our camp.'

The rudimentary track completed, they set off for Brunker Road, in Sydney. Cecil drove home.

Dad grinned. 'A half-tonne Ford second-hand. Four hundred pounds.'

The basic wage was about one pound a week.

Mum frowned. 'That's a lot of money.'

'The ute's hardly used, luv. Worth every penny.'

Victor pored over the knobs and bobs.

Daddy confessed, 'Vehicles seem alien to me. Barely controlled by humans. Suppose the ute gets out of control?'

Cecil laughed. 'No worries, mate. I'll show you everything.'

'That's the petrol cap. I can change the oil and top up the battery. What else?'

'Can you clean a carburettor? They're trouble.'

'Show me where the darned thing is first.' His big hands grasped a strand of wire, swilled petrol…'

'No parts over and in working order. Well done, Joly.'

Driving lessons began. Daddy clung to the steering wheel with white knuckles. Took off with kangaroo jumps. Crashed gears. Stalled the motor. Put the ute into reverse, by mistake, on a steep hill. His swear words were enough to put Mum into a tizz. Had she been there.

Boy, was I glad to reach home.

He said, 'I know the rules and regulations, luv. I'll go for my licence.'

'B-but you've only the haziest idea how to drive.'

He left with a wave and shriek of gears.

Mum met him on return. 'When do they want you back?'

'They granted me a licence on the spot.'

'They what?'

'I passed the oral test easily. The sergeant checked my vision. The right eye was perfect. I covered it to check my left. Couldn't see a thing. The sergeant chuckled. "You've pressed against the left eye, affecting your vision. With the sight in your right eye, I'd grant a licence anyway."'

'What did he say about your driving?'

Dad looked sheepish. 'He didn't check that.'

'So he doesn't know you can't… Oh, my hat! You'll have us all killed.'

Outside, Daddy winked at Victor, 'It took four rums to get my courage up.'

Mum's concerns switched to Poppy. 'I've sent two letters.'

'Most likely she's busy.'

'Who's not busy? It's damn rude not to reply.'

By then, Daddy drove on the roughest terrain. He missed boulders and stumps by inches. The ute tilted at scary angles. At any moment, we expected it to roll over.

Mum said, 'Wake up. You've gone from timid to reckless.'

More than once, we bailed out and walked home.

One matter puzzles me. Why did Mum delay announcing her pregnancy? A month before her due date, she confirmed what we already knew.

Awaiting her confinement, we rented a cottage in Gundy. Before British occupation, the hamlet had been an important Aboriginal ceremonial site. That's where whites settled. In the 1800s, travellers used it as a stopover. Gundy starred in *The Shiralee*, locals used as extras. Red Mill Club members drank a bottle of rum a day. The fifties would bring murder.

One detective said, 'Half the town are too drunk to answer questions. The other are half too stupid.'

Six members of one family suffered genetic defects.

Dad said, 'Harmless enough.'

At eight, I rushed past them and their dilapidated home.

The smithy tended his forge in a long, leather apron. His fire glowed at white heat. A hammer pinged against the anvil, pounding horseshoes into shape. Hot metal sizzled in cold water. 'Makes it strong. Tempering, we call it.' Draught horses pulled ploughs and carts. Saddle animals attended to stock work. Certain farmers used buggies for town. 'My skills are still needed.'

Shops facades gleamed with cream paint. The general store sold everything from petrol to food, and fencing supplies. Mr Brown, in white apron, scribbled notes on a pad. He rushed back and forth, pencil behind one ear. Customers told of bad legs and dicky hearts. Mr Brown cut portions of cheese with a wire. Weighed pounds of sugar. Large jars held musk sticks, conversation lollies, Minties. Boiled sweets came at ten a penny. My mouth watered.

'Yes, young lady? And what can I do for you?'

'A pennorth of bullseyes and jelly babies, please.'

'And you, young sir?'

Victor chose liquorice all sorts.

Tantalising aromas drew us to the baker's shop. Currant buns, cinnamon rolls and hot meat pies.

'Two standard-size loaves, please.'

'Wholemeal or white?'

'Wholemeal, thanks.'

Mum sliced them at home.

The butcher's shop smelt of death. Sawdust clung to my shoes.

The owner said, 'And how are your family?'

Mum chose a pound of fine mince. I loved her meatballs, a mix of spices and onion. Her thick, brown gravy was delicious with mash, beans and pumpkin.

A decade later, supermarkets would arrive in Scone. The general store and butcher's shop went first, paint-peeling facades. The baker's shop burnt to the ground. The Linga Longa Inn flourished. A little corner store took the smithy's spot. A post office occupied one corner, petrol a useful sideline.

Dad would say there was little capital tied up in stock. 'It'll survive.'

13

Mum worried about the Gundy school in 1948. Would Mr Kane give us proper tuition?

A parcel of hand-me-down clothing arrived from cousin Pat. Her old school uniform fitted me perfectly.

Auntie wrote, 'Suggest the kids call themselves Anglicans. It will save bother.'

Mr Kane made introductions, and pointed out the toilets. He showed a keen interest in every child's progress. And I borrowed enough books to start my own library.

Valerie, Susie, Enid and I played hopscotch and jump rope. John and Kevin enjoyed cricket and rounders with Victor. He won a prize for painting, an unexpected talent.

One morning, Enid's mum took aim at a snake in their garden. Bang! My friend ran into the firing line. Amputation of her foot meant home schooling. I missed her cheery face.

Curley demanded we call her Vivi.

Late August 1948, the two of us helped Mum carry her suitcase to the bus stop. She wore a bright pink maternity dress. Other passengers eyed her enormous bulge. I felt embarrassed.

Mum kissed us. 'Be a good girl, Dessie. Look after your sister.'

The bus misted from sight. We passed our cottage, its eyes squeezed shut. The house next door was empty, too. That mother had died of cancer. Her children seemed lost. Suppose our mum didn't come back?

Mrs Scamps wheezed as she shuffled her bulk along the concrete path. The mother of fourteen children, Daddy had paid her to mind us. 'You'll be in safe hands.' Victor stayed with him.

I breathed the red scent of roses. Bees buzzed on yesterday, today and tomorrow blossoms.

She glanced up, face creased into a smile. 'Mum get off all right?'

'Yes.'

At five, Vivi whimpered. 'How long will Mum be away?'

'Fourteen sleeps.'

'She'll be back before you know it, girls.'

The old lady bent over to pull weeds. She wore no knickers. I felt shocked. Best not to tell Mum.

Every hour dragged. Our nighties went missing. We slept in our dresses, wearing them day after day. My hairbrush grew thick with loose hairs. They defied removal. Ribbons hid in our case.

Vivi's curls challenged untangling. She shrieked, 'Stop. It's hurting.'

Our long shadows, hand in hand, made morning and afternoon pilgrimages to the post office.

No news.

A runny nose. My handkerchiefs went missing. Almost in despair, I found ironed ones at the bottom of my case. My eyes seemed gritty, looked red and felt sore. Reading became impossible. I dreaded mornings. Waking in terror, my eyelids glued shut. I groped my way to the laundry. Fumbling for the tap.

Footsteps padded on linoleum. A frantic 'Sis...'

'Laundry.'

My sister raced to my side. I doused my face and lids with ice-cold water. Removed dried crusts from my lids and eyelashes. Overwhelming relief. I can see, I can see.

Vivi whined for Mum. Would that blooming baby ever arrive?

Another fruitless mission to the post office. Two weeks? It seemed like a year.

Fathers' Day, 3 September. The dark-haired assistant waved a telegram. 'Congratulations, girls! A little brother.'

Daddy took us to see our baby. Druce's red, creased face reminded me of a butterfly which had just emerged from a chrysalis.

Mum beamed. 'Isn't he beautiful?'

We felt overjoyed to have Mum home. Even though she curbed our wandering. Even when she became cross. Even though Druce yowled – thank goodness he slept most of the time.

Mum prepared his Lactogen. 'They say it's better than breast milk.' She clucked over Vivi's hair. 'Your curls haven't been brushed properly since I left.' She cut out the knots.

Druce lay without nappy, kicking.

Mum beamed. 'Babies need ten minutes sunlight daily.'

We expected to attend a fete.

'Sorry, girls, I'm too tired.'

I howled.

'You selfish girl, thinking only of yourself.'

I cried all the louder.

Mum folded a towelling nappy into a double triangle. Wound a cloth binder around my brother's tummy. 'Stops problems with the belly button.' Supporting his head, she slipped on his singlet. A long dress, new matinee jacket, and fancy bonnet.

He looked cute. I loved the aroma of Johnson's baby powder.

She helped me lift Druce into the cane pram. Bought second-hand, and painted cream, it looked new. I adjusted the embroidered blanket, and took charge.

She held Vivi's hand. People stopped us to admire the baby.

One acquaintance asked, 'Is he really yours?

She bristled, 'Of course he's mine.'

At the School of Arts building, treasures of every sort met my delighted eyes. Old jewellery, crockery, flat irons, toys, books.

Mum handed over a shilling. 'Spend it wisely.'

I spotted a kaleidoscope. Spellbound by the variety of colourful shapes. Vivi tried to grab it.

'Get lost. It's mine.'

'Behave, you two.'

We sucked peppermint-flavoured pink and white striped bullseyes.

Victor bought Ginger Meggs comics and marbles. A jigsaw had parts missing. 'I like it anyway.'

Vivi selected a pretty pink necklace. And spent the rest on a doll with no arms.

Mum tutted. 'A waste of money.'

She treated us to Passiona. I spilt mine down the front of my dress.

She rubbed the stain with a hanky. 'Do be more careful.'

'It's time to feed Druce.'

One of the ladies smiled. 'That's a baby for you. Either wet or ready for a feed.'

We arrived home. Mum mixed Druce's formula.

Vivi jumped up and down. 'Mum… Mum!'

'Wait. Can't you see I'm busy?' Mum was either up to her elbows in the washtub, about to fix feeds, or with a broom in hand.

I was happy with my book. But I could see that not having her mother's time troubled Vivi.

Mum stamped. 'Jealous of a baby? It's wicked.'

Vivi hung her head.

Daddy arrived on a visit. 'I'll pop out for a while.'

'That darned pub. Your tea's almost ready.'

'Back in half an hour.'

An hour passed. Mum fed Druce, put him down. Gave us our meals. Picked at hers. Glanced at the clock. Two hours.

Seething, she scribbled a note. 'Give this to your father, Victor. He's to return home.'

We stood outside the bar. Daddy's laugh was louder than the rest. Finally Victor found someone to take our message. Come home. Immediately.

Daddy appeared, one arm around a scruffy little man with a red face. They stank of cigarette smoke and beer.

At the cottage, Daddy slurred, 'Me mate Sid Ashland. Down on his luck. Here for tea. And staying the night.'

Mum's voice was glacial. 'Your food is stone-cold, Joly.'

'I'm glad to share mine, Sid. I'll warm it up. Can't have a mate eat cold dinner. Plenty of bread and jam for afters.'

I felt embarrassed. How awful it would be without a home.

Sid finished his meatball and vegetables. He spread a thick slice of bread with butter and jam. Devoured a second one, Burped. 'That was dee-lich-es, missus. Delicious.' His sad eyes reminded me of a stray. 'I can doss down anywhere, missus. Beside the fire will be dandy.'

Dad put down the camping mattress, added linen. 'Pyjamas?'

'No thanks, Joly. I'll sleep in me undies.'

Morning dawned. The living room smelt like a toilet.

It surprised me that adults wet their beds. Dad helped Sid wash. Found a spare pair of long johns. Rolled up the bottoms, so they didn't show under his trousers.

After breakfast, Sid shared a bleary glance. 'I'm lookin' for work.'

Dad shook Sid's hand. 'I'll see what I can do.'

Mid-morning he slunk away.

Mum stamped her foot. 'Filthy animal. It's obvious he's a drunk. Work? You'd rue the day.'

'Genn, I hope someone would help me out if I was in trouble.'

'Don't think I'll wash his disgusting linen.'

'My dear, I wouldn't expect it.' Whistling, Daddy dunked the sheets and blankets in soapy water. Rinsed them twice.

We farewelled our Gundy friends. Linda Scamps stayed with her mother, awaiting the birth. Cecil joined her. He'd become an inspector with the Pastures Protection Board. Our family bagged the slab hut. A kitchen occupied one end, sleeping quarters the other.

Daddy eyed a tall kurrajong tree 'Doubtless it grew here by chance.'

Victor had attached a rope to one limb. I climbed to the top. The rope slid between my hands on the way down. I learned the hard way about friction burns and palm blisters.

I stacked crockery into the washing-up bowl. Victor rested a can of boiling water on the floor. Vivi rushed around the table. In the half-light, her foot plunged into scalding liquid. Her screams brought Mum running.

'Careless, silly boy. Never, ever, put boiled water down there.' She immersed Vivi's foot in cold water. 'Bring me the first-aid box, a towel – oh, and butter. That helps scalds.'

'I won't do it again, Mum. Honest.' Victor awkwardly patted Vivi's head.

Mum dried the injured foot, smeared it with butter. Added a bandage. And hugged the sobbing child. 'There, there.'

Dad put on his jacket. 'You mind the kids, Genn. I'll get Vivi to the doctor.'

Victor lifted a tear-stained face. 'Is she going to be all right, Mum?'
'We hope for the best.'

Daddy told me the story years later. 'I still felt nervous about driving in traffic. Distracted by Vivi's cries, I asked Harold Kergan to take the wheel. I comforted Vivi on the way. Harold's face was sombre. "Shame such a thing's happened. A lovely little girl like you, Vivi."'

Daddy cradled her in his arms. 'Be brave, sweetie. Doc will soon have you better.'

Harold changed gears. 'Your girls seemed neglected while your wife was in hospital. Nobody looks after kids like their own mother. Genn does a splendid job. I admire the way she copes.'

At Scone, the doctor examined the foot. 'Pass on my compliments to your wife. Her quick action reduced the damage. Cold water was the right treatment. The butter would've soothed it, too.'

Her foot had second and third-degree burns. He dressed the wounds with Ung-Vita. 'Have your wife dress the foot daily. Bring Vivi back should any problems develop.'

Every time I heard Vivi's cries that night, the horror of her accident rushed back. Ung-Vita settled the blisters.

Weeks later came the final check-up. 'Superb job, Mrs Wright. The wounds have healed beautifully. Scarring is almost non-existent.'

Sid Ashland repeated his request for work. 'Everyone deserves a trial, Genn.'

Mum stalked off.

Dad explained to Sid, 'Your job is to burn log heaps.'

Sid looked at him with rheumy eyes. 'Why?'

'They harbour rabbits.'

Sid bowed. 'As you wish, sir. One of nature's gentlemen.'

Days later, Daddy came home, chuckling. 'Lazy old devil. Not one log burnt today. Snoozing. Empty rum bottle beside him.'

'Why aren't I surprised?'

'My dear, I have to admit you were right.'

Daddy shaped number eight fencing wire into different-size frames. He smoothed and stretched moist skins to fit, placing them in the sun to be cured. A pile of skins awaited sale.

Daddy swore us to secrecy over one last task. 'Old bushies' sleight of hand. Buyers offer us much less for skins in Scone than Sydney. This ensures a good price.'

Mum nodded. 'Evens things our way.'

A warm summer evening. Moths fluttered around the hurricane lamp. Our shadows leapt in weird, elongated shapes. We raced up and down the field, placing cured skins on dew-laden grass. A few hours' exposure to the moisture brought softness to the fur.

Daddy grinned. 'Adds weight and value.'

Daddy took me with him next day. 'Dessie might soften the old devil's heart.'

Inside the huge warehouse, my nose wrinkled. The smell of old fat and rabbit skins was almost overwhelming.

Mr Rascle, the dealer, flashed his bought smile. 'Good morning, little girl. What's your name?'

Shyly, I told him.

'And how is your health, Joly?'

'Not so bad, not so bad.' Daddy rubbed his hands.

Mr Rascle made cheerful asides about the weather. All the while he stroked the soft fur. A gleam in his eyes. Quickly hidden. He sighed, naming a low figure.

'In Sydney they're offering...'

'Ah, yes, my friend. Those are the finest skins. These?' He shrugged.

Daddy lifted the price. Mr Rascle lowered it a bit. And so on. I was fascinated.

Mr Rascle made a show of hesitation. He upturned the palms of his hands. 'That's my absolute limit.'

Daddy paused. 'I'll take it.'

Business over, they parted with smiles and handshakes.

Outside, Daddy winked. 'Twice what he'd have paid if we hadn't... Old devil still makes a fair profit. We've done well.'

Daddy told me later the word was barter. I tasted it on my tongue.

At the fruit shop, his eyes fell on two big bunches of bananas. 'I'll have those thanks, mate. My favourite.'

The fruiterer laughed, and gave me an extra one.

Swinging my legs on a park bench beside Daddy, we drooled over our treat.

Mum looked pleased to hear things had gone well. 'Are we ready to go home?'

'Not yet, sweetheart. We need more savings.'

I'd long known that my father killed rabbits. Never expecting to be involved in their slaughter, I retained a surreal innocence. Delighted by their fluffy white tails and inquisitive eyes. And I read *Peter Rabbit*.

Victor and Daddy were off to town.

'You'll have to run the traps today, Dessie.'

My eyes widened. 'Me?'

His voice was matter-of-fact. 'Hit the rabbits on their heads with my mallet. It's not hard to kill them. Put them in this bag.' He held up a sack. 'It'll be heavy. I'll collect it this afternoon.'

I wouldn't step on an ant. 'No!'

'There'll be pocket money.' He jingled the coins in his pocket.

Mum glared. 'You're lazy. A big girl of eight. I trapped rabbits for my father when I was six.'

I hoped Daddy would change his mind.

His voice was gentle. 'We can't leave them to suffer in traps all day.'

The sack thumped against my back. Oh, why did magpies carol with such joy?

Dappled in blinding light, the rabbits rattled their shackles. I'd pretend the traps were empty. But Daddy would guess the truth. And Mum? Tears stung my eyes. A voice screamed, 'No, no…' A little girl floated somewhere outside of herself. And wept on the grass.

Ark! Ark! Ark! Dark shape. Skeletal tree. Stiletto beak. Crows find rabbits' eyes a delicacy.

I flung a rock, screaming, 'Go away.'

Black wings. Flap, whoosh. Crow settled on the highest branch. Waiting. How could I leave the rabbits to that?

Mutilated paws. Frightened eyes. I hit each one gently, hoping to avoid further pain. Placing one inert body after another in the sack. Caressed by my tears.

I caught my breath. The prettiest yellow rabbit I'd ever seen. A prince among his clan. He shimmered before my amazed eyes. In an instant, my mind was made up. 'I'll not kill you.'

Yellow Rabbit sat quietly. My hateful task finished, I flung aside the mallet. Prince made no attempt to escape. Miraculously, his leg was uninjured.

'You're my friend.'

He seemed to understand every word. Stroking his soft fur, I slipped Prince inside my woollen jacket. I didn't know the word, but the concept was clear enough. He would atone for all the others.

Mum met me at the door. 'Did you do the job?'

I hesitated. 'Yes.'

'What's the bulge under your coat?

Triumphantly, I brought him forth. 'My friend, Prince. Isn't he beautiful?'

Mum scowled. 'You can't keep that.'

'But, Mum...'

'No buts. It's a wonder the thing didn't scratch you to pieces. Kill it at once.'

'Kill him? Kill my friend?'

I looked at Prince. He stared back with trusting eyes. Mine swam and blurred.

Time has erased memory of the awful deed. Did I stare in shame at his betrayed and lifeless body? Or set him free, to take his chances? By a cruel twist of fate, Daddy found all the other rabbits alive. My blows had only stunned them.

Daddy's contract ended.

The landowner grinned. 'Strong fences, rabbit-free pastures. I couldn't be happier.'

The owner's wife chuckled agreement. 'Our wool cheque is a lottery win every year.'

'There's money in felling timber at Stewarts Brook.'

Uncle Charles planned to join Daddy.

Mum raised her eyebrows. 'What's he know about bush work?'

'He'll learn.'

I've never forgotten my first glimpse of Rose Hill Cottage.

Mum said, 'Just look at those windows.'

They glinted pure gold in the afternoon light.

Daddy grinned. 'A fitting image. The valley produced tons of the stuff.'

Trevor Rose, Dad's friend, arrived to greet us. My father was six feet six. Shorty topped him.

I liked his warm smile and kind eyes. 'Why are you called Shorty?'

Mum shushed me. 'It's rude to ask personal questions.'

Shorty ruffled my hair 'You didn't mean any harm, did you, Blondie?'

I blushed.

'It's a joke. Or people's idea of one. When you're very tall, they call you Shorty. A red-haired man is called Blue. Understand?'

I didn't, but nodded anyway.

Dad said, 'What about the jokes? How's the weather up there? Folk find that one hilarious.'

Shorty nodded. 'We hit our head on doorways, feet stick out of beds...'

Talk drifted to their first meeting.

'Volunteer Defence Corps. Old boys from the First World War sure knew how to get the best out of a bloke.'

'I feel exhausted just thinking of those training exercises.'

Shorty's eyes lit up. 'I'd love to throw a line into the Gummi River again. You can't beat the flavour of freshly caught trout.'

'Let's make it soon.' Daddy found his prospecting dish. 'Fancy some fossicking?'

Shorty chuckled. 'Why not? Old miners reckon there's still gold in them there hills.'

'Bound to be. Father was here when the rush was on.'

Victor's eyes shone. 'Did Grandfather strike it rich?'

'If only.'

Daddy told of Grandfather answering an ad to go mining. 'He paid two hundred pounds for a partnership.'

Shorty nodded. 'A fortune.'

'They investigated an old shaft. His new mate said, "Go down and take a look. I'll lower you on my rope." About to gather samples, hairs prickled on Father's neck. Stunned to see his partner holding a huge rock, Father gulped. "What are you going to do with that, mate?" A crazed look. "Drop it on your bloody head." "Best if I come up first. Then drop your rock down the shaft. Make sure it's heavy enough." The other man cackled. "Good idea."'

Mum scoffed. 'But – why would he agree?'

'He was crazy, luv. "Okay, old mate," Father says. "Haul me up." Reaching the surface, he thrashed his would-be assassin and retrieved his stake.'

Shorty whistled. 'I wonder how many poor beggars he lured to their deaths?'

'God knows.'

Dad's gaze drifted across pink and white blossoms of the orchard. Casuarina, clustered along the brook. Beyond, peaks met the cloudless sky. 'This small valley swarmed with prospectors in the 1800s. A city of tents and shanties. Nine hotels. Laughter and brawls, clink of glasses. Songs, the music of violins and piano.'

Shorty told of the clink of windlass and clunk of picks. 'Men struggled up those peaks to stake claims.'

'And were killed for a few pennyweights of gold.'

Mum shuddered. 'It looks so tranquil. It's hard to picture violence.'

Shorty said, 'All gone. Except for chimneys and scattered bricks.'

Dad picked up his prospecting dish. 'Let's go.'

We struggled up steep inclines, passing grass-covered heaps of mullock. They took samples.

I shuddered away from the murky depths of an abandoned mineshaft. Daddy dropped a stone to gauge the depth. It took ages to hit water.

'A little girl like you could disappear down there without trace.'

I needed no reminding.

We released Trixie from a cardboard travelling box. Her black body was set off to perfection with white paws and throat. She followed me everywhere in the garden, sniffing aromas.

Mum laughed. 'She's more like a dog than a cat.'

She kneaded my lap, never pricking me with her claws. She rarely left the yard, avoiding many dangers.

Daddy brought the mail. Mum recognised Poppy's scrawl.

She read the letter aloud.' I must apologise for not writing sooner...' Her face shone. 'Oh, how wonderful. A son, Brian, was born on 16 August 1948. The Stephens family is complete. He's one of the happiest of bubs, always smiling.'

Daddy grinned. 'Walt will be pleased.'

Mum read on, 'We've moved to Dry Creek. The house is basic, but will serve us well enough.' Her face clouded. 'Now for the bad news. At eighteen months, Georgie climbed to the top of a strainer post... Fell on her head... Rushed to hospital... Immediate operation... Coma for over a week... Thank the Lord she's alive... Her fits have stopped... Ongoing problems... Tell you more when we meet. Love, Poppy.'

'Gosh...poor Georgie.'

'Walt's lucky to have a woman like Poppy. Not the sort to crack.'

'When can we see them?'

'Let's go this week. I'm fine with driving now.'

Oh, the hugs and joyful greetings. Adults debated whom the babies most resembled. Brian was born a month before our Druce.

Daddy pumped Walt's hand. 'Put it there, mate. Congratulations.'

Walt gave his crooked grin. 'Same to you and your young 'un.'

My parents were shocked to see Georgie. Now a pallid, silent child, clinging to Poppy's side.

Tearful farewells. They promised to write.

We overheard snatches of parental conversations. Mum whispered, 'It's just too awful. Once a healthy tot... Swallows more pills than food. Won't manage normal school. Lucky to make fourteen.'

'Imagine that hanging over their heads.'

Daddy built fences at either end of adjacent hedges, enclosing a vegetable patch. Manure and compost improved the soil. A water tank supplied household needs. Mum coaxed along plants with grey water. Tomatoes, crisp lettuce, delicate cucumbers, squash and other produce flourished.

The property owner declared a mulberry tree to be off limits.

Daddy said later, 'The tree's loaded. More than enough for everyone. Eat your fill, kids. The birds will only pick them if we don't.'

Mum's mulberry pies were delicious.

The neglected flower garden responded to liquid fertiliser. Mock-orange burst into masses of white blossoms. The delicate aroma mingled with the wonderful perfume of old red roses, the language of flowers. Their first blooms for years. Near the broken gate, a clover plant yielded nothing but four-leaf ones. I pressed them between the pages of my books.

Cobweb-encrusted windows blurred the secrets of a crumbling storehouse.

Dad glimpsed broken furniture and rusting tools. 'A perfect spot for snakes and red-back spiders. Don't play there.'

Daddy began felling timber.

Mum frowned. 'It's not safe working on your own.'

'You're right. I'll be glad when Charles arrives.'

Fred, the mill owner, also expressed doubts. But not on safety issues. 'You'll never keep up with my machines.'

Daddy honed his axe. 'We'll see.'

Fred watched Daddy in action. 'You'd be a cinch in the Royal Easter Show.'

Daddy laughed. 'I've no interest in competitions.'

He confided his modus operandi to Victor. 'Seek a largish tree. blue gum, stringy-bark or box are good timber. Make a belly cut in the trunk, the side where you want it to fall. Drive wedges into the scarf cut opposite.'

Daddy sharpened his axe three or four times daily, using a whetstone and spit. The rhythmic sound of metal on timber echoed through the bush. Every muscle in his back and arms rippled. Chips flew. Forest giants thundered to earth. In no time, the mill had a huge pile of logs.

Fred wrung his hands. 'You're the fastest timber cutter I've ever seen. For God's sakes, man, take a break. Timber needs sawing into planks before it's dry.'

A truck driver manoeuvred trimmed logs with his bulldozer, one of the first in the district.

Victor watched, fascinated. 'I'll drive one of those someday.'

I chuckled. 'Yeah, sure.'

Uncle Charles arrived. 'I'm glad to be here.'

'Not half as glad as I am to have you. A mate helps spot risks.'

Daddy noticed a mass of shuddering leaves. Something was caught in the foliage of another tree. He shouted, 'Charles, quick! Move!' They leapt back.

Seconds later a massive limb thudded to earth.

'Missed us by inches.'

Their axes lopped off the tops of fallen trees. They used an old-fashioned cross-cut to saw the timber into lengths. It lacked self-cleaning teeth. Shorty's flair with a file kept it sharp.

Two days cutting saw enough felled timber to last a week. Shorty joined the brothers to fossick in the old workings.

Daddy told Mum, 'It's only a matter of time before we find a rich vein of gold.'

She raised her eyebrows.

Years later, Daddy told me, 'Charles lacked experience, but learned fast. Back then, there were no hard hats, or danger money. We received one shilling and sixpence per hundred super feet. About ten shillings per tree.'

A landowner barred entry to all prospectors. He lived some distance away. Daddy and Shorty longed to assess minerals on his property. Strangers to him, they devised a scheme to gain entry.

A tall, impressive man, supposedly from the Department of Agriculture, Daddy enthused over their project. 'Your land has been selected for the trial of a top secret product. We're testing a new fertiliser. Your crops will grow up to the bellies of your cattle.'

Shorty nodded. 'Grasses will grow even in drought.'

'With your permission, we need to take a few soil samples. And best not mention it to your neighbours. They'll be green with envy.'

The owner invited them to meals. Drove them over his property. Offered any help needed.

'We'll be in touch with the results.' Chuckling, Daddy drove away. 'We couldn't have had a better variety of samples.' Alas, they yielded no gold.

Did the owner wait in vain for that call? Or lick his wounds over offers that seem too good to be true? Probably both.

We attended Stewarts Brook School, our third in as many years. A massive rock face sheltered it from blazing summer sun. Pepper trees made lovely playground shade. The Education Department insisted they be planted to reduce flies.

I began third grade, wearing a blue silk dress. Mum made it from a wartime parachute. 'A real bargain.' Its humble origins were enhanced, she thought, by bodice embroidery.

Girls whispered, 'Wouldn't you think her mother would make her something decent?'

My cheeks burnt. Oh, why hadn't I worn my school-uniform?

A boy called Alan asked Victor his name.

My brother drew himself up to his full height. ' Victor Jolyon Wright.'

Alan, like most of the boys, barely realised he had a second name.

He gave an incorrect answer. Lucky Sharpe thumped a heavy dictionary against Victor's ear. It pained for hours. And I felt the sting of a ruler for writing errors.

'Hold your pencil with the index finger flat.'

I never mastered his method.

Still, learning had me beguiled. Thrilled by everything from the aroma of pencil shavings to the scent of new books. Afternoons, Lucky enthralled the class reading from *The Wind in the Willows*. We couldn't wait to hear the next chapter.

Pupils ranged from littlies to gangling adolescents. Older boys drove tractors and rounded up cattle on family properties. Blackfriars Correspondence School provided their lessons.

I reclined in the orchard. Dappled by apple or peach trees, I read *Milly Molly Mandy*, or *Dot and the Kangaroo*. Trixie purred her delight. I loved the *John Mystery Adventures*, was intrigued by the *Woolly Sisters, Pearl and Plain Jane*. I time travelled with giants, passing through *Pools of Recollections* into *The Land of Tomorrow*. *The Boys Own Annual* made it hard to decide whether to be a secret agent or midnight rider.

Summer holidays brought oppressive heat. We paddled in deep pools. School friend Robin, Pat, Clare or Vonnie joined us. Mum and Vivi shared the fun. Druce asleep in the shade.

A stifling evening. Thunder and torrential rain lashed Rose Cottage. Next morning, torrents of brown water raced down a gully.

Dad and Charles rushed for prospecting dishes. 'Alluvial gold might have been washed down from the old diggings.' They only found a few pennyweights.

Wading in the stream, a glitter caught my eye. I ran to Daddy with my find.

'Well done. This rock is rich with gold. You've done better than both of us.' I couldn't have been more thrilled had it been *The Welcome Stranger*. Clasping his shiny sixpence.

Robin joined us fishing.

Daddy had shown us a trick he learnt from an old Aboriginal. 'Throw earth into a stream. Discoloured water tricks fish into believing a flood is on the way. You'll catch a feed in no time.'

The boys dug out earth. I threw clods into the stream.

A horseman rode by. 'What are youse doing?'

Our explanation brought laughter. 'You'd believe anything.' He cantered away.

No sooner had he left than the fish began to bite. Each time we threw in a line, an eel or gudgeon took the bait.

Victor called, 'Watch this.' He made a back cast, rapidly bringing the rod forward.

The line flew free. Laughter turned to dismay. Victor's hook had snagged the fleshy part of Robin's thumb, almost up to the shaft.

I whimpered.

Victor told me to shut up. 'This is bad enough without you blubbering. We'll find Daddy.'

Daddy whistled. 'Give me those pliers.' He cut off the barbed part. The hook remained firmly embedded. The nearest doctor was thirty miles away. Daddy said, 'Reckon you could hold still while I open the wound out a bit?'

Ashen-faced, nine-year-old Robin nodded. In those days, folk did what was necessary to help someone else's child. The sharpest blade of Daddy's pocketknife sliced into flesh. Robin gritted his teeth. Not a sound escaped his lips.

Daddy squeezed Robin's shoulder. 'You're a very brave lad.'

His father thanked Dad. 'Jeeze, mate, in your place I'd have done the same.'

The wound healed without complication.

14

Dad worked away, up the brook. Mum missed adult company. One day, she put Druce in his pram. She walked the half-mile to a neighbour's house, Vivi at her side. Hoping for a chat or game of tennis, she arrived hot and thirsty. The ladies of the house received her on the doorstep. Not so much as a cold glass of water.

Mum seethed to Dad when he arrived home. 'I wasn't good enough for them.'

'That sort aren't worth worrying about.'

Shorty's mother popped by. They chatted recipes and gardening. 'Do come to see us, Genn. And if there's anything you need…' She told me to call her Auntie Violet. I loved her warm smile.

Mum was overwhelmed by her kindness.

On our first visit, Auntie Violet enfolded us in her arms, pecked cheeks. She served tea in bone china cups, decorated with roses.

Mum hesitated. 'These are so precious. I'd hate to break one.'

'Nonsense. Cups can always be replaced.'

Thick slices of wholemeal apple bread, and home-made butter added to our pleasure.

Her living room seemed to me like an Aladdin's cave. Light dappled a spotted dog, flower-decorated dishes, and antique lamps. We admired English cottage teapots, and green glass jugs decorated with white figures.

'I think it's Victorian Mary Gregory. Here's a ruby glass one as well.'

Auntie made feather-flowers in rainbow colours. 'Dyed with crêpe paper.'

One thing we learnt early: never admire an ornament. She invariably offered it as a gift.

Mum and Auntie wandered among hollyhocks, larkspurs, pinks, stocks, and carnations. They discussed the finer points of horticulture. In spring, the aroma of jasmine mingled with roses. Butterflies clustered on purple and white buddleia blossoms, the perfume tantalising.

Uncle Jim didn't let a club foot and limp stop him tending a vegetable garden. He kept large cages of canaries and budgies, whistling in perfect imitation of his passerine friends. I secretly felt sad to see winged creatures denied their freedom.

His Khaki Campbell duck fascinated me. They tipped back their heads, with clicking noises. Were they straining insects from the water? Mum had to call me three times to go home.

Uncle Jim chuckled. 'They'll be here on your next visit, love.'

Auntie loaded the pram with jars of home-made jam, eggs and vegetables.

'What a lovely couple, Joly.'

'The sort of neighbours who make life a pleasure.'

Auntie Violet had carried both her babies in a fabric sling. She had reservations about mechanical gadgets. One day. she minded Druce, arriving red-faced at Rose Cottage.

'How they can call these darn things labour-saving?' She mopped her brow. Violet had pushed the pram a quarter mile with the brake on. She didn't know it had one.

Daddy's Christmas tree glittered with foil, glass balls, and cotton-wool snow. We hung multicoloured paper chains and bells.

Vivi carried around her present for Mum. A smallish, cylindrical package. She bubbled with excitement. 'Guess what I'm giving you?'

Mum went along with the game. Finally, she snapped. 'Obviously, it's a pencil.'

My sister looked horribly disappointed.

On Christmas Eve, we put out sherry and Christmas cake.

Dad said, 'Go to bed. We don't the elves to pass you by.'

Santa brought me the toy stroller of my dreams. A rag doll called Helga wore a blue satin dress, her black hair plaited. And the shrill cry of a red and yellow plastic whistle reverberated all day. Adults clutched their heads. Mum banned it from the house.

Uncle Charles dodged Victor's water pistol. But didn't move fast enough. He groaned. 'Kids.' And changed his shirt. Twice.

Daddy's drop of white emerged from the icy depths of the well. He shared a festive drink or three with Shorty and Charles. Auntie Violet and Mum drank a shandy, pouring us soft drinks. Uncle Jim had stayed home with his Khaki Campbells. Dad's fossicking tales dripped gold.

Christmas crackers. Silly jokes. Laughter. A rainbow of paper crowns. I breathed in the crisp, golden aroma of baked chicken, potatoes, pumpkin. Biting into Auntie Violet's pudding, with fat currants, dark raisins, spices and brandy. Mum's thick custard added a yummy touch.

'Look!' I cried. 'Sixpence.'

Vivi found one, too. Adults cheered.

Shorty and Auntie Violet left for home.

Uncle Charles strolled outside. Victor drenched him. He laughed. But not for long.

He used a bad word. 'Give me that bloody water pistol.'

Victor teetered on the verge of tears. 'Please, Uncle, give it back. I won't do it again. Promise.'

Uncle shook his head. 'Nothing doing.'

We searched inside the house and out. Victor was heartbroken.

December slipped into January. My summer cold proved to be chickenpox. Blisters appeared, itchy scabs turned into pimples.

I whined, 'Let me play outside.'

Mum said, 'If you're a good girl and stay in bed, I'll give you your plastic whistle.' Somehow, she endured the racket.

Recovered, I couldn't bear the screech. It shivered with unpleasant memories.

Auntie Violet and Shorty joined us on a fishing holiday in the Mount Royal Ranges. Uncle Jim stayed to mind his canaries.

Auntie chuckled. 'This is an adventure.'

We camped near the Gummi River. The men spent an evening making fishing flies. They tied bright feathers to each hook.

Shorty said, 'Trout think they're tasty insects.'

Auntie Violet shared a tent with Vivi and me. She gave tips on camping. 'I've read it's a good idea to dig hollows matching the shape of one's body. They say it makes an excellent base for sleeping bags.'

We dug out clods of soil and grass, hers plump, mine tall and thin, Vivi's small and chubby.

Auntie blew out the lantern. I turned over. Loose earth and pebbles tumbled into my sleeping bag. The flashlight gleamed.

Auntie told of the Princess and a Pea. 'She'd never have coped with this.'

We laughed but not for long. Vivi drifted off, then wailed for help. Giggling, we threw out the unwelcome guests. Then it was Auntie's turn, another earthen onslaught. Giggles became groans.

At first light, we moved the tent, averting our eyes from the diggings.

On bush rambles, we picked yellow everlasting daisies.

Mum pointed out a robin, sitting on its nest. 'See, it's made of plant materials. Lined with cobwebs.'

The red-breasted mate trilled nearby,

I shuddered away from a tangle of spitfire caterpillars.

Auntie said, 'They cluster to avoid predators. And grow into sawflies, if they're lucky enough to escape wasps.'

Late in the afternoon, Auntie knitted and chatted to Mum. Vivi played with her dolls. The men went fishing. I sat on a tussock, knees tucked under my chin, I watched Shorty flick his lure across a pool. Frogs croaked.

Shorty warned me, 'Be very quiet. Mustn't frighten the fish.'

Tiny criss-cross ripples flashed shimmers of sunset. Insects darted and soared. In the golden light, Shorty's reel whirred. The shining line spun free A trout sped off, fighting hard to escape. Everyone gathered to watch.

Shorty's eyes gleamed. 'It's a big one.'

At last the struggle stopped.

He lifted out the pretty spotted fish with his landing net. 'Sure glad I brought this.'

Dad eyed the fish. 'Wow! It's a whopper.'

My pleasure mingled with sorrow. The poor creature wriggled and gulped for air. Shorty put it out of its misery. I wiped my eyes.

Daddy patted my shoulder, 'I know how you feel about killing such a lovely creature. But it is for food.'

Shorty wished we had scales. 'The biggest trout I've ever caught. What do you think it weighs, Joly?'

'Must be at least six pounds – if not more.'

Shorty grinned. 'After a beauty like this, I'm happy. Even if it's my last catch on the trip.'

Dad grinned. 'Don't put a hex on yourself, mate.'

Our family gathered around the campfire. Telling of big ones that swam away. Daddy cooked the trout in a wire contraption, made from number eight fencing wire. The aroma of grilling trout had me ravenous.

Mum served the moist and pinkish flesh with corn on the cob, baby potatoes and damper. Dad dropped a handful of tea leaves into bubbling water. He banged the billy side to help them settle. I liked the tea's unique taste. The aroma of gumleaves mingled with smoke.

The men told of other rivers. Of eels longer than your arm, of gudgeon and perch.

Aunt Violet winked. 'Never believe fishing tales.'

Kookaburras laughed in the gold-drenched eucalypts. We heard the whisper of leaves. Clouds drifted by, painted in red, yellow and purple. Mellow light and shadows crept over the landscape. A wallaby edged forward on front paws and elbows, nibbling sweet grass. Sunset turned to twilight.

Shorty refilled the billycan from Dad's canvas water-bag. 'I feel like another brew.'

Daddy fetched the lantern. They yarned into the night of gold-mining days. Recalled nuggets the size of boulders. I yawned and tried to keep my eyes open.

Auntie Violet sighed. 'Men! Dreaming of Eldorado.'

Next day, Vivi developed spots. Mum took one look and said, 'Oh, no! Chickenpox.'

Daddy set my sister up in her own tent. 'You're ill. Stay in there.'

She popped out every few minutes, spots or not, to dance and play. At last she fell asleep.

In the darkness, we heard the plangent cry of a dingo. A mopoke spoke his name. I burrowed deeper into my sleeping bag. Glad Auntie was there.

Shorty became the next victim.

Aunt Violet chuckled. 'Not a sign of any chickens, son, but more than your fair share of spots.'

Nobody laughed for long. Shorty's fever soared. Lesions appeared all over his body. Some even in his mouth and hair.

Mum sighed. 'He's too ill for tent nursing.'

Shorty could barely raise a smile. We packed picnic baskets, tents and fishing rods.

Dad put mining dishes into a corn bag. 'Shorty's words were prophetic. Guess he wasn't meant to catch another trout.'

I hated to abandon our holiday.

A treat awaited us near Rose Hill Cottage. Blackberries. They grew along every laneway. And covered acres of farming land, not yet declared a noxious weed.

A neighbour offered Victor and me a couple of shillings. 'Pick me a bucket of the best berries.'

We laboured in hot sun, scratched by lethal thorns, munching delicious fruit. Faces, hands and clothing stained purple.

Mum baked a delicious blackberry and apple pie with hers.

She made to take Druce for his walk in the pram.

I ran to her side. 'Please, let me.'

She hovered. 'Do be careful.'

I took a corner at speed. The pram overturned. Druce disappeared under a scream of blankets.

Mum gathered my brother in her arms. 'There, there, baby.' She glared at me. 'Must you be so darned silly?'

It took a while to get a second chance. Full of pride, I wheeled the pram at a sedate pace along the deserted road. Hoof beats. Glancing over my shoulder, I glimpsed a farmer driving a red bull. Narrow lane, retreat blocked. My only escape was through a wire fence. But I couldn't lift a heavy baby between those narrow strands. Nor was I strong or tall enough to lift him over. Anyway, barbed wire prevented that option.

It would be nice to say I stood my ground, cape in hand. Being no bull fighter, I parked the pram near the fence, the safest place for Druce. And took refuge on the other side. The bull passed without a glance. My craven deed amused our small community. Their chuckles faded into the whistle of our holiday train.

The Stephenses grew oranges at Gosford. Mum volunteered to help harvest peas, grown as a sideline. Row upon row stretched toward the horizon. Under the blaze of midday sun, I felt sticky and uncomfortable. Bush flies crawled and tormented. Exhausted, I slumped onto the dirt. A hand crept into the bucket. One pod melted in my mouth. Two… The feast was unstoppable.

Mum came to investigate. 'What's taking you so long?' She glimpsed a half-bucket of empty pods. Her eyes bulged. 'You greedy little girl.' Slap. 'We're all working hard. And you've gobbled the lot.'

We took several trains.

On the ferry for Taronga Zoo, Victor kept well clear of the rail. 'Suppose it sinks?'

Mum laughed. 'That's unlikely.'

Vivi gazed at the expanse of water. 'Gosh, this is a big creek.'

Mum chuckled. 'It's not a creek, silly. We're on Sydney Harbour.

Ripples winked. Yachts glided by. Sails billowed.

My eyes followed the yo-yo sellers. 'Mum, please, buy me one.'

'Two shillings! That's way too dear.'

'Mum, we're the only kids without…'

Sighing, she extracted coins from a worn purse. We played with pink, purple and orange yo-yos all the way round the zoo.

Mum studied the features of each animal and read about their habitat. I couldn't bear the way she lingered, racing from one cage to the next. 'For goodness sake. You won't see anything running ahead like that.'

I craved to absorb every image. The picture would only be complete when I reached my final destination. On the way home, our yo-yos fell apart. And so ended our holidays.

Our dusty road shimmered in the heat. Trudging back to school, I envied Trixie, curled up in the garden. Sunny afternoons brought the golden glitter of Rose Cottage windows. I donned play clothes, taking a *Milly Molly Mandy* book into the orchard. Trixie mewed, asking me where I'd been, settling on my lap.

Leaves turned to red, yellow and brown. They drifted, free at last.

Three hours to go at school, Mr Sharpe looked gloomy. He'd piloted a Spitfire in the Battle of Britain. One of the older lads asked about the war. The light of adventure leapt into Sir's eyes.

We donned imaginary flying suits. Piloted ghostly Spitfires. Lucky plotted a tenuous course. Visibility almost zero… Planes scream, and fall, in flames… Five hundred lost in one operation… Messerschmitt shot down. Enemy bullets hit our fuselage. Crippled aircraft limps back to base…

Alan put up his hand. 'Excuse me, sir. Home time.'

Lucky blinked. 'Already? Pack up your books. Leave quietly.'

We ran home.

Trixie didn't greet me. She seldom wandered.

We worried, searched and called, 'Trixie? Where are you Trixie?'

Dad asked our neighbours. Several days passed. We had almost given up hope.

Someone found her in a trap. Daddy carried her inside. One of her paws was mutilated and smelt horrible.

'It's a disgrace, leaving animals to suffer. People should check traps daily,'

I stroked my pet. Trixie's loud purr told us she was glad to be home.

Dad wiped his eyes. 'She knows we're helping her.'

Mum washed the wound with disinfectant, putting on a dressing. Trixie lapped milk. 'Thirsty, poor thing. How did she survive?'

Dad laid her in a cosy box. 'I'd say she licked dew from the grass.'

My voice broke. 'Mum, will she be all right?'

She hesitated. 'It's a terrible infection…'

Trixie died that very night.

I was inconsolable. We buried Trixie close to the four-leaf clover plant. My heart ached every time I walked by.

A raging torrent roared along Stewarts Brook. Victor and I plodded through mud, hunched against the rain. A suspension bridge loomed ahead. The only access to school with high water. Missing planks made it daunting.

Lorraine with her Shirley Temple curls started to cross. Big boys rocked the bridge back and forth. Lorraine screamed. She almost lost her balance. Miraculously, making the other side.

Victor's longer legs conquered spaces between missing planks.

My turn lurked. I bit my nails to the quick. One misstep… Surging currents… My body swept away.

The boys chanted, 'Scaredy cat…'

Mr Sharpe came to investigate. They ran off.

It took every shred of courage to complete my short journey.

Lucky Sharpe struggled to light the fire. Any child in that shivering classroom could have shown him how it was done. He poked at a flat bunch of kindling.

Alan coughed. 'If you lifted it a bit, sir...'

Lucky's eyes streamed. 'I'm doing this, Smith.'

We held handkerchiefs to our mouths.

Alan gasped. 'Sir, I make the fire at home.'

Gritted teeth. 'Did I ask for your help?'

A downdraft. Smoke billowed, filling the room. Lucky spluttered his way outside. Alan lifted the kindling. Feeble tongues of flame licked at twigs.

Lucky returned. 'Back to your desk, Alan.'

Sir whacked the pile of wood with the poker. Thick fumes, streaming eyes. 'The rain's cleared. I'll hold classes in the playground today. 'Don, Alan, help move the desks.'

Weak sunlight. Thank goodness for warm clothing.

15

Grass crackled underfoot.

Mum sent me along the brook to gather dry casuarina wood. 'It's the best fuel for baking. Ensures an even temperature.'

I blew out every candle of my ninth birthday cake, never guessing the delicious vanilla-flavoured confection would be the last of my childhood.

At school, a pyjama-clad figure bolted for the teacher's cottage. Lessons often began after ten. Or later. Lucky's hands would tremble sometimes, anguish on his face. Now and then he lost sentences in mid-explanation. Treatments were few for shell shock.

Parents declared late starts a disgrace. Nobody complained.

We awoke to a deep stillness. A glow on the ceiling.

Nine inches of snow had fallen overnight.

Dad said, 'Sixty years ago my parents witnessed the last fall. Fancy me seeing another.'

Drill, sums, writing… Nothing could compare with the perfection outside. We longed to build snowmen with pebble eyes. Shriek and throw handfuls of it.

Sir glanced away from the blackboard. Dusted chalk from his fingers. 'Who's for an excursion?'

The classroom exploded into whoops. Lucky dashed home for his bag. Chill air brought pink blotches to every cheek. Eyes shone. We crunched towards the summit. Laughter danced with chatter. Lucky distributed oranges. The fruit made a startling contrast to the whiteness all around. And had never tasted so delicious.

We gazed at long shadows and golden hues. The afternoon sun shone over the narrow valley. Crystalline magnificence hid mining - scarred hills. Even the boys seemed humbled by the vista.

We had never seen Lucky Sharpe look so serene.

'What did you learn today?' Our parents asked.

'Sir took us for a walk in the snow.'

Mum raised her eyebrows. 'When will he teach them something?'

Transcendence. Victor and I knew the feeling but not the word for it. Part of the universe itself.

We readied to leave Stewarts Brook. In October 1949, I breathed the pink and white orchard fragrance. Bees buzzed, laden with pollen. Twigs weaved into nests. I hated the thought of leaving Vonnie and Pat and Lorraine. They had all been sad to see me go.

Victor asked Uncle Charles for his precious water pistol. He indicated a loose board on the wall. We'd passed it every day since Christmas. Victor's hand dived into the space. He blanched. Fled.

'Wait for me!' Brambles scratched my legs. I found Victor skipping stones across the water.

'What's up?'

'It's ruined.' He showed me the perished rubber bulb. 'Oh, why did Uncle keep my water pistol so long?' He flung it into a deep pool, wiping his eyes.

Voices called us back to Rose Cottage. Empty rooms held echoes of laughter, fun and mischief. Never again would I see the windows glimmer like gold. Read *Milly Molly Mandy* in the orchard. Hold Trixie.

Victor rode off for Hunters Springs on Hungry. He led Dolly, following faint trails through mountain terrain.

Mum sighed. 'He'll be exhausted, poor kid. Tiring for a grown man. Let alone a boy of twelve.'

Vivi and I squeezed onto the back of our overloaded Ford. We set off for Hunters Springs, the place Mum called home.

Decades later I made a nostalgic visit to Stewarts Brook. Rose Cottage, the orchard and Mum's garden had vanished. I'd half expected to see my four-leaf-clover. A flaking sign proclaimed the year the school opened, but not the one it died. The empty classroom echoed with Lucky Sharpe's Spitfire stories and voices of school friends. Even after twenty years, the dusty stationery cupboard carried an aroma of chalk and pencil shavings.

In the playground, I held shrivelled leaf fronds, mourning the slaughter of pepper trees. Pink seed membranes brought a pungent aroma. Here, girls had skipped, played hopscotch and shared confidences. In branches above, adolescent boys had teased each other about the rise of manhood.

Garden stones, with hints of flaking whitewash, reminded me of neglected graves. Vegetables and flowers had given way to lank grass and Scotch thistles. And the long-abandoned bridge still swung, bringing a shudder.

Hunters Springs shivered back in 1949. Daddy's blazing fire brought the house to life, a warm welcome.

Mum mourned a paper trail of damage. Rodents had feasted on her prized books and book prizes. She was heartbroken. Daddy sealed up their entry points. We had no further problems.

He hung up the green zinc meat safe. Holes allowed air circulation. I was fascinated to see him set up our Coolgardie safe. He covered a wooden frame with burlap, from corn bags. Filled trays on top with water, and hung lamp wicks down each side. 'Evaporation produces cooling. It's imperative for milk and butter.'

Daddy asked a rhetorical question – a word I learned later. 'Where would a man be without burlap bags? Folded in half lengthways, they form a hood against rain. I've made them into saddlebags, and blankets for camping. Fixed across a bed frame, they form a mattress base. Useful as rough veranda mats, too.' He grinned. 'A humble object. Multiplicity of purposes.'

I gave Druce his bottle. Mum changed his nappy and put him down. She scoured the kitchen table. Dad unwrapped plates and cutlery from newspaper, carved cold lamb. I sliced tomatoes and cucumbers. After lunch, we donned rough clothes.

Dad brought steaming buckets of water, fragrant with eucalypts. 'Give everything a good scrub.'

A flurry of brooms and scrubbing brushes. Vivi wielded a cleaning rag, filthy from head to toe.

Mum chuckled. 'What an urchin.'

It reminded me of our first days at Ben More.

Everyone took a turn in the bath.

Dad pushed furniture back into place. 'Glad to be home, Genn?'

'What do you think?' Her eyes gleamed. 'We'll make something of this place. Get a herd…'

He laughed. 'You'll get your cattle. First, we've paddocks to clear.'

Grandfather had stored fifty-pound bags of flour in his pantry bin, and sacks of sugar, with space for rice, barley, split peas…

Mum said, 'When this house was built, wagons went to town twice yearly for supplies.' Using a Vacola bottling outfit, she began stocking shelves with preserved fruit, vegetables and soups.

Daddy loved her home-made jam. And green tomato pickle was a favourite with cold meat.

Mum's ginger plant foamed and bubbled. She daily added powdered ginger, and sugar. Sometimes bottles exploded – what a mess. The ginger beer proved well worth her efforts.

Freshly butchered carcasses hung in Grandfather's meat house. Screens excluded blowflies. Dad cut up and salted or smoked meat. Neighbours shared supplies. Nan had preserved legs of lamb in an airtight casing of hard fat. The meat remained edible for ages. Use-by-dates were unknown. People couldn't afford to throw away expensive food.

Mum sniffed raw meat for an unpleasant odour or a slimy surface. 'Hmm! slightly on the turn.' She soaked it in vinegar, or a strong saline solution, killing bacteria. 'Washed in clean, running water it's perfect.' She also rubbed eggs with Vaseline or preservative paste. They kept for months.

Bathrooms were luxuries. Ours boasted a long tin bath. An old-fashioned washstand held medications and first-aid equipment. It smelt of mercurochrome and eucalyptus disinfectant. Snake-bite treatment included cutting the skin, washing the site, and applying Candy's Crystals. A pressure bandage was applied and medical help sought.

Before Band-Aids, a supply of calico fingerstalls fixed minor injuries. Larger wounds required clean linen and bandaging. Rawleys Ointment treated superficial cuts and scratches. Mum cured outbreaks of boils with flowers of sulphur. She mixed enough powder to cover a sixpence, with golden syrup, taken for several days. It tasted delicious – and worked.

Purges were considered healthy. Constipation required castor oil, Epsom salts or *Cascara Sagrada*. Dosed with aperient, one risked long walks to the outside pit dunny, by torchlight. Red-back spiders another worry.

Sceptics said, 'Joly must be mad to think he can make anything of a small, hilly place like that, covered with scrub.'

He grinned, 'I hadn't the slightest doubt we'd make a go of it.'

Years later, Daddy me told me about the original purchase of our property. 'Grandfather Stephens took up the selection in 1925. Paid a pound an acre each year, until it became freehold. He owned a couple of horses, half a dozen cattle, a pig and a sheep or two. He and Geoff cleared the flat with mattocks, axes, and saws. They helped build the house, yard, and sheds. Acres of scrub remained. Grandfather Rick ran the mail. Your Uncle Geoff laboured on Tomalla station. And Nan loved her little shop, operating a small telephone exchange as well.'

Our Ferguson 135 tractor arrived. Dad reverently touched the red duco. 'Modern equipment – just hope it's worth the money,'

The truck driver grinned. 'You won't regret this, mate. It'll work harder than one twice its size.' And so it proved.

Dad had another worry. 'Our Ford cost a fortune in repairs last year.'

He farewelled it at a local car yard. 'Small trade-in, but I can't complain – years of service.' The duco shone on Dad's new purchase, a blue Austin ute. His smile widened. 'Here's to trouble-free motoring.'

He purchased a plough, harrows, bags of seed and fertiliser. Funds dwindled.

'We need a crop of potatoes to bring in cash. I'll employ a casual labourer. There's work enough for several men.'

Victor drove the tractor. He enjoyed being one of the men, little knowing his loss. At the end of sixth-grade, they obtained his school exemption. Daddy had become an extra pair of hands at a much younger age, like his father before him.

My brother bequeathed me his desk. In its previous life, it had been a packing case. Daddy added rickety legs. I concealed its humble origins with bright, varnished pictures, inside and out. It provided storage for my school books. Not an antique, but it was better than the dining table.

We welcomed a placid jersey cow, with a small calf. Ruby, our old one, had been sold.

Daddy named her Susie. 'Never kicks over the milk bucket, or has a tantrum in the bail. Chews her cud, glancing around with those long-lashed eyes. Wants to see whether I'm finished.'

Nothing equalled fresh milk and cream. Each spring, Susie produced a heifer calf.

Mum's heaven shimmered within reach. 'Breeding animals rapidly increase a herd.'

Daddy cleared paddocks. Skeletal eucalypts, ringbarked decades earlier, were the first to go. Magnificent specimens, even in death. I took their last photo with my small Kodak camera. *The Three Sisters* won first prize in the photography club at school.

Dad's axe bit into those long-dead giants. Grey chips flew. 'I'll grub out the stumps later.' He hand-sawed limbs into manageable lengths. 'Enough firewood for months.'

The tractor chain creaked from early morning until last light. Victor moved aside large rocks, and dragged logs into stacks for burning. The night air breezed thick smoke. Logs groaned and spat. Flames danced with red sparks. Plovers shrieked.

Heavy steel discs sliced into earth. I loved the aroma of buried vegetation. The harrow broke up clods.

'Look at this soil – soft and friable.' Dad's eyes shone. 'Two paddocks are ready.'

George Foxcroft helped plant spuds. A neighbour, he asked, 'How about a half-share in a few acres of spuds, on my property?'

'Great idea, George. It'll more than double my yield.'

They celebrated over a glass of wine. George left. Dad emptied the first bottle, opened another…

A week of booze became two. Dad's big hands shook.

'I've learnt my lesson, luv. Just one glass to get over it. You pour.'

Her eyes bulged. 'When will you curb this weakness?'

'I'm a good husband and provider. Can't you overlook the occasional binge?'

Uncle Geoff visited, bringing a new aunt, Ruby.

Vivi's eyes glittered. 'We had a cow called Ruby.'

Our new aunt managed a chuckle.

Geoff excitedly showed his bride the family property. He admired Dad's improvements. 'Astounding progress.'

Plans for future projects made for lively discussions. They avoided religion or politics.

Mum whispered to Dad, 'Ruby's had a rigid upbringing.'

'Given Geoff's a Jehovah's Witness, I fancy she won't notice much difference.'

Folk raved about my sister's blonde curls. It didn't worry me.

Years later, Ruby confided she used to feel sorry for me. 'Skinny little girl, hair straight as a pin. Didn't seem fair Vivi was getting all the attention.'

One day, Mum, Dad and Geoff left for town. Ruby called us for breakfast. Victor and I ate our porridge. Vivi failed to appear.

Auntie Ruby wrung her hands. 'I've called and called – Vivi must have something to eat.'

Victor chuckled. 'Auntie, Vivi's eating apples in the orchard. She's just naughty.'

No sooner had our visitors left than Alfred, a neighbour, rode up.

A lean chap with a dry sense of humour, he lived on the Gloucester side of the mountain.

Daddy offered him one tiny glass of sherry. 'All I have. Sorry, mate.'

Alfred eyed the pitiful amount. 'But what are you having?'

'Let this be my shout. Next time.'

Alfred postponed his pleasure, placing the glass on a table between them. Ever the victim, he drawled his latest disaster. Gales of laughter.

I dashed past, on some errand. My skirt brushed against Alfred's glass…

Daddy pulled up outside the Linga Longa Inn at Gundy. 'Be back in a minute.'

Mum pursed her lips.

Mrs Kergan brought her an overflowing glass of shandy. 'Hot enough for you, Missus Wright? This will cool you down.' She served behind the bar, the only woman allowed inside.

We kids sipped sticky lemonade.

An hour passed. Two. Scarcely a breath of air.

Mum's glass stood empty. A line of froth on the rim. Vivi and Druce grizzled. Victor stood kicking at pebbles.

I felt helpless and frustrated. 'When are we going to Scone, Mum?'

'How the hell would I know?'

Paddocks begged for rain. Daddy scanned cloudless skies. 'We need inches.' He felled timber, in our back paddock. Food in his big, red tuckerbox.

We set off to join him for a picnic. Mum strode ahead, Druce carried in a sling on her back.

She crossed our small stream. I stepped from one rock to another. Vivi's short legs just made it.

Ripples kissed pebbles. The crystal water tasted of moss and wild herbs. Mounds of sphagnum moss grew nearby. I made to caress it, but Mum pulled my hand away.

'Don't. Funnel-web spiders hide there.'

In the rainforest, palest green lichen hung from the limbs of tea trees. Some like unkempt beards of old men. Others clung to trunks, embossed wallpaper. Tree fern fronds arched above my head. I stroked the soft, red fur near the base of each leaf. They emerged, curled like snails.

We scrambled over rotting hulks of logs, covered with carpets of soft moss, found tiny red or purple fungi.

'Mum! Fairies' brollies.'

'So they are. Look, Druce.'

I plucked buttercups and white violets.

A single cloud drifted in the luminous sky. One large drop caught me by surprise. Others followed. They floated from the canopy, magnified by some trick of the light into huge, translucent balls. I sheltered on a moss-covered rock. Transfixed.

Druce giggled, his chubby hands intent on capture. The miracle ended.

Mum blinked. 'I've never seen anything so lovely.'

We couldn't wait to tell Dad and Victor.

Wait-a-while vines clawed at our legs. Jimmy Burn's pretty orange blossoms tempted closer inspection, hiding their prickles.

Vivi cried, 'Ouch.'

No quick cure. Nettles stung me. Crushed young leaves, rubbed on the spot, brought instant relief.

'For pity's sake, kids, watch out.'

Dad looked startled. 'Rain? You're dreaming. Not a drop here.'

Tiny pieces of manna nestled at the foot of a white gum tree. A sweet substance known in biblical times. We couldn't believe our luck.

Dad gestured towards the scrub. 'Useless for agriculture until it's cleared. No grass for native animals or cattle. In a few years, it will be valuable grazing land.'

Mum put down her bag. 'Mature eucalypts make valuable animal shelter.'

'Indeed. It'll be like a park.'

Victor looked dreamy. 'If only we had a bulldozer.'

'We're lucky to have the tractor.'

A giant towered above us.

Dad called, 'Stand back.' He spat on his hands. Swung his axe, grunting.

The blade sliced into eucalypt flesh. Red sap dripped. A shudder. Fibres ripped. A terrible groan.

The victim thundered to earth. Branches smashed in flight. Listering leaves silenced by the fall. Dust rose. Beetles and other insects took flight. Ants signalled news of the disaster. Some carried eggs Possums and gliders fled into the undergrowth. A lump constricted my throat.

Daddy's back muscles glistened in the sun. Man and white trunk seemed vulnerable and poignant. He stripped away the bark. His mallet drove steel wedges into the protest of timber. Its trunk split lengthwise along the grain. 'Ready to be sawn it into lengths. Thank the Lord, there's a ready market for fence posts.'

We scrambled around the fallen tree. The air was fragrant with the scent of bruised and broken leaves. Sap ran red.

Daddy rested his axe against the stump. 'I'm ravenous.' He put twigs into a pile, struck a match, and blew, fanning the flames with his stained felt hat. Added sticks, large and small. The fire blazed. He drove two forked limbs into the ground for posts. Poured water from a canvas container into the billy, slipping a straight stick through the handle and into the forks. Brewed tea.

We munched mutton, tomato and lettuce sandwiches.

Mum chatted about birds. 'As a girl, I pored over *What Bird is That?* I could identify most of them.'

She whistled up a willy-wagtail. It hopped closer, fluffing out its feathers, head on the side. Puzzlement in its eyes.

Dad told of lyrebirds. 'Imitate anything. Whips cracking, dogs barking, cattle lowing, stockmen calling. Even the click of a camera.' He threw away tea dregs. 'A man would swear a whole mob of cattle were coming over the ridge. Fooled me more than once.'

Lunch over, our parents took a snooze. Druce napped on a rug. Even Vivi fell asleep. Victor and I explored. A zigzag puff of white, of a rabbit taking flight. Feather flowers among the dull foliage of eucalypts, mountain louries, brought flashes of red and blue. The russet slink of a fox disappeared into brown bracken. In the sighing canopy above, wrens and robins twittered. Furry ears and noses on alert, a lope of kangaroos merged with the muted greys and greens of the trees.

What could shatter our quiet rural life?

A huge boom almost split our eardrums. We fled outside, fearing our house might collapse. A supersonic aircraft sped into the distance.

Mum trembled. 'Darned fools. They think scaring people is funny.'

George Foxcroft rode his big chestnut mare along the road. One of the monsters swooped, pursuing horse and rider. It took fright. George tumbled to earth. Cursing, but unhurt. On the same day, Dad was ploughing George's potato patch.

A deafening scream and whistle shattered the afternoon calm. Fearing the tractor was about to explode, Dad jumped off, rolling to safety. The supersonic jet roared off.

Dad shook his fist. 'Damn fools. Behaving like big kids. And with taxpayers' money.'

Far from the watchful eye of authority, air force pilots regularly broke the sound barrier over the Barrington Tops.

It never occurred to me we were poor. Poverty meant attics in faraway places like London. Patches gathered on Daddy's work trousers. His town ones were immaculate. Our shabby play clothes vanquished brambles and bracken on the farm.

Mum said, 'Bare feet are healthy. They need air.' She made sure we were spotless on outings to town, with shoes.

We missed having friends. On a hill a hundred yards away, two children lived in a modest farmhouse. The only other dwelling for miles. We glimpsed them from time to time.

Dad chuckled. 'Man's a snob. Grandson of English aristocrats sent out to make good in the colonies. Wife has connections with the social set in Melbourne.'

Mum giggled. 'Imagine. They've even retained the Victorian custom of calling each other Mr and Mrs. And I can't believe they serve workmen morning tea on the wood heap.'

Victor decided we'd pay a visit. Our parents knew nothing of our plans. 'We'll ask Rosemary and Archie to play.'

Their kitchen door stood wide-open. We wandered in. The lady of the house looked up in dismay. Two barefoot urchins. I fancy we were as welcome as dog poo on a shoe.

Rosemary, about my age, wore shiny shoes, a frilly frock, and big bow in her hair. She eyed us in surprise. 'Why for you wear no shoes?'

Archie sucked his thumb.

Their mother's plummy tones, and a candy jar, lured us outside. 'Here you are, children. Boiled lollies.'

We smiled at the finality of that slammed door.

Victor enjoyed his sweet. 'Rosemary talks like a baby. Doesn't know the fun of bare feet.'

'Or rolling down a grassy slope.'

Our parents shook with laughter. 'Good one, kids.'

Decades later, Druce assisted the landowner castrate his sheep. A table in the shed had replaced the wood heap of yesteryear. The boss even joined his employee for morning tea. The men were about to tuck into food. Blood, dirt and tissue covered their hands.

Druce said, 'First, I need a dish of water, soap and a towel.'

The boss raised his eyebrows. The older men would never have dared demand such a luxury. Afterwards, basic facilities became the norm.

16

Wirth's Circus arrived in town – and so did we. It took loads of persuasion to get us there.

Posters shouted 'World-class Performance'. Brightly lit entrances, a striped big top. Brilliant pennants danced excitement. Lively music set my feet tapping.

A red-haired lady raised a loudhailer. Oh, the bling and glitter of her dress. 'Roll up, roll up, folks. You've never seen anything like this before. Never likely to see it again.'

Daddy handed tickets to Mum. 'Join you directly.' That meant soon.

We admired dappled grey ponies and splendid white horses. Red ribbons plaited into manes. Big ears flapped, inquisitive trunks. Bits of straw clung to dusty hides, elephants tethered nearby.

I expected Daddy to appear at any minute.

Monkeys chattered in barred vans. My nose wrinkled at the rank smell. Burmese tigers paced back and forth in cramped prisons.

The show was about to begin.

I hoped, even then, that Daddy might appear.

Mum was the picture of suppressed rage. 'I'll not wait a moment longer.'

We filed into the big top, the last to sit down. I cringed from the empty seat beside us. Mum's lips pulled into a tight, bitter line. I clenched my fists. If only Daddy would appear, fit and well. With a logical reason for his absence.

A tumble of clowns cavorted in front of us. Red yellow and blue costumes, painted faces, red fake noses.

One beat a little drum. 'Why did the cowboy die with his boots on?'

The other did a funny walk. 'Dunno. Why did the cowboy die with his boots on?'

''Cause he didn't want to hurt his feet when he kicked the bucket.'

Ripples of laughter. I felt close to tears. Where's Daddy?

Spectacular high-wire acts. White horses and dappled ponies raced by. Leotard-glitter beauties stood on their backs. Crescendos of music and applause.

My excitement was obliterated by that tight, awful ache in my stomach. Foolish me. I'd hoped to meet my peers that night, make friends. But everyone sat in family groups.

The circus was over. I blinked, emotions frozen.

Mum gathered her things. 'Come along, kids.'

Druce had long since fallen asleep. She carried the leaden little boy in her arms.

'Where can your father be?' A break in her voice. 'Surely he isn't...'

Victor gulped. 'I'll scout around.'

Mum warned Vivi and me to stay close. We stood in a forlorn group. The crowd streamed from the tent.

I glimpsed Dad. Taller than everybody else, he misjudged every step. Bumped into people, slurring, 'Sorry.'

Mum said, 'Where the hell have you been? You've abandoned me and the kids, like always.'

He smelt of old beer and stale cigarettes, though he didn't smoke. He tried to focus on the woman he loved.

I felt nauseous.

'How much longer am I expected to put up with this?'

People sniggered.

My face burnt. I hated him. Hated the watchers. Someone said one of the tigers had shit through the bars onto a man outside his cage. His humiliation couldn't have been greater than mine.

'When will you grow up, Joly?'

Someone tittered. People hung around, watching developments.

I felt trapped in our collective misery. Dad mumbled apologies, Mum berated him in that loud, hard voice. Victor sullen and silent. Druce wide-eyed, clinging to Mum's hand, whimpering.

Someone was missing. 'Where's Vivi?'

Mum glanced around. Panic in her voice. 'Where's Curley?' She hadn't called my sister that in ages.

Dad swayed like a tall eucalypt in a gale. 'Can't be far away.'

'When the hell did she wander off?' Mum's question was rhetorical.

A chill breeze teased my bare knees. The crowd surged around us.

'Curley, Curley, Curley.'

The name spun around me. A whirlpool of disaster. Suppose she'd been kidnapped? Children disappeared for days, sometimes for ever. Only last week on the radio...

In the end, it was Dad who found Vivi. Or maybe she found him. I heard his greeting. 'There you are, chicken.'

People stared.

Dad stepped high, meaning to go forward, heading sideways. 'Whoops, there.' He adjusted direction. Burped. 'Hang onto me shirt.' The tail hung outside his trousers.

The little girl grasped her lifeline. Mum strode ahead. I guessed she didn't want to know any of us. If she'd had a stockwhip, it would've been wrapped around Dad's neck. Victor carried Druce.

In later years, Vivi asserted that Mum had left with her still missing. Gone to Shorty's place, where we were staying.

'Hang on, sis – Mum wasn't the sort of woman to do that.'

'But it happened. I remember.'

I tried to imagine what it must have felt like to a four-year-old. Abandoned in that melee of feet and legs. Mum never lightly cast off responsibility. But who am I to criticise? Vivi's burr-in-the shoe images of that unhappy night must seem real to her. God knows, I had enough painful recollections of my own. They melted the snows of memory.

We were all trapped like caged tigers. Once, they roamed free in distant jungles, far from the stink of cages and gawking faces in small towns, never knowing they'd be expected to perform on cue for hungry crowds. All they ever wanted was the thrill of the chase, a good meal, ripped from the bone. To lie back, sleek and well-fed, dozing in the tropical sun.

I'm sure Dad hadn't planned to drink the night away. Perhaps, even while he'd been thinking, not this time, his feet had sped him to the brightness and laughter which beckoned from the pub. Hungry like me for friendly faces and pats on the back and camaraderie. 'Just one won't hurt.'

Perhaps the sear of whisky healed some inner pain. Making bearable the drudgery and exhaustion of everyday life. Refilling his well of hopes and dreams. Making up for cloudless skies when crops screamed for rain.

Dad tapped rings on the tanks. Sighed. 'Barely enough water for the house.'

We coaxed vegetables along with grey water.

The slightest breeze whirled away ploughed earth. The potato plants looked worse every day.

Dad's shoulders slumped. 'Short of irrigation from the creek, nothing will save them. We could afford a second-hand pump. But pipes cost a fortune.'

That afternoon, he looked up from the paper. 'An auction, luv. Fire hose. Bound to go cheap.'

He arrived at the sale early, disappointed to see farmers crowded around the hose. Ready to leave, an idea flashed into his mind. Strolling over to the pipes, he made a pretence of examining the loops of canvas. Disgustedly threw them onto the ground. 'Well, they're no bloody good.'

Potential buyers drifted away.

The sole bidder, Daddy returned home in triumph. 'They cost next to nothing. Haven't a clue whether they're worth anything. Silly beggars thought I was an expert.'

Mum frowned. 'I hope you haven't wasted money.'

'We'll soon know.' He set up the pump and irrigation equipment. Seconds ticked by. Water rushed through the hose. Daddy whooped. 'No leakage. Not a drip. Put it there, Victor.' He hugged Mum.

The potatoes flourished. Dad couldn't hide his excitement. 'Prices are sky-high. We'll be laughing.'

Red and gold leaves scampered from orchard trees. Twiggy brown sticks of potato plants waited for harvest.

At dawn, Daddy milked the cow, and separated the milk. A whistle on his lips, he cooked bacon, sausages and eggs for the family.

Uncle Charles brought his bride. 'Meet your second Auntie Aileen.' He joined Dad and George gathering potatoes.

Our neighbour's white hair and curling moustache made him appear ancient.

Druce eyed his evil-smelling pipe. 'What's going to happen to your pipe when you die?'

George chortled. 'I'll leave it to you in my will, young fella.'

Auntie Aileen number two spent every day in her room. She emerged for meals. Perhaps she preferred her own company. Or had lost patience with our pranks. She engaged in a weekly ritual with pomade, setting her hair in huge, elaborate curls. She glimpsed two dogs fornicating in the locked position of their kind. Rushed out, hair half-done. 'Quick! We must do something. Those dogs are injured. Tangled up somehow.'

Victor and I giggled. 'They're pupping.'

We couldn't convince her. Our parents were away. Perhaps Uncle Charles set her straight.

Unseasonal heat continued. Long morning shadows followed the tractor. Furrows revealed hundreds of fine spuds. The men bent and straightened. Flung them into heaps. They cursed the broiling midday sun. Backs ached. Feet stumbled on clods.

In the half-light of evening, they bagged the best ones. Setting aside seconds for household use. Others became pig feed. In the half-light,

Daddy reached for a potato. He grabbed a funnel-web spider by mistake. Deadly fangs proved no match for his calloused palm.

Darkness came too soon and not soon enough. In the flicker of a hurricane lamp, the men sewed tops of lumpy jute bags, ready for the carrier. One weary day of harvest followed another.

Aunt Aileen number two left to give birth, her first baby. Uncle found a job at Newcastle. Charles recommended a couple of chaps to help out. They were expected soon.

Dad was devastated by Potato Marketing Board prices. They barely covered wages, seeds, bags, and cartage. Shop prices remained high.

Daddy said, 'We do the hard yakka. Middle men reap the rewards.'

Mum stamped her foot. 'It's a disgrace.'

'I'll save a few quid. Cart some in the Austin.'

Heat gave way to rain.

'Road's a quagmire – you'd never make it.'

'I'll leave before daybreak, while the earth's frozen.'

Daddy congratulated himself on crossing the mountain. Next moment, came a loud clunk. The barely run-in Austin utility jerked to a stop. 'What the...'

A neighbour took Dad and his potatoes to town. Towing costs and repairs to a broken differential chewed up the last profits. The diff failed every other month.

Daddy said, 'So much for trouble-free motoring. I need something reliable.'

December blazed. I counted sleeps.

Mum had warned, 'We can't afford Christmas this year.'

I didn't want to believe her. Recycled presents, like the wrapping paper, would be fine. I fell into a restless sleep.

Darkness loosened its grip on the wardrobe, my chair, and bed. The room pulsed with anticipation. Grey light dissolved into pearly pink.

Christmas Day. Hurray! Mum's words rushed back. My heart shrank. Rays of gleam peeped over the horizon.

Somehow, I convinced myself Mum had been joking. A bride doll would be perfect. Everyone had one – except me. Or a signet ring? That was on my list. A bike even? I had wanted one for so long.

I pictured the wrapping paper – which design would be mine this year? I'd rip it off. No, I'd open my present carefully. Smooth out the paper. My cream curtain billowed in agreement.

A cautious glance. No parcel at the foot of my bed. Nothing on my dressing table. I peered under the bed. Only a few balls of fluff. Santa never left anything in my wardrobe. I did look.

A plover wailed.

Ross Madison enjoyed a working holiday from New Zealand. 'Fancied a stint in the Australian highlands.'

I liked the crinkles around his blue eyes. Laughed at his jokes and riddles. Games of skill and chance each evening kept us intrigued. Animal, vegetable or mineral? What fun.

A few marks of his pencil and his sketches shimmered into life. Equipment, landscapes...

Victor snooped one day, discovering a drawing of a naked couple making love.

Ross snatched it away. 'Oops! Did that when I was drunk.' It was consumed by flames.

Years afterwards, he would write me a lovely letter. 'You were always academic, never had your head out of a book. Victor enjoyed learning, too. Young Vivi was full of fun, a flibbertigibbet. And I recall Druce roared like a young bull when he was taken away from his parents' room to a new bed.'

Mr Dave Ogle arrived, a former Pom. He hailed from Newcastle. 'I'll enjoy being away from the big smoke for a spell.'

The heroine of a radio soap opera had teased her admirer, mispronouncing his name. I did the same. 'How do you do, Mr Oogle.'

Everyone chuckled. Mum corrected my mistake. Nobody guessed.

He dismissed fifties' formality. 'Call me Dave.' Friendly eyes glittered behind dark-rimmed spectacles.

We thought him old. Mum guessed his age at forty.

Dave made a tour of the orchard. 'A single-strand electric fence? Looks flimsy – does it work?'

Victor grinned. 'Gives animals a little shock. Keeps 'em out of the garden all right. Touch it with this stick.'

Dave hesitated.

'Have a go. It won't hurt you.'

Dave reeled back, accusation in his dark eyes. 'Wouldn't hurt me?'

We exchanged guilty glances. Suppose he told Daddy?

Dave burst into laughter. 'Good one, Victor.' He didn't report our prank.

The men built a large dam on useless, swampy ground. 'It'll ensure good irrigation, whatever the season.' They built an earthen wall and overflow. Before many months, visitors marvelled at our huge lake. It mirrored the eucalypt-clad hillside.

Floating reed islands appeared.

In later years, Druce took Mum out in our small boat. He persuaded her to step onto one island. The pretext? 'There's a nest.' He rowed away.

Mum yelled, 'Come back.' Leaping up and down on the undulating island. Puce with rage.

The first trout hatchlings grew in spots and size. Platypus frolicked and played. The Barrington Fishing Club would become regulars. Daddy built them a lodge. On a subsequent visit, Uncle Geoff couldn't believe his eyes.

Bare branches shivered in frosts and rain. Sleet stung faces, and froze hands.

Dad scanned angry skies. 'Hope snow holds off until we finish the harvest.'

I felt glad to be indoors. Housework tasks might not be exciting, but I preferred them to toil in sleet and snow. My correspondence school teachers' comments made me feel they had my best interests at heart. I slotted schoolwork between soapies on the wireless, Read every book that came my way. Wrote poems and dreamed stories onto the page.

I celebrated my tenth birthday with a small present or two. Nobody appreciated the significance of double figures.

Mum simpered. 'Sorry. I forgot to bake you a cake.'

All the family enjoyed my birthday cakes. Surely she'd make me one next time?

George Foxcroft brought us a large box of second-hand books. I read everything from *Landtakers* to Wild West yarns, disappointed to learn American cowboys had swapped chaps for business suits. Autobiographies or memoir brought insights into other lives, places and times. I loved *The Story of an African Farm* by Olive Schreiner. Louisa M. Alcott's *Little Women* was another favourite.

Winter downpours made outside work impossible.

Daddy was almost in despair. 'Spuds rot in soaked paddocks.'

The men finished the harvest.

Daddy taught Ross and Dave how to cut timber. 'I'm impressed how quickly you've learnt.'

Relentless rain drove them into the shed. All three were amateur boxers. They compared the merits of famous fighters. The punching ball took a beating. Sparring matches ensued.

Dave took off his gloves. 'There's a dearth of good fighters. Lots of dough in it.'

Ross praised Daddy's skills. 'You handle yourself well. Thought of taking up the sport?'

Daddy made inquiries.

Mum blinked. 'A boxing bout? You're mad.'

'A fortune to be made. I'll get in and out quickly, before any damage.'

Mum pursed her lips. She fought her own battle: drying clothes in persistent rain.

The sun shone through sullen skies. She lit the outdoor copper. Vivi and I gathered soiled linen, trousers... Water bubbled and steamed. Mum grabbed her pot stick, a former broom handle. Lifted boiled sheets and pillowcases into concrete tubs. Blew tendrils of hair from her damp brow. Rough trousers and work shirts entered the cauldron.

We rinsed whites in Reckitt's blue. Wrung them by hand, the mangle having broken. Vivi and I pegged them out. Mum scrubbed chocolate soil from work clothes. A rinse… We adjusted the clothes prop.

She slumped into a chair, fanning herself with the *Advocate*. 'That's over, thank goodness.'

Daddy brought her a cup of tea. 'You need a washing machine.'

'Huh! When could we afford that?'

'All I need is one good win.'

Mum raised her eyebrows.

Swollen clouds gulped the sun.

Mum leapt to her feet. 'Quick, girls, it's about to pour.'

Big drops battered faces and arms. We ripped everything from the line. Mum draped half-dried clothes on chairs near the stove, in front of the open fire. We pegged sheets on a front veranda line.

Rain thundered on the corrugated-iron roof. Cascaded down windows. The deluge lasted for days.

Wireless news crackled. Maitland, lower down the Hunter, in flood. Rescues were underway. Roads were cut, except for four-wheel drive vehicles. For over a month, Dad ran the mail, bringing groceries and supplies with the tractor.

Daddy opened his paper. 'Traffic accident. Remember young Robin, from Stewarts Brook? Family truck overturned on a cutting. Killed his father, trapped his uncle.' Flung clear, the boy walked miles in the darkness for help. 'Saved the life of his injured uncle.' Dad shook his head, 'Brave lad. Not a sound when I cut out that fish hook. Deserved a medal.'

Mum smiled. 'He's got one now?'

Daddy chuckled. 'Says here, "Robin's award for bravery was presented by the wife of the NSW Governor. She asked, "Do you mind if I kiss you?" "I'd kiss a spider to get my medal."'

Dave chuckled. 'That's kids for you.'

Victor and I enjoyed a bush ramble. Huge, moss-covered rocks loomed above us. In a small vale, cream blossoms of native banksia, or honeysuckle, brought a delightful aroma. Clumps of bright yellow buttercups quivered in the breeze. Wild white violets, yellow bachelors' buttons and native blues peeped between clumps of grass. I dubbed it my valley.

After I'd left home, Mum would ride into that spot, nostalgic for an absent daughter.

Peggy trotted at our heels. Nose sniffing the air, she detected aromas humans couldn't even imagine. A few grey hairs had crept among the black. Her loyalty never wavered. At home, she made sport of shepherding sheep against Daddy's electric fence. Perhaps she liked to hear them bleat.

Mum shouted, 'Come behind!'

The dog slunk away, guilt in every paw. The moment Mum went inside, Peggy resumed her fun.

Daddy heard scratching at the door. Outside, Peggy whined, clearly agitated. 'What's up, old girl?' Tremors in her body and limbs. 'Quick, Genn. Some bastard's given her a bait.' He administered a salt and water emetic. Whirled her around. Induced vomiting. Miraculously, Daddy saved her a second time.

17

Dad made plans for his first boxing match at Newcastle. He won one, but was knocked out of two others.

Mum scowled. 'Huh! You're forty. Leave it to younger chaps.'

He shifted uneasily. 'Next bout, I'm bound to win.'

It was declared a draw. But Daddy hurt his hand. While it healed, he mulled over ideas.

'I need to build an audience. Reckon you could make me a fancy pair of shorts?'

'I'll think about it.'

He and Shorty plotted tactics for a heavyweight tussle. 'So far as the crowd's concerned, we haven't met. Shorty from Jerry's Plains versus Joly from Tomalla. The Battle of The Giants. How does that sound?'

Mum spluttered. 'You'll never get away with it. And suppose you're hurt?'

Hard bushwork saw them fitter than men half their age. They trained daily. Running, push-ups, weights, sparring sessions…

'You'll see, luv. I'll make a name for myself. Buy a reliable vehicle. Probably a Rolls.'

Mum put down her crochet. 'You and your silly ideas.'

Shorty said, 'We'll give the crowd their money's worth during the first few rounds.'

'And bring the bout to a dramatic end in the fourth. At my signal, protect yourself. I'll turn my head and spit into the bucket.'

Fight night. Locals in the packed stadium knew them both. Ready for the fun. The referee held open the ropes. Dad stepped through in blue silk shorts, made from the wartime parachute. Shorty, in green, ignored the narrow opening. He stepped over the top. The crowd roared.

Shorty and Dad shook hands, going to their corners. A bell rang. They sparred, ducked, and dodged around the ring. Ah, the fancy footwork, the cheers. Aficionados told them later they had given an excellent boxing exhibition. The pace quickened. By the third round, the crowd was half-standing in their seats, baying for blood.

The fourth began with rapid punch-ups. The referee separated them a number of times.

Daddy gave Shorty the signal, launching into the Fitsimmons Rip. A rapid succession of punches – left, left, right, left.

Shorty protected his solar plexus. His rapid action was missed by the crowd. His long frame collapsed, almost slow-motion. He hit the canvas. Gave a couple of spasmodic kicks. Lay still.

The crowd screamed. Everyone was on their feet, counting in time with the referee.

One, two, three… Shorty didn't stir.

The referee raised Dad's arm. Victory.

The crowd shouted, catcalled, banged feet on the floor. Showered them with pennies.

Mr Kergan rushed to offer congratulations. A boxer himself, he pumped Daddy's hand. 'Shorty thought he was good. But he's no match for you. I've seen a lot of boxers in my time. Let me tell you, Joly, you're the best.'

Dad flashed a modest smile. 'Thanks, mate.'

Shorty chuckled afterwards. 'Pure theatre! An exciting night's entertainment was had by all.'

They shared the prize, all three pounds of it.

Shorty chuckled. 'Doesn't even cover beer money. Let alone expenses.'

Auntie Violet glared. 'I'm ashamed of you both, rigging that fight. Think of all the poor souls who paid good money.'

Shorty abandoned his career.

Dad remained hopeful. 'It's not the time to quit yet, luv. I'll soon be able to name my own price.'

Mum raised her eyebrows. 'And cows will fly.'

He arranged another match.

His opponent took one look. 'I'm not bloody fightin' him. Seen what he done to that other poor bugger.'

No other heavyweight opponents came forward.

'It's over, luv. Anyway, I couldn't imagine a life beating someone's brains out. Sorry about the Rolls, though.'

'Rolls? The only fancy car you're likely to afford is a toy one.'

Ross enthralled me with tales of castles, cerulean blue Italian skies, and cumulus clouds. I'd seen prints from famous paintings. He told of olive groves and cypresses. Small villages, clusters of stone houses. One day, I'd visit those fascinating places.

He avoided mention of his time with the allies in World War Two. Maybe it was too painful.

One day, Ross scanned the library shelves.

I triumphantly drew forth a plain-covered volume. 'Mum told Daddy this book is a good one.'

He struggled to suppress a smile. 'Er, no thanks, Dessie.'

Puzzled, I put the *Book of Life* back in place.

I made to prepare my own garden.

Dave laughed. 'A seven-day wonder.'

His words spurred me into action. Soil preparation was nothing new. Remove rocks and litter. Break the ground with a mattock. Smash clods against the tines of a fork.

Mum gave me phlox, pansies, lupins and calendula. I loved the aroma of fresh earth, fine and friable. Carrots, peas and cabbage followed. I watered the beds regularly.

By December, Dave was no longer laughing. My garden bloomed. Vegetables hung on vines and plants.

Victor fed the dogs at dusk, and chained them for the night. Left free they wandered. 'Could get into trouble.'

In her old age, Peggy loathed the chain.

Victor yelled, 'Peggy! Come here.'

Mum whistled and shouted. 'Off on one of her rambles. I hope she's all right.'

Next morning, Peggy was still missing. Unusual for her.

Daddy feared the worst. He drove off, spotting a black body in the gutter. 'Poor old girl.' He gulped, stroking her fur. 'Heading home.' Telling Mum, 'Froth around her mouth. Distorted posture. Her third bait, poor beggar. Almost made it. Who would kill a good dog?'

'Someone with a sick mind.'

Dad buried Peggy under a cherry tree. I held Vivi and wept. We sometimes glanced around, half-expecting her to join us on an adventure.

Nan and Grandfather arrived. Devout Jehovah's Witnesses, they deplored Christmas, a pagan custom. And disliked Ross on sight. I was devastated.

Daddy avoided discussing politics.

A decade younger, Ross argued his left-wing beliefs with passion. 'Stalin will rescue the proletariat. Social justice for the common man.'

'How the blazes can you believe that?' Grandfather's eyes bulged. 'Stalin's had millions killed!'

In the History According to Ross, gulags, forced labour and killings were right-wing propaganda. Brutal actions were explained as necessity.

'Nice term that,' Grandfather said. 'Excuses anything. Even murder.'

'Excesses of the right are far more dangerous.'

Arguments became heated. Mum changed the subject.

Daddy chuckled afterwards. 'Spot fires continue to blaze.'

Nan wore enough jewellery and lace for a pagan princess. She disapproved of Mum's lipstick. 'A touch of Ponds cream is all you need, Genn.'

'I don't feel dressed without lipstick.'

Grandfather clucked. 'Powder and paint? You don't need it.'

'Dad, please!'

Mist shivered up the valley. The fire crackled bush stories, solace and companionship. Ross and Dave braved the damp weather wearing oilskins. Dad's finest axe felled a wild cherry tree.

Christmas glitter, baubles and fake snow chattered excitement.

Dave hung mistletoe, dreaming of cool Christmas mornings on the other side of the world. 'Gave English lads an excuse to kiss pretty girls until all the berries were picked off.'

Nan looked scandalised.

Mum's eyes reflected the glow of firelight. She paraded in Daddy's Christmas present, embossed riding boots.

Ross gave us boxes of paint and colouring books. Yippee!

Nan's gift? Perfumed soap, and pink washer, edged with crochet. Pretty – and useful. She said, 'And use it.' Did she have to make it seem an obligation?

At the children's table, I loathed half-hearing stories. Peeved at adult laughter. Mum's crisp fowl – not chicken, back then – was a treat. New potatoes, peas and carrots came from my garden.

'Hurrah!' I cried. 'Two threepences in my pudding.'

The oldies gathered around the fire. Tales were abruptly abandoned. Sideways glances towards our grandparents. Dave and Russ enjoyed a few glasses of beer. Our grandparents glared. Daddy didn't touch a drop.

Ross played his piano accordion. 'The Road to The Isles' and 'Bonnie Prince Charlie'. He launched into another.

Dave sang along to 'The Foggy, Foggy Dew'. Good baritone voice. 'And all night long, I held her in my arms, just to keep her from the foggy, foggy dew.'

Nan and Grandfather shocked. Daddy suppressing mirth.

Later, Victor told me, 'Nobody's allowed to sing it.'

'Why?'

'Maybe it's rude.'

Grandfather told of a few thousand Witnesses expected to gain eternal life. 'Suppose I'm not good enough?'

Mum said. 'But you don't lie, or swear, or cheat...'

'Not even over a halfpenny.'

Daddy added, 'If anyone gets there, Rick…' He told Mum later, 'Billions of humans have inhabited the earth. Defies logic that such a small number would become immortal.'

Mum sighed. 'I wish Mum had never joined that jolly sect. Dad endures terrible nightmares. He fears every storm is Armageddon – fires, brimstone, boulders flung about, screams of sinners…'

One night, thunder rolled around the hills.

Mum said, 'Dad lay awake for hours, expecting the final judgement.'

I imagined the terror sect children must feel.

Victor told of his dreams. 'Soon spaceships will reach the moon.'

Grandfather's eyes bulged. 'Jehovah would never allow it.'

Sputnik led the way into space. Goodness knows what believers thought.

Bible studies lured Nan and Grandfather home.

Mum said, 'I'm so glad you avoided alcohol, Joly.'

He looked miserable.

Dave returned to Newcastle. We missed him, glad Ross stayed on to help plant the new season's potatoes.

He built himself a bark hut in the back paddock. 'I want to experience life in the raw.'

Terrified of snakes, Ross carried a six-inch dagger in his belt.

Dad chuckled. 'Hope he's never bitten. He'd bleed to death.'

Neighbours arrived, a surprise visit.

Dad said, 'How about we make our friends a cup of tea?'

Mum muttered, 'I suppose I could.' I doubt if she meant to sound grudging.

After that, Dad asked Vivi and me to brew tea or make the lunch. We resented being treated as skivvies, with neither help nor guidance. Mum played the lady.

People sat down.

Then she took us to task. 'Can't I trust you girls to do anything? Why didn't you use a fresh tablecloth? This table isn't set correctly. Where's my knife, the one with the bone handle?' And so on.

We burned with embarrassment. Cracked cups, mismatched saucers and chipped plates added to our shame.

Mum regarded me as the good child. Not perfect like Victor, but quiet and amenable. I didn't argue with her decisions, knowing where it led.

Vivi proved my theory every time she questioned some edict.

Mum glared at her. 'Must you be so wicked and disobedient?'

Another strapping.

I lost myself in a mystery by Edgar Wallace, *The Clue of the Twisted Candle*. Read Marcus Clarke's *For the Term of His Natural Life*, *What Katy Did*, *Anne of Green Gables* and *Tales of the Arabian Nights*.

At ten, phrases in a foreign language fascinated me.

Ross said, 'It's French.'

Someday…

The Australian Journal, a monthly magazine of short stories and serials, spurred on my own writing ambitions. One day, I'd be a famous author. I scrawled an enquiry to Hodder and Stoughton about getting books published. Some editor in a busy London office must have chuckled at my childish scribble. With great courtesy, he advised me to try my work locally first.

I must have done something to incur Mum's extreme displeasure. She scowled. 'Wake up to yourself, or I'll send you to boarding school. They'll teach you proper behaviour.'

The worst punishment she could imagine shimmered before me. Yes, please! At boarding school I'd make friends, learn French… They lacked the money.

Daddy drilled us about the safe use of firearms. 'Unload rifles before storage. Treat any weapon as if it is loaded.' A stern glance. 'And never, ever, point a gun at anyone.' He even forbade the pointing of toy weapons.

Victor wriggled with irritation. 'But, Dad – it's only a game?'

'Guns aren't for play, son. Take care, even with toys. One day you might forget and point a real weapon.'

Victor grumbled, 'He treats me like a baby. I'll be a hundred before he allows me to handle the .22.'

Ross and the others set off for town.

Daddy had given Victor strict instructions. 'Look after your sister. And no mischief.'

I looked forward to the fun of a day on our own. The ute disappeared over the hill. Victor took the rifle from its rack.

'You're not allowed to touch that.'

'Why not?' He sighted along the barrel. Aiming it at my face.

Alarm bells shrilled. 'Don't point the gun at me. Daddy says...'

'It's not loaded, stupid.' He pointed it at the window. Squeezed the trigger.

BANG!

A hole splintered in the pane.

'My God.' Victor dropped the rifle.

I trembled. 'You could've killed me.'

Deathly pale. 'Don't tell! Promise you won't tell?'

'What about the broken window?'

'I'll think of something.' He put away the rifle.

I dreaded our parents' return.

Victor sauntered to meet them. 'We were playing tennis. Ball flew through...'

Mum glared. 'That was careless of you.'

Dad grinned. 'Kids and balls. Would you fix it, Ross?'

'Sure thing, Joly.' Ross held a tennis ball against the hole. He gave Victor a long look. Set to work with pliers, tacks, putty. You couldn't fool a soldier.

Ross returned to NZ. I mourned his fun and games. Snuggled in my bed at night, I pictured the moon shining over him. An invisible thread bound us together – an idea gleaned from stories of romance. I signed off a letter *Au revoir*, expecting Ross to be pleased.

His response? 'I was disappointed to see you putting on airs.'

My cheeks flamed. If only he'd written, 'It will be wonderful when you learn French. I can see you're keen to do so.' His lack of insight failed to dampen my enthusiasm.

Mum asked, 'What possible use is French to a child in the Australian bush?'

Even at ten, I planned to travel. And how wonderful it would be to speak with people in their own tongue. A lifetime later, a diploma in French from L'Alliance Français de Paris allowed me to achieve my ambition.

Six months passed. Not a single outing to town. Our interactions were confined, almost exclusively, to family. Vivi and I developed agonising shyness.

A car approached. I panicked. What would I say? Where could I look?

Vivi dived under a bed on the front veranda, horrified to see Mum taking our neighbour on a tour of the garden, feet away from her hiding spot.

'Vivi was here just minutes ago. Can't understand where…' Mum stopped in mid-sentence. 'What the… Why are you under that bed, Vivienne? Come out at once. Say hello to Gay.'

Vivi emerged. Faltered a greeting. Embarrassed at grubby clothes.

'Goodness, child, you're filthy. Wash and put on a clean frock at once.'

Vivi was a study in scarlet.

Leaping flames chuckled. The Tilley lamp hissed. Its strong illumination allowed Mum to crochet or knit, a big improvement on hurricane lamps. The wireless chatted stories and vibrated music. The ABC *Argonaut's Club* encouraged young people, aged up to eighteen, to write and paint. It brought art, drama, and literature to isolated families. I did achieve Dragon's Tooth Echo 35. Vivi's nom de plume eludes me.

Fog rolled up our small valley. Mum called it coastal weather. The wireless program crackled, and faded. Victor twiddled dials and fiddled with the aerial. We hated to miss episodes of soapies like *Blue Hills, Dr Paul, Life with Portia* and the enthralling *Search for the Golden Boomerang*. I also enjoyed *Dad and Dave*, a wacky version of Steele Rudd's *On Our Selection*.

Daddy frowned. 'They've ruined a good yarn.'

Pick a Box, a game show, starred Bob and Dolly Dyer. She awarded prizes, her sing-song voice breathless with feigned excitement.

Daddy loved the *Amateur Hour*. 'So many talented unknowns. My friend, Howard, auditioned. Beautiful tenor. Fear his rough clothes ruled him out.'

We played bobs, snakes and ladders or fiddlesticks. Mum waxed nostalgic over games of five hundred with her father.

She read us Jack London's *Call of the Wild*. Clustered around the fire, we listened spellbound. Kazan, the wolf, sleek and cunning, wandered pine forests, pitted against man. We begged for a second chapter. And another... Kazan died. Snowed in by our grief.

Mum assembled her brushes. I liked to see her paint. In her teens, she had copied old masters, developing certain technical skills. She favoured the naive style of landscape with Hereford cattle. Lifelike, in its narrowest interpretation, was her sole criterion. She lacked interest in art history. Couldn't appreciate the Impressionists. Mum sniffed. 'Can't abide modern art. A child of three could do better.'

Florence stepped from the up-country train. Our peachy gran, née FitzGerald, made an annual visit. She looked stunning in a well-cut suit, or costume, pearls at ears and throat. Her hug wafted with lavender. Mischievous eyes glittered behind thick spectacles. I envied her use of a lace handkerchief, ladylike and delicate. At twelve, I wanted to be like her.

We drooled over her pan curries, transformed from leftover roast. She swapped recipes with Mum. Having birthed eight children, Florrie must have had plenty of tips about child-raising. But had the nous to keep opinions to herself. She never criticised. Her role was to love, not raise us. At seventy-five, she had us chuckling over her jokes and sense of fun.

Once, she flung her skirts high and danced an Irish jig, singing, 'Bandy legs, bandy legs. Have you ever seen such bandy legs?'

We shrieked with laughter. Nobody else had a Gran like ours.

She brought sagas of bushrangers and bush picnics. Gold-rush towns of rough huts and tents appeared overnight, like mushrooms. 'I met your grandfather at Copeland.'

Gran said, 'We wandered hand-in-hand over hills splashed with violet morning-glory. Among the scent of golden wattle. Alas, a lovers' quarrel – I can't recall what about. I returned his ring with mixed feelings. A young man well over six feet tall and ever so handsome.'

We said, 'But you married?'

'Not so fast, girls! A big storm. The Copeland River flooded. I struggled through waist-high flood water, wading towards the shallows.'

'And?'

'"Stop!" Your grandfather frantically waved. He rushed to my side, clasping me in his arms. "Thank God you're safe, Florrie. You were headed for a mineshaft, hidden by the flood. I'll never let you go again." He saved my life. I loved him more than ever. We married soon afterwards.'

It seemed the most romantic story I'd ever heard.

Later, Daddy took us on a nostalgic visit to Copeland. A few fireplaces had survived. Huge trees grew in what had once been family homes.

Gran told of braving flood, fire and snakes during her time in the bush. 'I spent a lot of time alone with the children. Your grandfather was often away droving. One afternoon, a stranger appeared at our hut. I offered him tea and cake, as you do in the bush. Shadows lengthened. I didn't like the way he looked at me. Your grandfather wasn't expected home for weeks. How could I persuade him to leave?'

Vivi blinked. 'What did you do, Grandma?'

'I feigned a smile. "You'll have to excuse me now. My husband is expected home any minute. Gets upset if his tea isn't ready." He galloped off. I couldn't stop shaking. Kept a rifle at the ready all night. And no, girls, he didn't return.' She shared a complicit glance with Mum.

Gran told of childhood rambles in the bush. 'My sister and I loved to explore. One evening, we wandered further than usual. Twilight paths were gulped by darkness. We turned this way and that. Should we shelter in a hollow tree? Dreading the thought of spiders and centipedes.'

Dingoes howled. 'Creatures of the night shrieked and whooped. We clutched each other for comfort. Never had we felt so alone – or afraid. We glimpsed a brightly lit tent. Amazed to hear lively harmonica music. A voice called, "Ladies to the left, gents to the right." We giggled. Astonished. A square dance. Edging closer, I peeked inside. A gnome-like old man sat on an upturned packing case, playing to a non-existent audience. The gnome shared damper and cheese. Brought us a blanket. Next morning, our saviour led us to the edge of the forest. We turned to offer thanks. He had vanished. Mother and Father were about to mount a search. We never found him again.'

Gran told of parties. 'We children were meant to be asleep. Strains of "After the Ball" drifted upstairs. Ladies in fine gowns waltzed by. We dropped conversation lollies onto bald heads. Sent bedroom slippers whirling away on fashionable trains.'

People called Gran fey. 'I've had prophetic dreams and visions. Seen places and events on the other side of the world, though I've never travelled.' She read palms and teacups, told fortunes. 'All sorts of fancy cars used to drive up for a reading.' Her eyes glinted. 'Had to stop – too many busybodies.'

Mum suffered a headache. Gran laid on healing hands.

She inherited the FitzGerald love of writing. Descendants like Uncle Sid, Daddy, John Wright, Vivi and me have inherited this passion. It's as necessary to me as breathing.

The loss of her child, 'Florrie' – Florence Dorothy – still brought tears to her eyes, thirty years after her death. 'Your dad's playmate… God rest her soul.'

The horse with an empty saddle pained us, too.

The loss of Auntie Edna was more recent. I recall seeing her only once. A shadowy gathering at Gran's place. The silky feel of pyjamas against my skin. Auntie a plump and pretty young woman in powder-blue. She bent to kiss me goodnight, a hint of perfume. I never saw her again. She succumbed to bowel cancer, at only forty-two.

Daddy took a long, solitary walk in our back paddock. Men didn't cry.

18

We waved to Mum. 'Be back about four.' A visit to buy supplies in Scone.

Daddy chanced to meet Jack Rangers. They pumped hands.

'Great to see you, mate. It's been years.'

Jack eyed me in mock surprise. 'Dessie? My, haven't you grown.' He turned to my sister. 'Vivi? Never! A babe in arms last time I saw you.' He added, 'We've moved, Joly. House nearby.'

Dad grinned. 'Let's have a drink. Be right back, girls.'

They disappeared into the pub.

We waited. And waited. The sun took its leave.

At twilight, the men appeared. Their slurred chorus of 'When Irish Eyes Are Smiling' told me the worst.

Dad sat behind the wheel, Jack on the back of the ute.

'Daddy, aren't we going home?'

'We're staying the night.'

'But…Mum will worry.'

'Gotta catch up with Jack.'

Lydia welcomed us like invited guests, not strays dragged home by an inebriated husband. She fried extra sausages, boiled more vegetables. 'Seems only yesterday you stayed with us, Dessie. My Alec was born not long afterwards.'

We slept in our clothes. Next morning, the eight-year-olds, Alec and Vivi, shrieked and laughed over marbles. I helped with the housework. And worried about Mum. Twenty-four hours without news. She must be frantic.

The men finished a bottle of overproof rum. Opened another.

I swallowed. 'When are we leaving?'

Daddy swayed. 'Bye and bye.'

Day dragged into night. If only they had a phone, to let Mum know we were safe.

The fathers clinked glasses. They laughed at everything and nothing. Daddy stumbled outside, and threw up.

Next morning his hands shook. 'Hair of the dog.' He downed a rum. Jack poured a second.

Mum must be desperate. She wouldn't call anyone, afraid of revealing our family secret.

Three days. I despaired. Would we ever leave?

Daddy's eyes struggled to focus. 'I'm taking you girls home. Mustn't worry your mother.'

Lydia raised her eyebrows. 'Shouldn't you sober up first, Joly?'

'I'm fine. Bye and thanks. Great visit.'

I glared. 'You're drunk. I'm not going.'

He grabbed the ignition keys. 'Come along. Or I'll drive off and kill myself.'

I forced myself into the cabin, convinced we were about to die. Vivi whimpered beside me. We kangaroo-hopped through the gate. Missed the post by inches. Juddered along the road.

Where were the cops when you needed them?

He rambled. 'You girls don't know how much I love you. And your mother. The boys…'

Nothing felt less like love. Not with the ute weaving along the road. Not with my guts in knots. Not with my little sister rigid beside me.

A steep cutting.

'Please, Daddy. Take care.'

A maniacal laugh. 'Say your prayers, girls. Say your prayers.'

At this very spot our schoolfriend, Robin, had been in a crash. Walking miles in the darkness for help.

We made it round the first cutting. My mouth lost all moisture. Our ute dged around a second. A third…Vivi clutched my arm so tightly it ached.

Daddy lapsed into silence. Suppose he fell asleep? I talked non-stop.

Twilight gave way to darkness. Moonan Flat. Ahead, a treacherous road climbed into the mountains. Risky in daylight, with a sober driver. Suppose we met a timber jinker? I shuddered at the thought of Daddy backing up. On the outside of some steep cutting.

He turned off the main road. The ute jerked to a stop.

'Gotta see old Fred.'

I stepped out. My legs had been pressed hard against the floor for hours. They buckled under me. I grabbed the door for support, humiliated at the prospect of strangers seeing Daddy in that state.

He shook Fred Hunt's hand. 'Great to see you, old mate.'

'You, too, Joly.'

Fred's red face and slurred voice reassured me. Two of a kind.

Fred sloshed whisky into tumblers. Glasses clinked. Dad drank several for the road. He'd forgotten why he came – if he ever knew.

Fred said, 'Why not stay the night?'

'G...good idea.'

They drank to it.

Fred's boys appeared. Jake, almost fifteen. Tex a year older. Blond hair and lovely smile. 'Mum's away. We pretty much look after ourselves.'

They shared a meal of toast and jam with Vivi and me.

Bored with our drunken fathers, we left to explore under the house. It sat high on pylons.

Musty darkness. I brushed away cobwebs, trembling. Pale beams of Tex's flashlight illuminated old chairs and a table, a broken rocking horse.

'And there's my tricycle. Now only two wheels. A while since I rode that.'

Reality seemed at one remove, shadowed by the knowledge of Daddy drunk upstairs. Jokes dispelled hours of tension. It felt a miracle to be alive.

Footsteps. In the half-light, Fred shambled behind us, reeking of stale alcohol. 'Come and talk to me, sweetheart.' The look in his eyes made me uneasy.

Tex whispered, 'Be careful of the old man.'

Whatever that meant. I stepped out of Fred's reach. He wandered off.

'Dad drinks every day,' said Jake. 'How about yours?'

'Binges. Last longer now. Sicker, too.'

I heard water flowing near the veranda. 'Is it raining?'

The boys guffawed.

Embarrassed, I realised Daddy was peeing into the darkness. We went back inside. Daddy couldn't keep his eyes open. The boys found him a bed, helping remove his boots.

Vivi and I slept in a little room nearby.

The boys served breakfast cereals. Our fathers snored on.

Tex picked up Dad's ignition keys. 'Fancy a spin, girls?'

Bright light illuminated the hillside. He took the wheel, Jake and me beside him. Vivi rattled around like a pebble in a parcel on the back.

We tore around the hillside at full throttle, barely missing stumps and logs. Our driver slammed on the brakes. We shrieked hysterically. Vivi bounced three feet into the air.

Tex drove out onto the bitumen. 'Let's see what she can do.'

The speedo climbed, trees blurred, posts whipped by. He screeched to a stop. Spun the vehicle around. Whooping, we took off, tyres smoking.

He chuckled. 'Best get her back before your old man wakes up.'

Tex parked.

Jake opened the door. 'Yeah. Let's get to hell out of this ute. When Dad takes his first drink, there'll be hell to pay.'

They returned Dad's keys.

At noon, the oldies emerged. Dad blinked in the harsh light, eyes bloodshot. He skipped food, taking a rum or three for the road. 'Let's go, girls.'

With the sun at its zenith, we made our farewells.

Tex and I shared a long wave. What a dish!

I ignored Daddy's erratic driving, strangely tranquil. Itching for a bath and change of clothing.

Passes, bends and cuttings.

The ute made a wobbly progress down the last hill.

Mum fronted Daddy at the gate, shaking with rage. 'Where the hell have you been, Joly? Three days without a word. Three days! I've been worried sick. How dare you put our daughters through such risks. What sort of a man…'

He swayed before her.

She gave him a disgusted look. 'Oh, what's the use? Go to bed.'

Mum didn't quiz us about our whereabouts during those missing days. And I didn't mention Fred's stalking. Or Dad's driving, let alone our morning antics with the boys.

But I did share my news. 'Tex is my boyfriend. He asked me to give him a call.'

Mum's eyes bulged. 'Boyfriend? At twelve? I don't think so.' She berated Dad for placing us in moral danger.

'Mum, what's…'

'Never you mind.'

My dictionary was less than helpful. 'Virtuous, chaste, sinless.'

Sick to the stomach over Dad's drinking, I sought to discuss it with Mum.

She snapped, 'Be quiet. It's none of your business.'

She made me feel angry and resentful. 'We could have died, Vivi.'

So young, yet circumstances had brought a wisdom beyond her age. 'I know.'

Mum nagged and insulted almost everyone. We felt sorry for the perpetrator.

Only Victor remained beyond reproach.

Toots hopped into our lives. He stole hearts. The baby kangaroo had been orphaned by a traffic accident.

Daddy found him, huddled near his mother. 'Couldn't leave the little fella to die.'

We fed him milk every couple of hours. I can't recall whether it was full or half-strength. Mum used a pillowslip as a makeshift pouch and bed. He hopped inside, manipulating himself with his head between his long legs.

Dad said, 'My, that's clever.'

Toots talked to us in the clikkety sound of his kind. He enjoyed the occasional sweet. We chuckled at his posture: eyes closed and paws clasped as if in prayer, sucking like mad. He more than doubled in size, nibbling sweet grass. Milk was off the menu.

Dad said, 'The time has come to return him to the wild.'

We knew it had to come. A meadow with kangaroos seemed ideal. Toots hopped free. We drove away. Heartbroken at leaving him to his fate. I'll never forget that empty feeling.

Shorty noticed an advert for a five-ton Bedford lorry. 'At Newcastle. Only a few years old, Joly. Given excellent service. Owner no longer needs it.'

Daddy's eyes glittered. 'A lorry would save a fortune in cartage. And I'd be rid of the ute.'

They left early, Shorty driving. At Maitland, busy traffic kept them trapped on a side road.

Shorty groaned. 'Will there ever be a break?'

Daddy pulled on his brother's old police jacket. 'Thought this might come in handy.' A few authoritative strides. In the centre of the busy intersection, he directed traffic, waving the Austin through.

Shorty drew over. He waited and waited. Daddy guided streams of vehicles.

Finally, he hopped back into the passenger seat. 'I've a flair for it. Could have gone on all day.'

The Bedford had every feature Daddy needed. 'Excellent trade-in for the ute. Small bank loan's covered the difference. All I need now is a heavy vehicle licence. Can't wait to cart my own spuds.

Shorty took the wheel. 'You'll not know yourself, Joly.'

On the way home, the Bedford's radiator boiled.

Shorty said, 'We need a belt to help unscrew the cap.'

Neither wore one. Daddy spied a motorcycle policeman.

The cop unbuckled his belt. Next moment, he roared after some hoon.

Dad clutched not only the belt, but handcuffs and a pistol as well. 'Reckon these are ours to keep?'

They fell about laughing. The policeman returned, and grabbed his equipment. A cheery wave.

Daddy sighed. 'Hope to God that radiator boil wasn't an ill omen.'

His heavy-vehicle licence in hand, he made discreet enquires. Café owners and householders were happy to buy potatoes direct from the grower.

Daddy finished loading over a hundred bags of spuds, aching in every muscle. He thought, Thank God that's over. I couldn't lift another thing.

In fading light, the motor groaned into life. He pictured a hot bath. His favourite armchair. A tasty meal.

Headlights illuminated the rutted track. Crossing a swampy gully, the heavily laden vehicle's wheels lost traction, spun…

'Bogged! Bloody hell.'

Somehow he found the energy to remove half the load. Drove the vehicle over the wet spot. Carried the bags across, hefting each one back onto the lorry.

Well after dark, Daddy staggered home. 'I'm all in, luv. Barely enough energy for a bath.' Gulping a meal, he fell into bed.

The alarm screeched at three a.m. He groped for his clothing. The lorry grumbled into life.

He told Mum, 'Stars glittered as I spun along the frozen road. A lopsided moon hung low on the horizon.' He parked in a shadowed back street, to avoid busybodies. 'Homeless alcoholics stumbled from sleeping places in pig pens at the sales yard.' He wondered what drove the poor beggars from normal society.

In pink light, Daddy made the first restaurant deliveries. He hefted heavy bags up rickety steps to storage areas. Staggered into cramped attics. Teetered around narrow corners. Stepped down shaky stairs, into musty cellars…

He told Mum, 'I'm buggered.' On the plus side, prices were excellent. 'We've made a profit, first time ever. No more Potato Marketing Board for me.'

He bought a pre-war kerosene model Hallstrom refrigerator. A large timber chest, with a motor assembly at the side, and enamel interior. A tiny freezing compartment made Dad's eyes gleam. 'I'll make lots of ice cream.'

Mum chuckled. 'You and your ice cream.'

We loved his delicious confection of custard and fresh cream.

He built a laundry and new bathroom. Moved the copper indoors. Designed storage for stove wood. 'And there, my dear, new concrete tubs. And now, an even better surprise.' He whipped away a cover.

Mum gaped. 'A Breville washing machine.'

Pumping a plunger forced soapy water through heavily soiled clothes. 'Much easier than scrubbing them by hand.'

They hugged.

A McCormick-Deering separator stood next to the copper. Dad wore gumboots, patched work trousers and check, long-sleeved shirt. He poured foamy milk into the large bowl. Whistled 'Lily of The Lamplight'. Turned the handle slowly. The motor reached the correct revolutions. A bell rang, yellowish cream poured from one spout, milk from the other.

Frothy skimmed milk fed our pigs. They fought over it at the trough.

I made the butter. A pinch of salt and I whipped the rich cream. Fats separated from buttermilk. A wash removed impurities. Lightly salted, I slapped it into shape with decorative grooved paddles. Home-made butter looked and tasted delicious – nothing like the bought variety.

Mum blushed, handing me a booklet on puberty.

Tiny, mobile circles swelled into breasts. Late in my twelfth year, our lorry laboured up the mountain. Sitting on the back, deep red embers of sunset glowed above the landscape of childhood. Blood above and blood below.

In secret, I savoured my first period, excited to join the sisterhood of women, from Mona Lisa to Marilyn Monroe. I expected Mum to welcome my news.

She went into shock. 'But you're so young.' Her menses had begun at fifteen. She couldn't accept that girls were reaching puberty earlier. 'So young.'

I longed for cute elastic belts, nylon slot fasteners, and modern peri-pads.

At two shillings a packet, Mum said, 'They're too dear.'

I hadn't money to buy my own.

She gave me rectangles of towelling – the only choice in her day. An unbleached calico belt and two enormous safety pins completed the ensemble.

I knew how a horse felt in harness.

Mum made no special effort to celebrate my thirteenth birthday.

I longed to shout, 'I'm a teenager. Take notice!'

Vivi and I counted the days until Auntie Aileen's visit.

Mum grumbled. 'She'll be a bad influence on the girls.'

Daddy shrugged. 'Gets her away from that dreary room, luv. It can't be much fun for my sister on an invalid pension. Hasn't been easy since her divorce.'

Auntie stepped from the train, a vision in well-pressed maroon costume, sparkly brooch on the lapel. Rouge emphasised high cheekbones. She hugged us. I felt the frail strength of her arms, smelt the aroma of 4711.

'So glad to see you again, girls.'

That night, her raven hair gleamed in the light. Could the rumour of a Spanish count ancestor be true? I blew out the lantern.

Her cigarette glowed in the darkness. 'Tobacco companies hooked me as a young woman. Back then, it made one socially acceptable. I used to say a man isn't a man unless he smoked – silly me. Never take up the habit, girls.'

Given her asthma, I felt amazed she smoked.

Auntie told us, 'At fourteen, I narrowly survived a bout of pneumonia. Journeyed through rain and flood.'

Her stories and jokes kept us chuckling. We were meant to be asleep. She told of her latest grievances at her lodgings. 'They like the money but don't want you in their home when you're sick.'

Supported by high pillows, she wheezed, gasping for air. Ventolin puffers and nebulisers were yet to be invented.

Ulcer pain racked her emaciated body.

'I'm afraid to eat,' she told Mum, 'Just a glass of milk will do.'

Like many women of that era, she swallowed Bex powders for pain, little knowing they caused both migraines and ulcers. At times she lay across the bed, like a child's abandoned doll. Clutching her throbbing brow.

Intelligent eyes aglow, she recounted vignettes of her life – pearls we strung along the memory of her visits. 'A friend and I worked as a doctor's home help,' she told us. 'One evening a group of lads clustered outside our bedroom window. They handed us a packet of aniseed balls. Teasing, we refused to hand them back. The boys chanted, "Give us back our balls! We want our balls!" The doctor knocked. "Give the boys back their balls, girls. And go to bed."'

Vivi and I fell about with laughter.

Auntie smiled. 'You're quite the young lady now, Dessie.'

I groaned about the downside of periods. 'I hate washing and hanging towelling strips on the line. Suppose someone guesses?'

Auntie said, 'I felt the same. Called it washing the meat rags.'

'I put them to soak in a covered dish under my bed. Daddy chose that day to fix wire supports under the mattress. He must have smelt…'

'Oh, you poor darling.'

My curves drew male glances. I vacillated between irritation, exhilaration and amusement.

One man's risqué jokes had us laughing. He asked, 'Heard of the man who offered to buy his girlfriend new panties? So long as she let him try them on.'

The sensual gaiety in Auntie's dark eyes sped George Foxcroft back to his vanished youth. He touched her knee.

Aileen giggled. 'You are awful.' She winked at me. At fifty, she enjoyed being found attractive. And I thought, why not? She told me later, 'Dirty old devil. They're all after one thing.'

Mum said, 'I can't bear the way your sister flirts.'

Dad shrugged. 'Harmless enough.'

'She'll fill the girls' heads with all sorts of nonsense.'

'I'm sure it's not as bad as you think.'

Over lunch, Aileen recalled a prank with her siblings. 'Mother left to have a baby. Sid started a fight. I brought out the .22 rifle. Sid hid behind a tree. He poked his head out one side. I took aim. Bang! Then he peeked out the other side. Bang! Bill persuaded us to shake hands.'

Mum said, 'I'd thrash any child of mine who behaved like that.'

We retreated to our bedroom. One funny tale led to another.

Auntie said, 'Keep the door open. We can't have your mother thinking I'm a bad influence.' She shared risqué jokes.

Mum strode by, frowning.

Aileen told us later, 'Your mother has never forgiven me. Awaiting your birth, Dessie, she stayed at my place.' Auntie went on, 'In 1940 young men exchanged civilian clothes for uniforms. For many it was their first job after the Great Depression. So young, and facing the ultimate sacrifice. Jack and I held parties to give them a happy farewell.'

It was the first we'd heard of it.

'The lads were all bravado. Your mum saw only brash young men drinking to excess. She told off one poor lad. "You're drunk. It's a disgrace…" I was furious. "Laugh, Genn, even if you don't get their jokes. Have a glass of lemonade, or a shandy. And no more lectures."' Auntie smiled, 'Afterwards, your mother would put on her prettiest dress.'

A sad expression crossed her classic face. 'So many boys never came back.'

Auntie's holiday drew to an end. She strolled with us in the garden, whispering, 'Penny royal. Women use the leaves to induce abortions.'

I guessed she was hinting at Mum's secret. Poppy had told us the same tale. I doubted its veracity.

Auntie added, 'Your mother may be suspicious of my letters. I'll enclose a separate piece of paper for anything private.'

We removed her vignettes about boys, or the latest jokes. Giving Mum the letters.

Clouds gathered from all points of the compass. Only to vanish.

Dad groaned. 'Not a drop – nature likes to taunt a man. Lucky I can irrigate the spuds and gardens.' He tapped the rings of our tanks. 'We're going to run out of house water.'

Mum frowned. 'Can't we use some from the big dam?'

'We need better quality water.' He looked thoughtful. 'A multitude of springs keeps the creek flowing, even in the worst drought. Crystal-clear water. Suppose I trench around the hillside? Bring it into a holding dam. Pipe it to the house.'

'How long would a job like that take?'

'A fortnight. Month at most.'

'Huh! With all that clearing?'

Dad and Victor pegged out the route. They made diversions around boulders and trees. The chain saw screamed through logs. Using the tractor, Victor dragged them away. He cleared undergrowth.

Dad moved huge rocks into place as if they were marbles. 'Strengthens the earth wall.'

His pick bit into hard ground, pinged on rock. Bushflies crawled and harried.

'Beggars know when your hands are busy.'

The trench inched forward. Days dragged into weeks. Our afternoon tea visit raised Dad's flagging spirits.

Until Mum said, 'Will this jolly thing ever be finished?'

'We're almost there, luv. ' Dad bit into fresh scones, face lined with exhaustion. He drank sweet black tea, dumped the dregs. Grabbed the shovel. 'No rest for…'

Whistling, he dumped soil onto the lower side of the trench. Hacked through tough roots with an axe. Dad fanned himself with his stained hat. His brow dripped. He drank from a canvas water bag. 'Ahh, that's good.'

A month passed, two. The ditch snaked down the last hill. He and Victor had gouged out a holding dam. We piled into Dad's four-wheel drive. He grabbed a long-handled shovel. The trench stopped two feet from the bubbling creek.

'Hope to God my levels are correct.'

His shovel bit into swampy earth. It released an aroma of moss and wild herbs. Stones splashed into the stream.

One question teased. Would the water flow?

Earth crumbled. The last barrier. Tendrils of liquid explored dust, merged. Rushed along the trench. A torrent swept aside leaves, insects and debris. Rounded a curve of the hill. Disappeared.

Daddy shouted, 'Let's see how far it goes.'

He gunned the motor. We jolted down the rough track. Water poured into the dam, levels slowly rising.

Dad threw his hat in the air. 'Bloody beauty!' He said, 'No more worries over tank water. Nature's storehouse.'

I boiled the copper. A sybarite even then, I wallowed in a deep, scented bath. My parents had ridden away, checking cattle. They couldn't upbraid me over wasting wireless batteries. I turned it to full volume, humming the latest pop songs. After an hour, I indulged in the caress of a warmed towel.

Mum's quick dips amused me. 'Five minutes in the bath is enough. I couldn't bear longer.'

Once, my little brother Druce lingered in the bathroom.

Dad shouted, 'Come out of there. I mean now.'

Mum shivered. 'What does that boy do in there?'

Their aversion to long baths puzzled me. Did it date to days when cold baths were a punishment? Or to quench the fires of desire?

Problems emerged with the water supply. Cattle squelched around the dam, making the water cloudy.

Daddy groaned. 'A fence will keep the beggars away.'

Leaves and dirt blocked the inlet pipe, which required frequent cleaning.

Mum grumbled, 'Your father should have done a better job.'

Her lack of appreciation annoyed me. She applauded her father and Victor for any job. Failures belonged to Dad. He had needed grit, determination and physical strength to finish the project. The water system functioned for years. A bulldozer finally gave Victor the opportunity to trench new pipes to the house. Mum praised his wonderful effort, ignoring Dad's marathon a decade earlier.

19

Victor spouted the current *Tribune* views. 'Reports of Soviet injustice? Propaganda. Victims? Criminals – they deserve punishment. University degrees? A waste of time.'

I couldn't bear the notion that one must remain a victim, or become a traitor to class.

Mum glowed. 'You understand these things so well, son.'

I agreed with him about Joseph McCarthy. In the fifties, he wreaked havoc among writers and intellectuals. The Rosenbergs were executed on my birthday. They proclaimed their innocence until their deaths. I felt sad for their two orphaned boys.

Clearly, Communism destroyed freedom and took lives. But totalitarian regimes of left or right encouraged neighbour to spy on neighbour, with a murderous, ripple effect.

Dread of nuclear war shadowed my childhood. Arguably, the Bomb prevented a third world war, lacking safe havens for the elite. Experts touted nuclear power as the preferred option for a life of luxury. Chernobyl and Fukushima Daicchi would later convince many it was unsafe.

British nuclear tests at Maralinga in 1956–57 saw Indigenous folk moved from their lands. Witnesses have long since died from related illness. A wind change blew contaminated red dust across the continent.

Dad was excited to find a patch of pink snow. 'Only later did I realise its significance.'

Red stars glittered in Victor's eyes for years. I once accompanied him to a gathering of the Soviet Friendship Society in Sydney. The Russian ambassador was guest of honour. We helped distribute supper. My brother bustled back and forth serving the VIPs, stolid as Napoleon, George Orwell's horse. Beatific expressions lit the faces of believers, some draped in the Soviet and Eureka flags.

I grabbed a platter of smoked salmon, salami, caviar and cocktail frankfurts, asking Victor, 'Shall I put these savouries on our table?'

He drew back in horror. 'Oh no. Those are for the official table.'

I laughed. Rat-trap cheese and shallots were good enough for us.

Daddy asked Vivi and me to gather spuds missed during harvest. 'You'll make a tenner a bag.'

The first, painful day of my period, I staggered along behind the harrows. Frozen hands and face made a fitting adjunct to gut cramps. Embarrassment prevented me from telling him.

Later, I laughed about it with Auntie Aileen. 'Next time, girl, speak up.'

In the darkness of our room, she shared stories about dating and boys. Funny experiences. Foiled seductions. And one poignant tale of lost love. She nurtured a healthy attitude to sex. 'An enjoyable yet often funny part of being human.'

Mum never discussed such matters. Double entendres went right over her head. The whole family would be chuckling. She'd glance around. 'What's so funny? If it's the sort of thing I suspect, you should all be ashamed.' Her remark brought fresh gales of mirth.

Dad offered one piece of advice. 'Beware of men with soft hands. Never done a day's work in their lives. A few calluses on his palms, and you'll know he's dinky-di.'

I guessed Mum never had many boyfriends.

Auntie laughed. 'Your mother was very pretty. Had many admirers. Two neighbours were in love with her. Of course, she dated your father from sixteen, so he had the advantage.'

I dreaded Auntie witnessing the daily breakfast scenario. It varied only in minor details.

Dad shouted, 'Druce! Get up. I mean it.'

A sleepy grunt from my four-year-old brother. I fancy he cuddled tighter into his cocoon of sleep.

'Your breakfast is on the table.'

A note of hysteria in Mum's voice. 'Come here at once. Your food will be cold.' She sniffed, 'Oh, why doesn't that boy come when he's called?'

Dad pounded on Druce's door. 'If you aren't here in five minutes, I'll have the belt to you.'

My gut twisted. Why not let him miss breakfast? Hunger would teach him to arrive earlier.

Sullen and pale, Druce slumped down in his chair.

Mum fixed him with a glare. 'Go wash and tidy up.'

Dad snapped,. 'A boy your age shouldn't have to be reminded to comb hair his hair.'

Druce returned. Glum, hair slicked down.

Mum shoved a plate his way. 'Eat this.'

A tremor in my brother's voice. 'I'm not hungry.'

'Nonsense. Everyone's hungry at breakfast.'

Auntie and I exchanged a troubled glance.

He took one look. 'Yuk. Egg.'

Mum slapped him. Hard. 'Don't dare say such things. 'She fed him, spoonful by spoonful. 'You must learn to like all foods.'

He vomited. Trembling into sobs.

Mum jumped to her feet. 'A dish, somebody. Quickly.'

Dad brought water, soap, a towel.

Mum washed and dried him. 'Selfish, wicked child.' Roughly, she pulled on his clothes. 'My meal is ruined. Oh, my poor digestion.'

Dad loomed over Druce. 'You should be ashamed of yourself. Upsetting your mother.

Mum raved on and on. The pallid child shrank into his chair.

My appetite vanished. Anger simmered. When would Mum shut up? A silent vow: I'd never, ever subject my children to such abuse.

Later, Auntie shook her head. 'Food should be given for hunger, not stuffed down throats. Kids learn to eat three meals a day, despite their parents. It would be useless for me to tell them.'

Mum shrieked, 'Wicked, careless child!'

A broken vase. Her tirade continued. A glazed expression entered Vivi's eyes. Perhaps she drifted into an out-of-body state. A tremor, and reality seemed to flood back.

Auntie hugged the troubled child. 'Don't take your mother's fussing to heart, pet. It was an accident. Between you and me, it was an ugly old thing.'

I rolled my eyes. 'Ah, yes! But Victor gave it to her.'

Mum tackled Dad. 'The girls are so careless. Especially Vivi. A wicked, disobedient child. What am I to do?'

His relaxed posture hinted at the need to forgive human frailty.

'Well, aren't you going to back me up?'

I suspect he felt her harangues were enough for both of them.

I returned to the bedroom. 'Oh, when will Mum shut up?'

Auntie winked. 'Saints make life so hard. Aren't sinners a blessing?'

We laughed.

Auntie added, 'That said, a lesser woman might have left your father, given his drinking. She has your interests at heart. Corrects your English. Encourages a wide vocabulary and pride in your appearance.'

Mum yelled, 'You girls haven't said goodnight.'

Hugging Dad brought a warm glow. Mum's embrace brought me no pleasure.

Druce made to slip away.

'It's a dreadful thing if a boy won't kiss his mother.' Mum smothered her baby in kisses.

My sister finished the ritual quickly.

Victor's turn.

Mum gazed at him with adoration. 'Goodnight, boy.'

He took off.

Mum gave a cloying smile. 'From the back, Victor looks like my father. And such small feet.'

'And such small feet,' Vivi mimicked. 'You'd think Victor's feet are some feat.'

I giggled. 'The other day I told her they were small for a man. Mum was taken aback.

Vivi's internecine warfare with Mum brought ongoing distress. 'Why must I do such and such?'

'Because I say so.'

'I don't want to.'

Another strapping. My sister defiant. I swallowed anger. Not daring to intervene.

Mum mistook my silence for acquiescence. She would hold out her arms. 'You must love your mother.'

A lifetime later, I suffered clinical depression and breakdown. Anger internalised once too often?

Auntie glimpsed the nervous twist to my sister's mouth. She skated across quicksands of the problem. 'Goodness. Your mother does pick on you. You do know it isn't entirely your fault, pet?'

Vivi looked surprised. She recalled those words years later. 'Auntie gave me the first inkling my problems didn't spring from wickedness. Mum saw my questions as disobedience. Children were meant to be seen, not heard. I craved love. Often, she didn't even seem to like me.'

My sister sobbed in her sleep.

Auntie shook her awake. 'There, there pet. It's all right.'

Her holiday ended. 'I'd like to say something to your mother. But it could make things worse.' She promised to write. 'Keep your spirits up, girls. You're always in my thoughts.'

Later, Dad confided, 'I always expected your mother to have a heart attack during one of her rages.'

As an adult, I would wonder if she had suffered from intermittent explosive disorder. Her harangues did prove excellent preparation for workplace bullying. Psychology? Mum declared she never needed it.'

Much later, when Vivi married, I was astounded to hear of the letter Mum wrote to her fiancé, a man years older, 'I cannot recommend my second daughter as a wife. She has always been wicked and disobedient. I doubt she will change now.'

I suspected Dad had prepared the bullet for Mum to fire. But that chapter awaited a few more of life's pages.

I turned fourteen. Mum made plans for the two of us to visit Nan and Grandfather. Their gloomy take on life didn't promise much fun. I did look forward a few days with Uncle Bill and my peachy Gran, at Warners Bay.

I had outgrown my winter topcoat.

Mum frowned. 'New ones are so dear.'

A parcel of used clothing arrived from Aunt Aileen.

Mum held up a sorry-looking garment. 'A bit of dye and this overcoat will look like new.'

Brilliant green emphasised every worn thread. Huge canary-yellow buttons, from a cereal packet, didn't help.

'These really give it a finish.'

Finish was the word.

'Uh… Thanks, Mum.' Vivi would have refused to wear it. I'd solve the problem some other way.

Newcastle shivered in a southerly. I looked forward to an outing with my cousin, Len and wife, Vera.

She smiled. 'Which topcoat shall I wear, darling? The red or the grey?' Both were equally smart. She slipped on the red.

I longed to borrow her other one, lacking the courage to ask.

We wandered towards the cinema. Wind blew straight through my grey woollen dress. I kept the green overcoat draped over one arm. My teeth jittered. I snuggled into a red velvet seat. Warmth slowly crept back.

Len offered me a chocolate.

'Thanks, no. I don't like chocolates.'

He raised his eyebrows. 'What'll you do when your boyfriend buys you some?'

His recipe for social success? Dancing, tennis and a golden tan. Alas,

I lacked all three. Audrey Hepburn swept me into a magic world of music and fun of *Three Coins in a Fountain*. Oh, for movies at home.

Gran made me feel very grown-up, taking tea and chatting. We even sipped a small sherry.

Uncle Bill, a TPI pensioner, was legally blind. His limited eyesight meant he carried a white cane. That July in 1954, I travelled for free, his escort on a bus to Broadmeadow station. I rushed for a seat.

He caught up with me, his smile forced. 'Next time, let me take your arm.'

His lively sense of humour dissipated my embarrassment.

'You'll have lots of fun when you're older.' Uncle expelled his breath, in a long sibilant 'Yes-s-s.' It hinted at all manner of forbidden delights.

I took my place in the Gosford-bound train, smug at travelling alone. Two exuberant ladies dripped gold jewellery. They talked of a world cruise. I eyed the P& O tags on their luggage. My journey paled into insignificance.

Welcoming hugs and kisses.

At the Springfield house, Aunt Ruby said, 'I'm expecting in November.' David wasn't yet at school. 'Pregnancy complications. I must rest until baby arrives.'

Mum had added, 'You'll stay for the next six months. Helping in the house and on the poultry farm. You'll study by correspondence.'

I felt stunned.

Nan had suffered from nerves for years. She managed light household duties. Later, I realised her problems were depression and acute anxiety. She must have endured hell.

I'd left a laissez-faire farm. The rigidity of the Stephens household took me by surprise. They waited until the clock chimed noon – not a second before or after – and Uncle said grace. Only then could we begin lunch.

Uncle Geoff made scrambled eggs, omelettes or fried eggs. Cracked shells, or double-yolkers didn't sell. His poached eggs were awful. He crammed so many into the pan, vestiges of slime remained. Nobody else noticed.

Mondays, Grandfather lit the copper. We scrubbed soiled clothing and linen by hand, and put it through the mangle. I helped peg it on the line.

Tuesday mornings, Uncle Geoff shopped.

Wednesday afternoons, and all day Saturday, the family walked miles, in pouring rain or blazing sun. Proselytising for the Jehovah's Witness faith. I refused to join them.

Fridays, I cleaned and polished every room. Studies took second place. A slight relaxation of standards might have allowed time for my education.

Grandfather helped me wash dishes at night. Hot water triggered his rhinitis. A drop of moisture would appear at the tip of his nose. In horrified fascination, I watched it become huge and translucent, plopping into the sudsy water. Grandfather paid no attention.

We'd be eating from those plates the following morning.

In Gosford, I gazed at high-school students through a plate-glass barrier of impossible dreams. I yearned to be among them, making friends. Learning a wide range of subjects – including French.

I lost my black shopping bag, a gift from Vivi. Expected Nan's commiseration. Suggestions how to find it.

She glowered. 'How can you be so careless?'

Grandfather said, 'You must pay attention. Be responsible.'

I struck back. 'Probably I'll lose things hundreds of times yet.'

Nan glared. 'What a wicked attitude.'

Grandfather added, 'It's disgusting to be proud of your mistakes.'

Devastated by the loss, I scarcely slept. And retraced my steps without luck. I waited disconsolately at the bus stop.

A newsagency assistant ran towards me. 'Have you mislaid a black bag?'

I could have hugged her.

A lovely smile. 'These things happen.'

Grandfather seized the last word. 'Let it be a lesson to you.'

I endured Nan and Grandfather's favourite Sunday religious broadcast. The pseudonyms, Frank and Earnest, hint at the level of debate. Add narrow views, halting delivery…

'It says in the Bible, Frank…'

'Yes, Earnest, but we must remember…'

'I see, Frank, but…'

Sunday afternoons, Nan insisted I attend the Jehovah's Witness service. The sermons were laden with portents of disaster, and emotional appeals to be saved. 'Eternal damnation awaits non-believers.'

Eternity with critical people seemed more like hell than heaven.

At night, I played songs like Alan Freed's 'Sincerely'. And 'Autumn Leaves' from Nat King Cole. Overwhelmed by loneliness. Would I ever experience love of my own?

My grandparents swallowed vitamin pills by the score. Rubbed embrocation on aching joints. And Grandfather drank copious quantities of an evil-smelling, dark mixture – brewed, I suspect, in a witch's cauldron.

'What's that for, Grandfather?

'What's it for? Blazing everything.'

Murmurs crept from Ruby and Geoff's room.

Nan feared she might be the subject of their conversation, saying, 'Anything which need to be discussed, should be said at the table.'

Even at fourteen, I guessed tender words in a marital bed should be private.

Nan said, 'In all our married life, I've never undressed in front of Grandfather.' What she termed the 'marital act' took place in the dark. 'Not discussed before or after.'

Her strict parents had forbidden outings. 'One night, at eighteen, I crept out a window. My girlfriend and I went dancing. Oh, what a lovely evening. Mother waited for my return. You should have heard the explosion. I never dared to do it again. Dreamed of being a teacher.

Mother thought education a waste for girls. She kept me busy in the house.'

'How did you meet Grandfather?'

'I was a penfriend of Linda, one of Rick's sisters. Went to Tomalla on holiday.' Thirteen years her senior, Rick visited her in Sydney. 'We became engaged. On my wedding day, I was about to leave in my bridal dress. Mother asked, "Are you going through with it?"'

In the nuptial photo both look scared. Nan stands far away from her new husband, stretching a hand towards his shoulder. Rick is seated, a hat clamped on his bald pate.

Nan told of her difficulties, a bride of nineteen. 'Isolated at Tomalla Station, away from home, brothers and sisters.'

I guessed that Grandfather's personal and caustic attempts at humour didn't help. And Nan's strict religious upbringing ensured guilt over sexual matters, even when sanctioned by the church.

Rick was equally inexperienced. I sensed Nan had found the whole thing distasteful – even scary.

She said, 'I never recovered my health after your mother came to town.'

The highlight of 1954 for Uncle Geoff was the Redex Trial, a 15,000-kilometre car rally around Australia. He traced the route on the front pages of the tabloids. At night, we gathered around the large wireless. Gelignite Jack Murray, in his Grey Ghost 1947 Ford, the favourite, battled dust and potholes. He dodged kangaroos, forded flooded creeks, survived rockslides and collisions.

Uncle Geoff hushed us into silence. I guessed he sat right there in that car, mile after mile, shaking his head at Jack's latest disaster. Counted among the thousands who cheered his arrival in large towns. This colourful Aussie emerged hero of the hour.

Uncle Geoff shouted, 'Hurray! Gelignite Jack's won.'

It was the most excited I'd ever seen him.

A later interview paid tribute to those dramatic years. Jack recounted an experience in another rally, 'I heard my navigator say, "Go fast." Stepped on the gas. Next thing I know, we shoot out into space at a sharp corner. Straight over a wire fence. And landed – God knows how – on all four wheels. Funny thing is, had I not increased speed, we'd not have survived. My navigator had actually said, "Oh, blast."'

I laughed and laughed.

Geoff paid me a few pounds each week. I put an overcoat on lay-by, plotting how to dispose of the old one. My problem was almost constant surveillance.

Opportunity presented itself. The laundry finished, Grandfather strolled down the paddock. I glanced around. Nan, Ruby and David busied themselves somewhere in the house. Uncle had gone shopping.

I grabbed a large pair of scissors. Slash, slash, slash! Off came the sleeves. The collar followed. Gleefully, I cut the body into quarters. I'd destroy it bit by bit, over several weeks.

I threw the sleeves into the smouldering laundry fire. Green wool sizzled into ash. The sight brought a sort of blood lust. A quick glance. Nobody around. Dare I burn the remainder? I raced back to my room. Grabbed every piece, bundling them, onto the fire. The fabric flamed, flared. Withered. And died. I stared in grim satisfaction.

A gruff voice made me jump. 'What are you up to?'

'Watching the fire.'

The flames should have died down long before. Grandfather poked at the embers. The glowing coals kept their secrets. For some reason, he didn't question me further.

Nan shared other tales of married life at Tomalla station, 'Snow drifted through cracks between the weatherboards. Little drifts formed near the walls. Bare floors, tiny windows.'

Grandfather kipped on a straw mattress on the floor. Nan occupied his single bed. Did this reflect an ambivalence about his new status? Or underline his innocence? Why didn't he buy a double bed before his bride arrived, or make his own? Daddy had chopped down a few saplings, stripped bark…

Nan chuckled. 'Mother wrote, asking me about my house. How many rooms? What size was my living-room? Did I have carpets, a nice bedroom?' She clipped a picture of a glamorous bedroom from a magazine, and sent it off. "This is very much like mine." Mother was satisfied – luckily, she never came to visit.'

Ruby lumbered around the house. I guessed that birth was near. One November night, headlights knifed through darkness, disappearing into the valley below. Tomorrow, I'd welcome a new cousin.

Mid-morning, Nan grew anxious. 'Hope everything's all right. We should have heard by now.'

Just before lunch, Uncle Geoff returned. Jubilant but haggard. 'I've a baby daughter.'

At the hospital, he stood aside to allow me through a doorway. Shy and conspicuous, I froze. Unsure what to do.

He was plainly annoyed. 'Go on.'

Ruby purred, the epitome of maternal pride. I gazed at my cousin Janette, a delightful baby. My only disappointment? They hadn't named her after me. Luckily, the thought never occurred to them.

Gossips later reached entirely the wrong conclusion about my six-month absence.

20

Auntie Ruby shouted me a trip to Sydney. A treat for helping out. Her mother minded baby Jan. Five-year-old David stayed with his father.

I glimpsed the magnificent harbour and bridge. Gaped at big department stores like Farmers and David Jones. And the NSW Art Gallery took my breath away. Awed to think N.C. Piggott had achieved those wonderful pink clouds effects of *Flood in the Darling*, 1890–95. Sky reflections alive with ibis and other waterbirds. Another favourite was Elioth Gruner's *Spring Frost*, 1919. I loved those long morning shadows of cattle, the atmosphere damp with mist and ice.

We tramped around galleries for hours. Our feet and legs screamed for mercy.

In stockinged feet, we limped through the Arts and Science Museum, delighting over a replica of the Strasbourg Clock. Richard Bartholomew Smith created this engineering masterpiece in gilt and green, from 1887–89. It shows phases of the moon, lunar eclipses, transit of Venus. The transparent woman made me burn with embarrassment. A replica of me, and my intimate bodily functions. It served as a sex education aid.

At June Millinery, customers sat on stools around a basement carrousel. They waited for hatters to create confections of flowers and lace.

Ruby said, 'They're a fraction of prices you'd pay in big stores. Let's take a closer look.'

She glided towards the basement on an escalator, the first I'd seen. Afraid to step aboard, I baulked. Halfway down, she noticed my absence. A tentative step. I felt an utter fool.

Ruby pointed out straw shapes, ribbons, flowers and net. 'That huge hat is probably for the races. This one's for street wear – elegant and refined. And here's something for a cocktail party or wedding – all froth and frivolity. Your mum would kill to visit a place like this.'

'She says, "No woman is dressed without a hat and gloves."'

Ruby laughed.

The excuse for a rest, we saw *Gone with the Wind*. I drooled over Rhett Butler, the most exciting, sexy man I'd ever seen. Most girls of the era fell for him.

Auntie Ruby said, 'Read Margaret Mitchell's book. You'll love the romances. Though the American Civil War is sad.'

We paid the price for a week's sightseeing in a few hours.

Next morning, I could hardly walk.

Ruby grimaced at every step, a smile never far from her face. 'That was my best holiday ever.'

Fifty years later, in her seventies, she would confide it had been the happiest day of her life.

I was touched by Nan and Grandfather's parting gift, an inscribed gold watch.

Nobody ever knew how I longed to stay and attend Gosford High School, dreading the resumption of solitary studies. Friendless.

Mist swirled up our valley, eucalypt-covered hillsides cloaked in drizzle. And I'd almost forgotten Mum's gift for turning trivial incidents into catastrophes. My finger traced patterns on the fogged windowpane. Rivulets of frustration crept down the glass. No bus here to speed me on a ride into town or to a movie. What madness drove my ancestors into these brooding mountains? Poverty, the search for arable land?

The fire leapt and crackled. Daddy warmed his big hands. 'I hate this gloomy weather. A man wants to finish harvesting the darn spuds.'

Daddy's new worker, Sasha Davis, echoed his concerns. Treated as one of the family, he seemed a lively sort of chap.

Years later, Daddy confided, 'Neighbours advised me not employ Sasha, a drinker. Away from the bottle, he was a model worker.' He gained the best from his employees by example, encouragement and respect.

The log fire chuckled over Dad's yarns. 'Neighbour Tom's a legend. Catches rainbow trout as big as whales from the Barrington River – the Snowy is a creek by comparison. He leaps onto the backs of brumby stallions. Tames them at a single ride.'

Sasha grinned. 'Superman in jodhpurs.'

My pen stopped in mid schoolwork. I couldn't stop laughing.

A new log sent showers of red sparks up the chimney.

Dad said, 'One winter, Tom reported snow fifteen inches deep. He encountered a group of kangaroos, snap-frozen in mid-hop. Others lay like fallen statues. He snapped off their ears on walking past. He'd make a fortune from fiction.'

General laughter.

Mum glared. 'So what if Tom believes his fabrications? A lie is a lie.'

We chuckled all the louder.

Teachers criticised my untidy work. Ink blots spoilt the pages. And I envied Mum's handwriting. It never varied. Mine changed all the time.

Dad looked thoughtful. 'You need one of those new biros. Bics don't leave stains. Trouble is, they cost ten quid.'

Mum snorted. 'Blackfriars School wouldn't approve of them.'

Victor nodded. 'And banks ban biros. Too easy for cheque fraud.'

Sasha took a Mont Blanc from his pocket. 'I hope we never lose quality fountain pens like these.'

Dad consulted the newsagency man in town. 'He showed me how to roll a refill within a cylinder of glued paper. And here it is, my Bic pen – at a fraction of the cost. And not a single blot.'

Mum began supervising correspondence lessons when she was twelve. Nan was in Sydney for surgery, Geoff, her ten-year-old brother, her student. In the 1940s, it was Victor's turn. By 1954, she had taught four of us. I fancy Druce was one child too many.

Mum glanced outside. Plants to be dead-headed or pruned. 'Will you hurry, son?' She pushed her face into his. 'Think, boy – you know the answer.

Druce hunched into his seat, giggling. One could have cut his anxiety with a knife.

Mum slapped him. 'Stop that nonsense. Get on with it.'

He burst into tears. She unleashed a string of abuse. Provided answers.

I felt helpless. My kid brother's confidence seemed at zero. In adulthood, his thinking processes would freeze over instructions, distorted by memory of a looming authority figure.

Dad glared at him. 'Stop giving your mother a hard time.'

Lessons over, she grabbed gardening gloves and secateurs. Her regular companion, a kookaburra, waited on the handle of her garden fork. Sharp eyes, a worm wriggle. A beak plunged into loam.

House alterations took place in 1954. Dad's extensions upset Nan. She declared he had ruined her design. We thought the indoor septic toilet bliss – no more torchlight excursions up the yard on freezing nights. Nan's former telephone exchange had become Dad's office. I recalled brown Bakelite telephones, and swapped silver plugs, to facilitate calls.

My return brought the flat iron exterior, single, smoking chimney and undulations in the tar-paper lining into stark focus. Threadbare mats covered linoleum holes.

I ran a hand over the knobbly, yet smooth, texture of the embossed-glass front door. The child in me loved it. Gumboots left muddy offerings on the back veranda. Oilskin raincoats dripped water. Stockwhips readied for action. Logs waited beside kerosene and kindling, to light fires. Ten-foot ceilings hinted at Nan's aspirations.

During the Great Depression, an Austrian called Joe Gabboer had arrived at Tomalla in search of gold. He had worked as a skilled artisan at Tokapei, the finest Ottoman palace in Istanbul. Using a variety of timbers, he helped restore intricately patterned parquet floors. Guards wouldn't allow him to souvenir the tiniest chip.

In 1925, Grandfather employed Joe to build the humble cottage at

Hunters Springs. He moved to other projects. The Second World War stopped building. Joe established a tropical fruits plantation in Queensland.

Dad said, 'Every year until his death, he sent a box of bananas.'

Mum told me about Nan leaving for her hysterectomy. 'At twelve I ran the house at Tomalla Station, Uncle Geoff's little mother. I carried picnic lunches to Dad in the back paddock. He praised the way I was handling my responsibilities. I worked half a dozen busy party lines of the telephone exchange, shivering until all hours. Subscribers rang at the last minute, hoping for off-peak rates. Once, long after the exchange should have been closed, a subscriber shouted, "Put me through. Immediately." Another caller said, "Don't be like that. She's only a little girl." Nan spent a year in Sydney. I felt anxious and confused, wondering whether she'd ever return. I suspect she had some sort of breakdown.'

Mum insisted we girls wear hats to town.

'Other teenagers think we're hicks.'

'Who cares what others think?'

Pester power won.

Stabbing a hatpin into her latest floral creation, she would sigh. 'You'd both look so much nicer in hats.'

Vivi reached her menses. 'Thank God. Now Mum won't strap me.'

She marched into the pharmacy, purchasing sanitary products on Dad's account. I continued to use towelling pads.

Mum raged. 'Our family is far from rich.' Words like selfish and extravagance spun around the room.

My sister didn't budge.

We took the measure of our busts.

Mum eyed our antics. 'Give me that tape.' Amazingly, her bust size increased at the same rate of as ours.

Self-confidence faltered. At fifteen, my feet felt out of proportion to my body. I gritted my teeth over silly comments: 'You've got a good grip on Australia.' Tucked my aristocratic feet under chairs. Dropped, bumped, or fell over things.

Victor always encouraged me. 'You're so clumsy.'

I quaked on strolling across a public room. Lacking the courage to glance at people, I failed to recall facial details, let alone names. It gave me the reputation of being stuck-up.

Victor, our third parent, would snigger. 'You walk like a lame duck. Straighten up – one shoulder's lower than the other.'

No doctor ever diagnosed minor scoliosis. A surgical vest might have corrected the problem.

Mum seemed to feel willpower was enough. 'Don't hunch your back.'

I used my best voice to converse.

Later, Victor accosted me. 'You make me sick when you speak in that affected way.'

Mum nodded. 'It's never nice to put on airs.'

I could have killed them both.

Mail-order catalogues arrived twice yearly from Anthony Horderns and Grace Brothers, Broadway. Glamorous dresses never fitted like fashion page photos, doubtless pinned at the back. We made our own.

On outings to town, Vivi selected and discarded a dozen garments. 'Nothing looks good on me. Skin eruptions, huge nose…' As for her curls, they just weren't in vogue.

Dad fumed. 'Why can't that girl ever be on time?'

At the last moment, she washed her favourite bra.

Mum yelled, 'You'll never get it dry.'

'Don't worry, Mum.' My sister popped it into the oven. Went to iron her dress.

Dad sniffed. 'Something's burning.'

She flung open the oven door. Smoke swirled, baked brown fabric crumbled under her fingers, leaving two metal rings. The first woman to burn her bra. Long before women's liberation.

We rode on the back of the Bedford. Belting out Buddy Holly and Big Bopper songs. Covered with clouds of dust from passing vehicles.

Vivi raced me upstairs to the Ladies Room of Campbell's department store. Fifty miles of sun and wind had chapped lips, reddened cheeks. Hair was barbed wire.

My voice echoed under high ceilings. 'I'll never get a comb through this.'

'Ouch! Mine is full of knots, too.'

We changed dresses. I despaired of my skin. 'Mum, can't I use a little make-up? To hide the damage?'

'You're too young.

Downstairs, Mum bought a few yards of material. 'For a new dress.'

Miss Lee gushed, 'Goodness, Mrs Wright. Haven't your girls grown? You could be sisters.'

Mum looked pleased. I hated being taken for the sibling of someone decades my senior.

Fashion dictated three-tiered, full skirts. Five yards of fabric were gathered onto a waistband. Stiffened petticoats added a bouffant effect.

Shop-window undergarments dripped lace and ribbons.

Vivi drooled. 'I want one.'

Mum glared. 'They're too dear.'

Soon a pile of unbleached calico hung over Mum's sewing machine.

'Vivi, I've made you some petticoats – and you're going to wear them.'

Vivi examined the ugly garments. 'They're horrible.'

'You ungrateful hussy. After all my work.'

My sister burst into sobs.

Mum banged the table. 'Take these petticoats to your room. At once.'

Vivi flung them into the bottom of her wardrobe. And there they stayed.

The fifties rocked with the raw sounds of Sh-Boom. Hormones pulsated. Rock spelt rebellion, exuberance, suppressed sexuality – and excitement. We'd transcend dull and conformist society.

Dad flapped his newspaper. 'You girls are wasting batteries with that racket. Yeah, yeah, yeah, You love me babe, Yeah, yeah. They call that garbage music?' Dad's favourite program was the news. Gruesome tales of war, bombs and crimes fascinated our parents.

Bill Haley and the Comets brought 'Shake Rattle and Roll'. Cliff Richard's 'Livin' Doll', promised love, belonging and fulfilment. Elvis Presley gave us 'Heartbreak Hotel'. Buddy Holly and the Big Bopper sang 'All I Have to Do Is Dream' and 'That'll Be the Day'. Tragically, they were killed at the height of their popularity.

Perry Como's easy melodies evoked romantic pictures of snowy sleigh rides. Dad grinned. 'Now, that's real music.' Bing Crosby also met his approval.

Hit parades offered prizes for putting songs into order of popularity. The top eight morphed into the Top Twenty. Soon we rocked to the Top Forty. The wild tempo hinted at the thrill of scientific advances, speeding mankind towards frontiers of Space. Hunters Springs awaited electricity.

Victor pushed Druce away from the wireless, switching off his program. 'Never again let me find you listening to that American rubbish.'

Druce crept to his room. Attacked by his adored elder brother.

Mum hated that unbearable din. We would giggle on hearing her hum one of the catchy tunes.

She said, 'You girls can't be the only ones to hear the radio. Victor must have his choice of program.'

Victor looked smug. He changed stations and twiddled knobs. Just to prevent us hearing our stuff.

I must be the only girl of fifteen without a boyfriend. And feared nobody would ever be attracted to me, let alone fall in love. Sasha happened to be walking by the window. I'd never thought of him in a romantic way. Definitely not husband material. But his mischievous sense of humour and boyish looks appealed. He acted younger than Victor, despite being a decade older.

He rose to the bait like a hungry trout on a warm summer's evening. Boldly, I returned his glances.

He whispered compliments over a new haircut. 'Wow. I'll really go for you now. You're pretty.'

My self-esteem soared.

Sasha helped us wash the dishes each night.

Dad said, 'It's very kind of you, after a hard day's work. Helping children with their chores.'

In the sitting room, the ABC news absorbed our parents.

Our chore became an interlude of jokes and laughter. Flirtatious remarks, exchanged glances. He pretended not to like me, bringing a quiver to my tummy.

A foursome at euchre, Sasha and I took opposite sides. Chairs side by side, his thigh stroked mine. I read somewhere, we made love with longing glance, and knees 'neath table.

Victor enjoyed these euchre sessions. Oblivious of the main game. Someone cried, 'Euchre!' Slapped winning cards on the table.

Time for bed. We girls filled three hot-water bottles, one for Sasha. He slept on the glacial veranda. I cuddled up to mine, thinking of him.

Next morning, he rose first, and lit the fire. I toasted bread above the glowing coals. He whispered tender words. My cheeks flushed.

Mum rose, delighted to find the table set. 'I'm so pleased you're getting things going for breakfast.'

I was suitably modest. 'That's OK.'

A brightness lit the ceiling. Snow had brought an unearthly stillness. Every vista was transformed.

Breakfast over, Sasha, Vivi and I rushed outside. Icy missiles flew back and forth. 'Take that.' We shrieked with laughter. 'And that.'

Victor's face glowered through a windowpane.

'Who's for snowballs?'

We crushed snow into small heaps. Rolled them down the hill, gathering new layers with every turn. They were enormous. Vivi made a snowman with button eyes, adding a mop for hair.

Sasha helped me fashion ours into an igloo. He whispered, 'Let's live here. Alone. All winter.'

I floated somewhere above the landscape. 'Why not?' My eyes met his. Shaky laughter.

Wet through and exhilarated, I shivered out of my coat. We stamped snow off our boots.

Mum glared. 'You're all mad – out there in the cold. Victor wouldn't dream of such foolishness.'

Victor flashed a smug smile. He'd never know how sorry I felt for him. Nineteen and out of fun.

Dry top and jeans. I thawed frozen hands in front of the fire. Bowls of hot vegetable soup made a perfect end.

Sasha found me alone on the front veranda. He caressed my cheek. A long, gentle kiss – my first adult embrace. A second, not gentle nor innocent. Footsteps. We sprang apart.

He whispered, 'Stolen fruit are the sweetest.'

We reached Scone under leaden skies. I admired a water set, decorated with yellow and red poppies.

Sasha appeared at the gift shop window. 'Would you like that?'

'Yes. It's lovely.'

'Come Christmas, it'll be yours.'

We set off for home. A late afternoon downpour sent windscreen wipers racing. Visibility reached almost zero. Dad invited Sasha into the cabin. I sat on his knee. Mum nursed Druce. In the darkness, he hugged me. His chin caressed the back of my neck. I admired the way he carried on a conversation with my parents. Shivers zinged through my body.

Daddy peered through the fog. 'A terrible night for mountain roads.'

Sasha said, 'Mum's away. Stay the night at her place.'

'An excellent idea.'

Dad limped inside. His hip had worried him for a while. He started a fire. 'Boy, that's good.'

We soaked up the warmth. Sasha's eyes burnt into mine. He rustled up hot baked beans on toast.

Desultory conversation. I savoured the intimacy of the past hour. Fearing the risk of a solitary bed in a strange house. 'Druce can sleep with me.'

Sasha helped harvest the last of our potatoes. He arranged to work for our neighbour, George. The last morning. He entered my room, on the pretext of getting his suitcase. Vivi appeared to be asleep.

'Goodbye, sweetness.' His lips caressed mine. Then he was gone.

She sat bolt upright. 'He kissed you.'

I laughed. 'Don't be silly. He just bent down to – say goodbye.'

Sasha's motorcycle bumped away over the rough road. My heart felt tattered. This wasn't part of my plan.

I gagged over the stink of manure and urine mixed with mud in the milking yard, struggling to wrestle a cow's feisty calf to his pen. Bucket between my knees, I squeezed Susie's teats. She flicked mud from her tail into my face – I'd forgotten to hitch it out of the way.

Sasha invented a string of excuses to visit Dad. He asked my father's advice. Talked of his achievements. Invited himself to dinner. A foursome at cards, his fingers lingered on my wrist. Fire in my belly.

After he'd gone, Mum said, 'Heavens, that Sasha is a boaster. Why did he come?'

Dad sighed. 'God knows.'

My romance with Sasha must end. That much was clear. But my future looked bleak. Not one eligible boy for miles. In vivid technicolour dreams, I saved the handsome pilot of a crashed aircraft. The *coup de foudre* – love at first sight. And, decades before *Dr Who*, dreamed of a glittering space craft in the lower paddock. 'A Martian lover spirited me away.'

Vivi chuckled. 'Men from Mars will visit one day. I'm sure of it.'

21

Ruby arrived on holiday. Her air of amused superiority stuck in my craw. She made Mum's grumbles and criticisms even more unbearable.

Poppy and Walt Stephens planned to visit. We craved their jokes and laughter.

Dad told Ruby, 'Walt's father was a cousin of Rick Stephens. Dreadful poverty. They almost lived under hedges in England. Australian members of the family helped him emigrate. My mate for years. Rat of Tobruk in the war.'

Ruby smiled. 'Gracious – what a hard life. And his wife?'

'Poppy is from a large family. Worked at everything from shop assistant to cook before she married Walt. Do anything for you. Has the gift for friendship. A joke, a laugh, and perfect strangers tell their secrets.'

'Gosh! I'd better watch out.'

My sister and I prepared their room. Flowers from Mum's garden added a final touch. We slipped on starched petticoats, and floral skirts. My blouse white, Vivi's blue.

'We'll stroll over to meet them.'

Aunt Ruby smiled. 'A walk? Mind if I join you?'

We exchanged a dismayed glance. 'Uh – no, of course not.'

Skipping along the deserted road, we spied the familiar green FJ Holden.

I winked at Vivi. 'I'm tired of walking. Let's leg a lift.'

We hitched skirts well above our knees.

Ruby paled. 'Girls, girls – stop that at once. You don't know who it is.'

Vivi laughed. 'It's Poppy.'

'How can you be sure?'

The Holden stopped in a cloud of dust.

'Any chance of a lift?'

Walt and Poppy chuckled. Our cousin moved her plump body across the seat.

'Sit here – Ruby, isn't it? Genn told us all about you. There's no doubt about these girls. Always up to something.'

Ruby fanned herself with a lace handkerchief. 'It could've been anyone.'

We squeezed into the back seat with Brian and Georgie.

Poppy winked. 'Luckily, the girls know our car.'

At home, Poppy unloaded fruit, vegetables jams and pickles.

Vivi and I offered to pick her cherries. 'We've a bumper crop.'

Mum said, 'You do everything for other people –'

'We'll bring some for you, too.'

That evening, Mum chatted, knitting with Ruby.

Poppy helped us prepare the meal, a laugh in every saucepan. Georgie clung to her, pale and listless.

Poppy said, 'She finds it hard to learn – don't you, pet? Handles her limitations well.'

Brian, a strong, cheerful boy, charged around with Druce.

We giggled over Poppy's risqué jokes, the others out of earshot. She helped with the dishes, shared secrets. Boy-talk seemed a normal part of conversation.

'You need to meet lads of your own age.'

Chuckling, we joined the others. Poppy and Walt's stories made the room shake with mirth. Even Mum enjoyed their humour.

Ruby wiped her eyes. 'Oh, Poppy – you really are a tonic.'

Vivi and I climbed into the cherry trees.

Poppy plucked fruit from lower limbs. 'I'll make jam with these. And Walt loves pies.'

Georgie a shadow at her side. Boisterous puppies, the boys tumbled and played.

Soft green leaves teased my fingers, cherries luscious in my mouth. Buckets brimful, we put three into Poppy's box.

Mum hovered. 'Oh, why give her such a lot?'

Dad limped to the table. 'There's oodles left, luv. And here's some for you.'

Tiger Bay starred John Mills and his daughter, Hayley.

Poppy offered to take us. 'By the way, Genn, Victor's coming.'

Mum gave a tight little smile. ' Victor shouldn't be made to go if he doesn't want…'

Poppy chuckled. 'He's looking forward to it.'

Mum blinked.

Later, Poppy grinned. 'That took the wind out of her sails, no mistake.'

Walt took a short contract on a local property. Their house lacked a telephone. One afternoon, the mailman dropped Druce off at her new address.

Poppy puzzled. 'Have you a note?'

Druce said no.

The boys played for hours.

That evening, Poppy discovered Mum's letter in my brother's suitcase: 'Joly is being driven mad with pain in his right hip. The Moree mineral springs are worth a try. We'll be away for a week. Thanks for minding Druce until we return.' She chuckled. 'Only too pleased to help out. If only the little beggar had told me why he was there.'

Gran suffered a severe gastric haemorrhage. In January 1956, Daddy and I rushed the hundred and fifty miles to Newcastle by taxi, having missed the express. Sombre family members had gathered at Newcastle hospital.

Cousins, aunts and uncles embraced me, united in silent fear of impending loss. I struggled to quell tears.

Grandpa and Daddy towered over everyone, faces glum. They discussed Grandma's chances. 'Doc says 50-50. Lost at least a pint of blood.'

Daddy recalled a time Aunt Lulu had nursed an invalid in her spare room. He grinned at her. 'You told me, "Don't make any noise, Joly. Ivy's not well."' He went on, 'I assumed it was a sick friend. Your patient was a chook.'

She giggled like one.

Sister allowed us to enter the ward in twos. 'Only stay a few minutes. She is gravely ill.'

I gagged at the antiseptic smell and odour of old blood. Gran's colour matched the white sheets. She opened her eyes briefly. Tears in mine. I recalled her dancing the Irish jig. Her blood transfusion made a red, drip, drip, drip. I felt queasy.

Nurses sped back and forth. Noiseless. Lacy caps. Smart uniforms.

'Like angels, aren't they?' Auntie Lulu said. 'You'd make a wonderful nurse.'

I blushed. 'Me? A nurse?' I observed their good humour and calm. Saw them plump up pillows, lend a hand to those in walkers or on crutches, push wheelchairs. These girls seemed little older than me. Coping with grace and maturity.

Dad and I made our farewells.

Aunt Aileen whispered, 'Think about nursing, pet. Pay not bad. Free accommodation. But for God's sake don't tell your mother it's my idea.'

I gave her a special hug.

Dad took me to visit Dave at Adamstown. I'd been ten the last time we'd met at the farm. His pal, Alec, and his twenty-something daughter, Pamela, nicknamed John, were strangers to me.

I suddenly felt overwhelming shyness, avoiding their eyes. My home-sewn dress and matching fabric-covered handbag seemed the epitome of bad taste.

Pamela smiled at me. 'Like to see the garden?'

I leapt at the chance.

'I could see you were miserable in there. I've been admiring your handbag.'

'I made it myself.'

'How wonderful – and you sewed the dress too? Wish I could do that.'

I relaxed under her warm sun of understanding. 'Your nickname puzzles me…'

She laughed. 'Father wanted a son. I've always been John.'

'You don't mind?'

She shrugged.

'I don't know what came over me.'

'Perhaps the trauma of seeing your gran so ill?' She told of being a secretary. 'Any plans for after school?

'Maybe nursing. My auntie's idea…'

'Excellent. You could travel when you finish.'

'Uncle Bill says it's a ticket to see the world. Not a whisper of this to Daddy.'

A conspiratorial smile. 'I won't breathe a word.'

Inside, John brewed tea. I balanced my cup and nibbled poppy-seed cake. Smiling, confident, thinking of life as a nurse. Two years before making a decision.

The following week, a letter from Aunt Aileen brought wonderful news. 'Gran is up and about. Drinks her glass of sherry after dinner as usual. I'll visit you later this year.'

Vivi and I could hardly wait.

My parents presented Druce with a second-hand tricycle. Watching his glee, my unfulfilled longing for a bicycle rushed back. Sixteen – and I flamed with irrational jealousy. The reaction shocked me.

Graziers trotted fine horses in the rodeo ring. Wide-brimmed hats and moleskins. Cattle parade. Young men chanced their lives on buck-jumpers in clouds of dust.

Mum had once wanted to compete in the camp draft. Dad 's brow had creased. 'It's way too dangerous.'

He shared yarns with men at the bar.

Our cousin, a farmer's wife, said, 'Love your maroon corduroy trousers and white blouse, Dessie. The Peter Pan collar is so cute.'

I blushed.

Mum upbraided Vivi over some trivial offence.

The cousin said, 'My word, Genn. You're a cranky old thing.'

Mum giggled. They chatted about the dry weather, the price of cattle.

My sister and I slipped away, seeking flirtation and excitement. Perhaps some dishy lad might invite me to the dance.

Jimmy Sharman's boxing troupe matched fists with local hopefuls. A bloodied nose. Black eye.

I shuddered. 'Let's get out of here.'

'Roll up, roll up. Shoot the ball into a mouth.' A row of clowns. Red plastic mouths gaped. 'Balls ten a penny. Roll up, roll up.'

I chuckled. 'Can you believe we once sought these garish prizes?'

'And bought cheap trinkets from the lucky dip.'

Fairy floss attracted a queue of littlies. We succumbed to tinsel dolls on sticks and pink monkeys.

'Perfect beside the posters of Yul Brynner and Marilyn Monroe.'

The circuit finished, we exchanged disappointed glances. 'Not one sexy boy.'

Then I saw Sasha. Not a boy, but boyish. His easy smile and ready quips made me smile. Smart grey slacks and a striped shirt. Luscious geometric tie. His glance was a caress.

'Going to the dance?'

I shook my head.

'Please do – I'll teach you a few steps.'

Dad expressed gratitude. Imagine a man of mature years helping his little girl improve her dancing.

Mum seemed equally impressed. 'Only, girls don't dance in trousers.'

Sasha smiled. 'I'll ask a friend of mine, Mrs James. She'll lend Dessie one.'

We walked towards her house.

In the darkness, an arm slid around my shoulders, his voice husky, 'You're mine. My special girl.'

We kissed. My blood tingled.

Mrs James's dress fitted me perfectly.

Sasha whistled. 'Wow!'

On the way to the hall, hugs. Kisses.

I longed to linger. 'They'll worry if we aren't back.'

He claimed every dance. I'm sure gossips had us engaged. My head spun silken threads of fantasy and desire.

'You're sweetness itself. My lovely girlfriend.'

A voice in my head whispered, careful! You'll get infatuated. Sasha continued to drop by, visiting Dad. The putter of his motorcycle sent my pulses racing.

If he didn't appear for a few days. I moped.

Mum said, 'Are you ill?'

'No, no – I'm fine.'

'For heaven's sake, find something to do.'

Victor groomed his big chestnut mare. He usually tightened the girth a notch or two, and cantered off.

I narrowed my eyes. 'Wow! He's shining the saddle.'

'Have you seen his riding boots? Buffed within an inch of their life.'

At nineteen, a man for quick baths, he lingered. Emerging in a cloud of aftershave. Hair slicked back with brilliantine.

We eyed his new shirt and moleskins. 'Anyone special?'

Victor turned brick-red. A lass happened to be visiting our neighbour's farm.

Vivi grinned. 'You're off to see your girlfriend? Do tell.'

Mum jumped as if she'd been struck. 'Don't be so damn silly. Victor hasn't a girlfriend.' She flashed Victor a sickly smile. Clamped him in her arms. 'Don't forget your old mother.'

He looked embarrassed. 'Uh, gotta go.'

Her saccharin voice. 'Don't be late home, will you, son?'

He escaped. Mum looked desolate.

In the privacy of our room, I shuddered. 'Rifts with Dad. Emotional support from her sainted elder son.

'Surrogate husband. The stolid one who doesn't drink.'

Week after week, the visits continued. About to leave, Victor would be trapped in the prison of Mum's arms.

'Visiting her again, son? Is she nice?'

He shifted uncomfortably.

I glanced out the window. 'Your nag looks restless, Victor.'

He shot me a grateful glance. 'I'd best go.'

We never did learn why the romance ended.

Mum looked relieved.

It embarrassed me to visit town. At sixteen, I said, 'Please, Mum. Let me wear make-up. Younger girls are dolled-up with everything from rouge to fake lashes.'

She pursed her lips. 'That doesn't mean you need to follow suit.'

I groaned to my sister, 'Mum seems to think lipstick would make some man race me behind the nearest bush.'

'And have his wicked way? Bound to.'

Vivi was only twelve but mixed almost exclusively with adults. It brought a maturity beyond her years.

Finally, Mum agreed. 'Very well. Just a hint of lipstick.'

My sister thought my permission gave her the same privilege. She bought foundation, blusher, eyeliner and mascara. All on Dad's account. And looked at least seventeen.

Mum's eyes bulged. 'Oh, you selfish, wicked girl. You're far too young.' Her protests fell on frosty ground.

Aunt Aileen arrived, frailer than ever, her spirit undaunted. Jokes in letters paled beside bedroom chuckles. We basked in the warm sun of her approval.

'Have you thought any more about nursing, pet?'

'Yes, but – I've a phobia over blood.'

'You're strong enough to beat that.'

She thought it perfectly understandable that we missed teenage company. Detta, a neighbour's sister, was visiting from Newcastle.

'We'd love her to stay a few days.'

'Surely your mother wouldn't mind?'

Mum frowned. 'It's inconvenient with Auntie here.'

Aileen feigned deafness.

'We'll help with chores, Mum.'

She sighed. 'I was hoping to paint the kitchen.'

'Detta's a whizz at painting.' Exaggeration? Complete fabrication. She'd need coaching.

She pursed her lips. 'Very well, but you'd better behave yourselves.'

Detta arrived. Bubbly, cute dimples. Victor lifted his face from a book, long enough to say hello.

In the bedroom, Auntie conversed about boys and make-up. Discussed wonderful possibilities for our future.

Detta gave a mysterious smile. 'Does your brother have a girlfriend?'

'Victor? Had one. It fizzled.'

She brushed back short auburn hair. 'He'd be quite nice if someone thawed him out.'

We showed Detta how to stoke up the woodstove for baking. 'Flue adjustments make it warmer or cooler.'

Mum said, 'Put a hand into the oven to judge the temperature.' I preferred to use a piece of white kitchen paper. 'Golden-brown indicates a moderate oven, dark a hot one.'

Detta produced chocolate cakes and passionfruit sponges, oozing cream. Victor ate them without a word.

Desperate for his approval, Detta helped paint the kitchen.

Mum bided her time. Victor sat nearby. She went in for the kill. 'You've done a very poor job here, Detta. Missed this spot – and that. It's useless doing half a job. You'll have to paint the whole wall again.'

Detta flushed scarlet.

'And, by the way,' Mum twisted the knife, 'if you must cook, make it something simple. I'm sick of expensive cakes.'

Detta slunk into the bedroom. 'I nearly died from humiliation. Victor heard the whole thing. I don't think she likes me.'

We all laughed. 'Mum dislikes any girl who fancies Victor.'

'Well, I'm through with cooking. And your Mum can jolly well paint the kitchen herself.'

Vivi smiled. 'Good for you.'

Our friend's last night. We racked our brains, desperate for excitement.

I said, 'How about a midnight feast? Boarding schools in *Girls' Own Annual* make them sound wonderful. If only we had someone else to ask.'

Detta's eyes glittered. 'How about Victor?'

We chorused, 'You must be kidding.'

She giggled. 'He'll come.'

Aileen helped hide food in our bedroom. We kept our feast secret, to avoid Mum's veto. She shot suspicious glances at our forays back and forth from the kitchen. But our plans remained undetected.

Auntie shook me awake at three a.m.

Detta said, 'Wow. Isn't your auntie a brick?'

Victor had refused to join us. She couldn't believe he was so dreary. We sat on logs in the old shed, shivering.

Detta said, 'Are there many spiders?'

'No.'

Torchlight beamed on corrugated iron, festooned with cobwebs.

We made feeble witticisms. Laughed. Drank mugs of tea from Mum's thermos. Crammed our mouths with cake, apple pie and sandwiches. None of us felt hungry. An owl hooted. Very close and really loud.

Detta stifled a scream. 'I'm no hero. Let's go.'

We made to return things.

Mum shouted, 'Stop that noise. Some people need their sleep. Why are you girls racing up and down the corridor?'

My mind whirled. 'We...er...went to the toilet.'

Rushing for bed, Vivi fell. Horrified to hear the clink of broken glass. She burst into tears. 'Mum's expensive thermos. What'll I tell her?'

Detta patted her shoulder. 'It's OK. I'll get Victor to cover for us.'

Victor pretended he'd dropped the thermos from his tractor. We were amazed. He'd acted like a brother, instead of a third parent.

George telephoned.

Auntie's eyes danced. 'I'm an old friend. Guess who?' He rode over, as Auntie put it, 'With moustache twitching.'

'Aileen. How delightful to see you.' He greeted her with a smacking kiss.

Aileen was over fifty, George in his mid-seventies.

Mum was shocked.

Dad hobbled around. 'I'm in agony from my arthritic hip. Thermal baths at Moree helped last time. Aileen can mind the girls.'

Mum sniffed. 'Aileen?'

I don't know what was said but Dad, Mum and Druce drove away.

Vivi shouted, 'Yippee. The house to ourselves.'

News of the departure brought George and Sasha riding by. The log fire leapt to jokes and laughter.

Victor sat bolt upright, unsmiling, arms crossed.

Later, Auntie said, 'It's sad to see a young chap take life so seriously.'

I frowned. 'Maybe Dad told him to keep an eye on me.'

Aileen put a hand on my shoulder. 'I'm concerned Sasha's taking such an interest. There's no future…'

'It's just been – fun. I wouldn't do anything silly.'

'I'm sure you won't.'

'Most girls of sixteen have boyfriends. Sasha was the only berry on the bush.'

She giggled. 'And you decided to test your wiles?' Her eyes sparkled. 'Oh, my dear. It's only natural you long for male company. When you leave this lonely place, you'll meet suitable boys. Be patient.'

It seemed the hardest advice I'd ever follow.

The sun played hide and seek with roiling clouds. Victor rode off to check the cattle.

The boys ted up their horses. Vivi and Auntie chatted to George at the fireside.

Sasha and I wandered outside. A bridal veil of cherry blossom fluttered on the breeze. I climbed into a fork, my glances daring him to follow. He swung beside me, desire in his eyes. The scent of Californian poppy in his hair.

'My lovely girl. I'm very fond of you.' His lips caressed mine.

Victor rode home. We strolled towards the house.

My brother scowled. After our guests left, he warned me, 'Be careful of Sasha.'

A bright Miss Innocent smile. 'What exactly would he do?'

Victor flushed scarlet.

Daddy returned. Auntie alerted him to the situation.

He was astonished. 'Sasha will never set foot in this house again.' Daddy's reputation as a boxer ensured no man needed a second warning.

Loneliness ached in my gut. Screamed with the plovers. Thundered with rain on the tin roof.

I recalled my brother Druce saying to Sasha, 'I'm like you. I'll not marry when I grow up.'

He'd given a secret smile. 'You'll change your mind when you meet the right girl.'

I missed the thrill of stolen fruit.

22

People crowded around electrical store windows in November 1956. Drawn by the miracle of TV, they watched the opening ceremony of the Melbourne Olympic Games. Australia's first modern transmissions had begun earlier that month. At about a thousand pounds, few could afford a set. At Hunters Springs we watched our wireless, still lacking electricity. Thrilled by the roar of crowds, we pored over newspaper pictures. Arrival of the Olympic torch from Athens brought excitement, the glimpse of an ancient world.

Sasha gifted my beautiful water set to Mum and Dad, in tasteful Christmas wrapping.

She looked puzzled. 'Why's he sent us this?'

I shrugged.

Cousin Pat invited my sister and me to Newcastle on holiday. We felt surprised our parents let us accept. I envied Pat's smart clothes, make-up and perfect nails. Shopping in Hunter Street was a treat. We nibbled sandwiches with her and Auntie. Surf thundered in the background, a lovely briny interlude. Pat drove us in her Jaguar to a beer garden. We sipped cherry brandies, feeling very sophisticated.

My future as a nurse topped the agenda.

'I also want to write stories.'

Auntie smiled. 'Just like Grandma Florence? Good for you.' She told us enjoy yourselves in the pool. 'We'll sit and chat.'

We swam into friendship with some boys. Laughed and exchanged stories.

'There's a party next week. We'd love to have you girls along.'

Vivi's face fell. 'Oh, no! We're off home tomorrow.'

Pat worked as the Bradford Cotton Mill's night supervisor. David squired us to *The King and I*. Deborah Kerr's charm contrasted with Yul Brynner's smouldering sexuality.

We parked in the glitter at King Edward Park, a popular smooching site.

Munching his treat, banana fritters, David chuckled. 'Now I've got to follow Pat's advice. Do you mind?' He kissed me, long and hard.

Did Pat think her husband would initiate me into the gentle art? I surged with bitter sweet memories.

Vivi said, 'Cut it out, you two.'

We drove home, singing 'Getting to Know You' and 'Shall We Dance?'

I told Mum, ' I went to the movies with David.' I omitted the kiss. And didn't mention Vivi.

Stunned, Mum said carefully, 'And – did he hold your hand?'

I faked astonishment. 'Oh, no, Mum.'

Her face flooded with relief.

Dad snaffled a road contract, to augment farm income. Broken pieces of rock around drill holes had convinced rivals to bid high. 'They feared hitting rock, with increased costs.' Daddy expected the job to take three months.

We girls chopped firewood. Slammed it into the wheelbarrow. Shoulders ached and fingers bled. Spiders, beetles and pet ants fled. Trees fell on fences. We hacked through timber, using axes and saws. Twisted wires together, fingers numb.

Mum said, 'Temporary repair. Job for the men.'

Her petrol-driven washing machine broke down. We washed by hand.

Piglets dug out of their pen. We raced off in pursuit. Cursing nettles and wait-a-while vines. Porkers squealed, dogs barked. We scraped shins on logs, darted through fences. Only to lose them in wattle and bracken.

Afternoons, Mum yelled, 'Vivi! Have you locked up the calves? Must I remind you?'

Mornings found calves desperate to feed. I attempted to latch one to Dottie's teat. She kicked and bellowed. Wrong animal. They looked identical to me. I allowed her calf a brief suckle – it brought down the milk. Wrestled him back into his pen. Time to squeeze teats.

Mum raged. 'How could you think that was Dottie's calf? Markings are completely different. You have to learn these things.'

I curbed a shout. 'Come eighteen, I'm out of here.'

Mum called every one of her cattle by name, her friends, cheerfully sending them to slaughter. This dichotomy puzzled me.

For years, Susie had been our best milker. We regarded her with great affection. Advanced age meant no calves.

Dad couldn't afford to put a valuable animal out to pasture. 'Can't bear to slaughter her, either.' He sold her to our neighbours for that purpose.

Vivi visited them for lunch.

Dad looked concerned. 'You didn't eat meat?'

We could see by her face she had.

'How could you? It was probably Susie.'

Vivi rushed outside to be sick.

My face became swollen and distorted. It had started with red, sensitive eyes. A macular rash and sniffle confirmed measles. Druce, Vivi and me ended up being nursed in the same room.

Druce would yell, 'Stop coughing my way. Don't want your silly germs.'

My fever subsided. Mum fell ill. Nursing her proved perfect preparation for difficult patients. The soup was too hot or too cold. It lacked flavour.

'This tea's undrinkable. What have you done to it?'

'Illness has altered your perception of taste.'

'Rubbish.'

We were too noisy or too quiet. Her bed felt uncomfortable.

'Can't you even do one simple task?'

Ragged from her impossible demands, I spilt her chamber pot. Urine flooded the floor.

'You're so clumsy. Get a cloth and clean it up.' She made me wring it out with bare hands. I hated having her pee on my skin, scrubbing it until they it was nearly raw.

My social calendar? At seventeen, depressingly empty. I begged, 'Take us to the football dance.'

'We'll see' meant 'No.'

Geographically impossible. No boys, no dates.

'I'll learn to drive.'

Dad shook his head. 'Insurance premiums go through the roof for a novice.'

Mum glowered. 'Even if you could drive, we'd not allow you to run all over the countryside. Victor doesn't pester us to go out. Why can't you be like him?'

Words unspoken. 'You mean dull and dreary?'

Poppy and Walt stopped by. We shared our frustrations.

Poppy said, 'I don't care about the dance. But you girls need some fun.' She winked. 'Leave it to me. Walt and I are going to the dance, Genn. Sounds fun. A shame you'll miss out.'

Mum gulped. 'Of course I'll go.'

Outmanoeuvred, Dad grumbled, 'If we must...'

I told Poppy, 'I know Daddy's tired. But it's the price country people pay to give their teenagers a life.'

She laughed. 'You're right there.'

I wore a white dress with a simple scooped neckline. Vivi glowed in a dusty pink polished cotton. We looked a similar age.

In the weatherboard hall, the band struck up with 'Pride of Erin'. The quickstep and jazz waltzes followed. Piano accordions wheezed lively tunes. One old chap played a fiddle. And there on stage, Sasha, clacking away with bones.

Chatter and laughter, edged with anxiety. Vivi waltzed off. Only one other young woman. And me.

'Dance?' Laughing blue eyes, lopsided grin, tanned face.

'I don't dance very well.' Annoyed at my own words.

'Nor I.'

We got into the swing of it.

'The name's Arthur. And yours?'

'Dessie.' King Arthur and the Knights of the Round Table. His Queen Guinevere?

'Dessie. I like that.' His lips caressed my name, as never before or since. 'How come I've never seen you at any of these dances?'

'We're on a farm. Daddy rarely brings us.'

'I'm sure glad you made it tonight.'

He told of working in the fruit-growing areas in Victoria. 'The wheels of our utility spun away the miles. Little farms shimmered out of the distance.' Laden apple trees, emerald-green hills, drystone fences. 'Adventure lured us from town to town, farm to farm. We strummed guitars under the stars. Sang the latest songs. Sleeping beside a camp-fire.'

'It sounds amazing.'

Sasha stole a dance. My head no longer spun from his compliments.

Arthur claimed the next one, and all those to follow. I told him of my dreams. A nurse's certificate, learn French, travel. Not adding, 'And you would be the cherry on my cake.'

Supper over, he touched my shoulder. 'It's been a terrific evening. Will your dad to bring you to the next one?'

'I hope so.'

'I'm determined to see you again.'

Daddy had an air of disapproval. Arthur waved. Our Land Rover sped away.

I floated to the beat of music, a lopsided grin.

'He's a lot older than you, Dessie.' Dad added, 'Leads a gipsy life.'

'Dad! I'm not planning to marry him.'

Mum clucked, 'I hear he's had more than one girlfriend.'

I laughed. 'At twenty-four? I should hope so.' I imagined the sort of boy they'd choose: some dull fellow like Victor.

Mum sniffed. 'None of the young men asked me to dance.'

Vivi and I stifled giggles. A grumpy woman twice their age?

Mum grabbed her stockwhip. She rattled off a string of instructions. 'Strip the beds, do the washing and ironing, mop the floors…' She rode off to inspect cattle.

My heart purred. A boyfriend – at long last.

We washed sheets and towels. Blue-bags for the whitest whites. Colours hung inside-out to reduce fading. Sun-drenched linen billowed like my happiness. Dishes done, beds made, floors mopped. Pop songs gave our heels wings. We buffed up Queen Bee wax on linoleum. How it shone.

Time for the ironing. 'I'm so glad we ditched the flat irons.'

Vivi nodded. 'Even after we wiped away soot from the stove, they left marks.'

Our ethanol iron hissed. Gliding over pillowcases, tablecloths, dresses. We put everything away.

'Finished at last – what a morning.'

The gate creaked. Mum hung her stockwhip and felt hat on the veranda peg. Years of hot sun and wind had marked her hands and face.

Vivi darted me a glance. 'She'll not find anything wrong?'

'Nah. She'll be pleased.'

Mum took in the kitchen clock and bare table. She glowered. 'Midday. Where's my lunch?'

The corner of Vivi's mouth twitched.

I said, 'Mum – we've been busy.'

'Busy? You girls wouldn't know what the word means. I've ridden all morning. When I come home, I expect to find my meal ready. Oh, you useless pair.' She slammed wood into the stove.

I picked at my lunch. Mum gobbled cold meat and tomatoes. Stormed into her garden.

'Ungrateful bitch. I can't wait to leave.'

Vivi groaned. 'How will I bear it after you're gone?

We buried ourselves in a frenzy of rock and roll.

Dad arrived home. He tuned the wireless to the ABC. Prepared his meal of cold mutton and salad, humming to a Perry Como tune. Listened to *Blue Hills* in his favourite armchair. The cat purred on his knee, pooled by sunlight. Buzz, Buzz. Summer blowies crashed against the pane.

His siesta ended. 'I'll build an attic for you to write out my stories.'

My jaw dropped. His stories?

Daddy had published a number in country newspapers. One had appeared in the *London Argosy*. Another in *The Teaching of English*. He'd won a *Woman's Day* short story contest with 'Indira', a tale of an Indian hawker and his horse.

But what of my ambitions?

The road contract stretched into four months. The men took breaks. Victor fixed the washer and lawnmower. Dad adjusted fences.

I had one thing on my mind: the next dance.

Mum's eyes bulged. 'You girls are so selfish.'

In our room, Vivi stamped her foot. 'Most teenagers go out once a week. At sixteen, Mum rode to dances with Daddy. Not a parent in sight!'

'They must take us. Arthur's asked me.'

'Reckon that's why they won't take you.'

'What?' Ice chilled my veins. 'They couldn't be so mean.'

Uncle Bill visited. He flashed a wicked grin. 'If your father won't take you to the dance, I'll pretend to have toothache. Then he'll go to town.' He substituted toothache for pig-iron, from a current hit, 'I've got toothache. Toothache. Al-l-l-l toothache.'

We hummed Bill's ditty, falling about with laughter.

He said, 'I'm glad you've decided on nursing, Dessie. There's no future for you here. Told your parents?'

'It's far too early for that.'

We'd never know what Uncle said to Daddy. But the dance was on. In the hall, I felt overwhelming shyness. Avoided glances.

A touch on my arm. I looked up, expecting to greet Arthur. My spirits plummeted.

Uncle Bill's wobbly eyes beamed through thick lenses. 'Your dad asked me improve your dancing.'

'He what?' I pictured the scenario. Uncle Bill with the best of intentions. My father confiding I was smitten with the wrong sort of guy.

'It's easy once you get the hang of it, luv. One, two three. Follow the beat.'

I faked a smile.

Uncle claimed every dance. I wanted to say a meeting had been arranged. But suppose Arthur wasn't there? Or had brought someone else?

We left before supper. I sobbed myself to sleep. My parents offered neither explanation nor apology.

I received an invitation for Peter Wilkins's twenty-first birthday party in April 1957. His mother was a friend of Auntie Violet. I'd only met them once, which added to my delight. Mrs Wilkins promised to take good care of me, should I be allowed to attend.

Mum held the letter with the tips of her fingers. 'There's so much work to do here.'

'Please, Mum. I'll meet people of my age. It's only three days.'

'It's not fair that you should be the only one enjoying yourself.'

I blinked. Jealous of her seventeen-year-old daughter?

Mum wrote a cold note to Peter's mother. It made me feel like a stray parcel. 'Dessie may go, providing she is home on the Tuesday mail car.'

Vivi danced me around the bedroom. 'Off to the Central Coast? I'm so pleased for you, sis.'

Dad arrived home with a mysterious box. 'See what you think.'

A strapless turquoise organza. Diamante scattered over the draped bodice.

I hugged him. Almost speechless with delight.' It's…it's – a gown of dreams.'

Afterwards, I wondered, was it an apology for his behaviour over Arthur?

Mum's face was a study of disapproval. 'Must have cost a fortune. And so bare. Be sure to wear the bolero.'

Sunset shone on Central Coast beaches. Sea breezes, pelicans, lakes with every ripple painted red. I could scarcely believe my luck at being part of the carefree Wilkins clan.

I gaped at the function room. Chandeliers, thick carpets, wide, curving staircase. A set from some Hollywood movie.

One of the girls helped me do up my zipper. I omitted the bolero.

Mrs Wilkins stood back. 'A stunner, no mistake.'

A blush warmed my cheeks. Other girls wore simple dresses, mine a tad too formal. Still…

We sang 'For He's a Joly Good Fellow'. Female relatives and friends rushed to kiss Peter.

He looked startled at my peck on the cheek. And kept glancing my way.

Surprise, surprise – Peter drove me back to the house. He seemed shy and hesitant. I squeezed his arm. We kissed. I recalled Mum's six-month rule about kissing a boy.

He chuckled. 'That's a good one.' Peter adjusted his tie. 'We'd better join the party.'

We crept around the back, hoping nobody would notice – and into a huddle of amused relatives.

Peter's father roared with laughter. 'Aha! Sneaking in the back way.'

I winked. 'The car broke down.'

Mr Wilkins grinned. 'Told you we wouldn't be responsible after arriving home.'

Guests came and went. I soaked up the jokes and laughter. Sang along to pop music like 'All I Have to Do is Dream'. Danced into the early hours. Falling asleep in a double bed between two of his aunts.

Peter drove his old jalopy to Norah Head beach. A golden autumn day, we walked hand in hand, breathing in briny air. A cool breeze made us abandon the idea of a swim.

'Let's build a sandcastle.'

I'd missed out as a child. Peter helped me add turrets and a moat.

We abandoned our artwork to the waves. Walking around the rocks, we photographed the lighthouse and each other.

For hours that night, we played records. Everything from rock and roll to the classics and opera. In the early hours, Mrs Wilkins shooed us off to our beds. I pictured the fuss I'd have endured at home.

On the way back to Scone, we chuckled at old jokes and new. Sang 'Que Sera, Sera', and the Everly brothers, 'Bye, Bye, Love'.

I floated home, high on songs, jokes and laughter.

Victor and Mum's melancholy fell on me like a sack of potatoes.

'We've all had terrible colds.' She sniffed. 'A lot of jobs weren't done with you away. It's time to pull your weight.'

I shared one of Peter's jokes, hoping to lift their mood.

Mum sniggered. 'Laugh, Victor, Laugh. Wasn't that funny?'

'I couldn't laugh and be a hypocrite.'

Mum beamed. 'Of course you couldn't, son.'

I slammed into my room. I'd never, ever share a joke with them again.

Vivi recalled a time the three of us had enjoyed a radio play, It happened one night. 'First time around, Victor laughed fit to split his breeches.'

I nodded. 'We wanted to share the fun with our parents. They didn't even chuckle at the repeat performance. And Victor said, "Damn silly thing."'

My sister enjoyed every detail of my party fun. Nobody else asked.

Uncle Arthur visited from Melbourne. His given name was Godfrey, but relatives in NSW called him Arthur. In years to come, I would marvel at his restoration of a cedar dressing-table and other antiques.

We welcomed Cousin John, a month older than me. Our first meeting had been as twelve-year-olds. Now he stood a tall and dishy seventeen. I could only agree when Vivi sighed, 'Damn! He would be our cousin.' He recounted jokes and riddles.

Oh the joy of having another young person appreciate the lighter side of life.

I'd forgotten what we ate for dinner.

Years later, John chuckled about it. 'We endured the toughest meat I've ever eaten – casserole of parrot. Victor shot the bird in the orchard. Your Mum felt it might be a treat. Father and I suffered the worst indigestion ever.'

During the meal, Mum made some comment about electricity.

John grinned. 'Must be all the live wires around the table.'

We girls chuckled. Mum and Victor didn't even crack a smile.

After the visit, he declared, 'John has a lot to learn.'

Vivi raised her eyebrows. 'Who's talking?'

Dad made a return visit. Arthur held one of the top positions in the Victorian police force.

Sightseeing in his Pontiac, Uncle tried to overtake the car ahead. Hoons gave him the finger, blocking his way. They hooted with laughter.

'Hold on, Joly. I'll give these fools a fright.'

Pontiacs are large, heavy cars. Arthur roared alongside the smaller vehicle, nudging it to the side of the road. He hardly caused a scratch.

The louts screamed and yelled abuse.

Arthur and Dad stood at well over six feet, dressed in smart business suits. Dad expected violence.

Arthur flashed his police ID.

In the stunned silence, he delivered a scathing lecture. Wrote down their details. 'You'll hear from us.'

Driving away, Arthur chuckled. 'They'll expect a summons. Sweat over it for months. I wager they won't try that again.'

23

Week followed dreary week. Where would we have been without our saviour, Cousin Poppy?

'Walt and I are off to the Carnival Ball, Genn.'

Surprise! Surprise! Mum began choosing what to wear.

I lazed in a bubble bath. Painted toe- and fingernails. Combed my hair into the latest style.

The Victoria Hotel changing room. Teenagers jostled for space at the foxed mirror. Oh, the laughter, the heady perfumes. Girls donned bright nylon dresses with safe necklines. They gasped over my turquoise organza strapless. And the looks on their mothers' faces made me smile. I pirouetted around the room in my new silver sandals, enchanted by the swirl of the flared skirt.

Mum frowned. 'Stop showing off, will you? And stand still while I zip you up.' Mum bit her lip. 'It's way too bare.' She held out the bolero. 'Put this on.'

'Mum – it's 1957 not 1857.'

'That's all very well. For a girl of seventeen.'

'Mum, people can only see my shoulders.'

She had her way.

Vivi pouted, 'I might as well go home.'

'Nonsense, sis. You look lovely.'

Moonlit fields. I breathed in the petrichor aroma after morning rain. Huge stars glittered in a velvet sky. I longed to gather handfuls, adding them to the diamanté on my bodice. Waltz music floated from the small weatherboard hall.

Mum called. 'Come along, will you?'

Light dappled a pack of young men, clustered at the doorway.

Mum planned to sit beside us. We pictured embarrassment. She'd listen to every word. Disapproving of boys' carefree banter.

Poppy waved. 'She looks lonely, Mum. Why don't you join her?'

'But I thought – oh, all right.'

Bright conversation, fake smiles. I tapped my feet to the music. Ruddy-faced graziers in moleskins and checked shirts worked wheezing accordions. The schoolteacher, a red-haired spinster, all arm and bow, coaxed tunes from her fiddle. And there sat Sasha, clacking away with the bones. He hadn't seen me yet.

Vivi danced off. Suppose nobody asked me?

I removed my bolero. It had an electrifying effect. A stranger whirled me away. A different boy. Then another. I giggled with delight.

One asked, 'How do you keep the top up?'

'Magic. Isn't it obvious?'

Oldies shot scandalised glances my way. Probably the first strapless seen at Moonan Flat.

One boy grinned. 'Come with me to the movies on Saturday night, princess?'

'Alas, I'm geographically impossible.'

Sasha held me close. A tinge of nostalgia. 'You're still my lovely girl.'

I blushed.

A stranger smiled. 'Shame there isn't a competition. You'd be Belle of the Ball.'

Matt told of snow-capped peaks reflected in pristine lakes, of braided rivers. 'They surge across meadows of smooth stones in the spring melt.'

Vivi danced with his friend, Ray. The boys were on a working holiday from New Zealand.

Matt smiled. 'We'd love to take you home.'

Vivi looked at me. 'We're spending the night with Poppy at Dry Creek. Why not? We'll ask our parents.'

Our rare opportunity to enjoy a normal date. We sought out Dad.

'Ask your mother.'

She said, 'Ask Dad.'

I smiled. 'We'll bring the boys to meet you.'

One dance whirled into another. We felt reluctant to miss a minute of the fun.

Poppy told us later, 'Gossips had a field day over your dress. It worried your mother.

'The girls were going to introduce them. Where are they?'

Poppy had laughed. 'The night's young, Genn.'

The progressive barn dance. I found myself in Arthur's arms.

His eyes glowed with mingled shock and pleasure. 'Dessie! I didn't expect to see you here.'

I managed a sexy chuckle. 'You never know when I'll turn up.'

That lopsided grin did things to my tummy. 'I can see that.' He held me seconds longer than necessary.

I didn't have the courage to ask about that other dance.

Arthur was with a Scone girl. Almost every time I looked up, his glance met mine.

Matt and Ray took us to supper. They marvelled at the sponges, lamingtons, scones, slices, and apple pies. And who should be sitting opposite? Arthur. He glanced at Matt with an expression of pure jealousy.

Afterwards, the tempo of numbers sped up. Oh, the whirl and frenzy of flying fee. The laughter and joy. The music faded.

Matt wiped his brow. 'What an evening.'

Children from the sleeping annexe, grabbed balloons, entangled in paper streamers. I was dizzy with exhilaration.

We strolled outside.

'Meet our friends – Mat, Ray.'

Dad crossed his arms. Voice glacial. 'What are your surnames?'

The interrogation dragged on. And on. Acutely embarrassed, I craved friendly chit-chat. An invitation to the farm?

'Very well. You may drive the girls home.'

There was a caveat: he and Mum would occupy the first vehicle. Us in the middle. Poppy and Walt's car at the rear.

The boys shook their heads. 'It's a convoy.'

We made our way outside. A familiar voice made derogatory remarks to the Kiwis. Illuminated by the headlights, I glimpsed Arthur. Why had he spoken with such vitriol?

Our convoy was the talk of the town. One of the locals, driving past, shouted, 'Good on yer, Kiwis.'

Matt gave a triumphant blast on the horn.

A friendly kiss. They drove off, declining our invitation to coffee.

We learnt later, Daddy had told Walt, 'If they don't drive straight back past the cabin,' where he and Mum were staying, 'I'll investigate.'

Poppy laughed over Arthur's behaviour. 'Just quietly, I think he's jealous.'

The Kiwis had promised to call when they started work at Tomalla Station.

Our Bedford crawled down a long, steep incline. At that spot, I always pictured the Indian tea man, part of myth and legend. Not for any achievements in his life, but for the manner of his death, years before I was born.

Vivi rode on the back. She sang Buddy Holly songs at the top of her lungs.

My legs tensed against the floor. Our five-ton truck groaned along in low gear. Not far ahead, a hairpin bend. It had claimed a number of victims, including the Indian tea man. His vehicle had slewed around in loose gravel. Plunging him to his doom.

Daddy frantically pumped a pedal. 'God help us. No brakes.' He gripped the steering wheel. 'Handbrake not strong enough to stop a heavy vehicle.'

The Bedford gathered speed.

I guessed my life was over. The vehicle would become a mad, uncontrollable beast. Jolt and bounce. Overturn. Smash our bodies on rocks and logs.

A terrible note in Dad's voice. 'Only one chance. I'll put her into this tree.'

Seconds twisted into hours. The truck hurtled towards a small eucalypt. I had no memory of the impact. Amazed to find myself alive. Dizzy, but alive.

Druce moaned, clutching his knees. Mum sat speechless.

Deathly white, Dad rushed to check on Vivi. Bright blood ran from a wound on her nose. He dabbed it with a clean handkerchief. 'Thank God you're all right.'

She laughed. 'Just before the crash, the theme of a popular song spun around in my head, It was crazy. Crazy. Just a crazy dream.'

Daddy checked the vehicle. 'Water leak, large dent in the core.' He whistled. 'Engine's displaced at least an inch. Any more speed…'

I shuddered.

A local vicar stopped by. 'Nobody badly hurt? Thank the Lord for that. Can I drive you somewhere?'

He drove Dad, Mum and Druce to the camp. There wasn't room for us.

We directed vehicles past the obstruction, relieved when Victor appeared. Our Ferguson tractor towed our Bedford out of the way.

Cousin Poppy arrived in her FJ Holden. 'You girls will do anything for a bit of publicity.'

Laughter. 'So the accident was our fault?

'Of course.'

Poppy made us delicious toasted sandwiches with her jaffle iron. The fire leapt with jokes and laughter.

'Heard of the fellow who said to his girlfriend, "Let's get married or something"? "Let's get married or nothing."'

We wiped our eyes. 'Who thinks of these gags?'

Poppy asked about the dance. 'Seen anything of the Kiwis?'

I shook my head. 'Dad regards them as adventurers.'

'Locals say they're polite, lovely lads. Just quietly, I don't think any boy will be good enough for your dad.'

Poppy drove our parents to town. A golden morning. I grinned. 'Yippee! A whole day to ourselves. Up to the challenge?'

'Sure am.'

Just hundreds of yards away crouched the Sugarloaf, an extinct volcano. A huge beast, it dwarfed surrounding hills. We scrambled through a barbed-wire fence. The peak shimmered in rising heat.

Our goal proved elusive. Nearby one minute, distant the next. The sun was almost at its zenith before we reached the steep flanks. I took the first, eager steps, grasping at every handhold.

On and on we climbed, gasping for air. A swarm of hitchhikers clung to my damp shirt.

I grumbled, 'Feel like the old man of the sea. Only I'm carrying a whole bunch of critters.'

Halfway to the top. Bushflies invaded ears, teased eyes... I blew them away from my mouth, whisked them off my head with a small, leafy branch.

Energy and enthusiasm waned. We struggled from shade to shade, my legs aching. I paused to catch my breath.

Vivi surged ahead. She looked back with a cheeky grin. 'What's taking so long?'

I couldn't let my kid sister reach the summit first. Rushed to catch up.

Time for lunch. We reclined in dappled shadow under a kurrajong tree. I admired pale, bell-shaped blossoms. 'I read about these trees the other day. The name comes from the Dharuk language. Garrajun means fishing-line – they also used the kurrajong bark to make nets.'

Vivi stroked the bark. 'How did they discover these things?'

'Experimentation, I guess. Soft, spongy wood made shields.'

'Amazing the stuff they used from around the bush. Not only survived, but thrived.'

We drank tea from our thermos. Munched corned beef sandwiches, devoured apples, shared a last banana.

'All gone. Hunger only half-satisfied.'

Shadows tempted us to linger. A breeze took the edge off that heat. Vivi stood up. 'Let's go.'

The mountain seemed a parable for life itself. Challenging, difficult. Often not much fun. Just there, to be tackled and overcome. A bit like grasping for freedom. Or choosing a fulfilling career.

Our sneakers sent light shale pinging away, a metallic ring. The summit seemed no closer.

Stunted trees with large, shiny leaves struggled in the stony environment. We pushed aside dogwood bushes. The stink lingered on our hands. Knife-edged grass and prickly pear slashed at our trousers.

We battled on, lungs gasping for mercy.

Vivi cried, 'Hurrah, here we are.'

A cairn of stones and black direction indicator marked the summit. 'What's that?'

Daddy had explained it to me. 'It's a triangulation, or trig station. Governments put survey marks on high hills, or mountains. Hikers use them for navigation.'

'What do they survey?

'Land boundaries. Roads, bridges...'

Sweet pretty creature. 'Oh, look – a willy-wagtail. Dancing our sarabande of victory.'

'Who could ask for anything more?'

We gazed at twisting roads and rivers. Patchwork quilt fields. Shrunken farmhouses. I recalled Ross telling of Italian peaks with spectacular views. 'A castle perched on top. When I'm old and very rich, I'll build a castle up here.'

She laughed. 'Make it two – you live in one, I'll have the other.'

Blue to violet hills. Purple and indigo. Grey to chalky white. Evening beckoned us home. Muscles ached. We'd pay the price tomorrow. But neither of us cared.

The moon walked us to the cabin. We longed to share our excitement.

My sister said, 'Guess what? We climbed the Sugarloaf.'

Victor blinked. 'Our parents are delayed in town for a day or so. Poppy's away, too. Gay and Lizzie Blenkins have offered accommodation.'

I said, 'Let's stay with Mrs Blenkins. Her house is next to Poppy's. It'll be easy to collect our nighties.'

We made Victor's meal and washed the dishes. Tired but buoyed up by exuberance, we set off along the moonlit road, singing and laughing.

I sighed. 'Do you reckon Victor's jealous? Us climbing mountains while he works.'

'You're right. He didn't even comment.'

We hugged Lizzie Blenkins.

Her husband Albert frowned. 'We hard about your accident. Anyone hurt?'

Vivi showed the scar on her nose.

'Aha, nothing serious.'

Lizzy brushed back a mane of red, crinkled hair. 'It could have been a disaster.'

Our grandparents once lived in a cottage close by.

Albert grinned. 'We got up to all sorts of pranks. Egged on by those wicked Wright boys. Remember, Lizzie, when you, Aileen, and the boys decided to snitch one of old Mr Frost's watermelons? Kind old man. Huge white moustache. He liked children.'

'Until we got stuck into his melons.' Lizzie chuckled. 'We cut the first melon open. It wasn't ripe. So we stole a second. A third.'

Vivi and I exchanged a horrified glance.'

'Tried every melon. Late that afternoon, a bundle of greenery trotted down the road.' Lizzie wiped her eyes. 'With legs.'

Albert stoked the fire. 'Mr Frost carried a huge load of melon-vines in his arms. He threw it into the Wrights' yard, face empurpled. "You've taken my bloody melons. Now you can have the vines." Your Gran was shocked. "Did you steal his melons, boys?" They solemnly shook their heads. "In that case, old Frost can jolly well have those vines back. Take them to his place at once." And they did.'

Lizzie shook with mirth.' Poor man. It's a miracle we didn't get into serious trouble.' Unexpectedly sombre, she told about the loss of Dad's sister, Florence. 'We all felt for your dad. Such a lovely little girl.'

Vivi told of our climb.

Lizzie gaped. 'The Sugarloaf? I've lived here all my life and never climbed it.'

It was all I could do to stifle my yawns. Vivi's eyes kept closing.

Lizzie looked guilty. 'Gracious, what am I thinking? You poor girls must be exhausted.'

In our room, I gazed at delicate floral wallpaper. An antique cedar dressing table, with swivel mirror and the patina of ages. We slipped into a four-poster bed, with sprigged white muslin curtains. The Victorian Cranberry lamp had a clear shade. Sandblasted in a leaf design, and fluted edges. I stroked the brass base. 'So pretty. Wish it were mine.'

'Love ruby glass. Someday I'll have beautiful things.'

A caress of soft sheets. Sleep.

On awakening, I was shocked. 'Vivi, wake up. It's eleven a.m.'

We dressed in haste, anxious not to inconvenience our hostess. A note from Lizzie Blenkins: 'Popped out. Table laid. Help yourselves to breakfast.'

Lizzie Blenkins returned. 'It's horrible out there, girls. Bitterly cold. Summer to winter in twenty-four hours.' Through the windows, Lizzie pointed out a cloth of gold rose. 'Grew it with a slip from your Gran's place.'

A pale sun played hide and seek with scudding clouds. A gale shrieked around the house.

'I couldn't bear walking to the cabin in this.'

Lizzie shivered. 'Don't blame you. Stay and keep me company, girls.'

We gossiped and laughed the day away, warmed by a blazing fire.

The postman arrived. I collected our mailbag, putting Poppy's bread and mail on the table. The gale had blown open her doors, scattering clothes and papers. A curtain brushing a lamp to the floor. Spilt kerosene and broken glass. There wasn't time to tidy things. Vivi fed the chickens and dogs. I closed Poppy's doors. We hurried back to Lizzie's house.

I completed a short story assignment in time for the return post.

Mrs Blenkins urged us to stay another night.

We let Poppy know. 'We'll stay with Lizzie again.'

'Righto, girls. But, just quietly, your mum and dad are a bit worried about you.'

Vivi and I shot her a puzzled glance. 'Why?'

'Well, Victor hadn't seen you all day. And Gay didn't know where you were. Your dad was a bit annoyed.'

'But Victor knew we'd chosen Lizzie Blenkins' place?'

'Maybe he forgot. But don't worry,' Poppy chuckled 'I said you'd probably run off with the Kiwis.'

The three of us shook with laughter, little knowing Poppy's jest would come back to bite us.

Another evening of jokes and laughter.

Way past midnight, Lizzie wiped her eyes. 'Gee! Look at the time. It's so good to have young people around.'

Everyone rose late. A leisurely breakfast, sharing anecdotes and jokes. We made the bed, lent a hand to sweep and wash-up.

Hugging Lizzie in farewell, 'Thank you so much. It's been wonderful.'

Lizzie's huge smile. 'The thanks are entirely mine. Ages since I've enjoyed myself so much. Come any time.'

A leisurely stroll towards the camp. We skipped flat stones across pools in the river. Sang off-key renditions of 'Diana', 'Party Doll' and 'All I Have to Do is Dream'. Dreading a return to carping and criticism.

A midday arrival. The cabin sheltered under a native apple tree.

I shivered: some foreboding of disaster. 'They'll probably blow us up for being late. But I don't care.'

Vivi grinned. 'Nor I.'

I yelled, 'Get up, everyone. It's late.'

We opened the door.

Mum shrieked like a mad woman. 'How dare you go running all over the place. Where have you been?'

I took a step back. Stunned at the ferocity of her attack. 'Lizzie Blenkins…'

An accusation of faces glared at us. Dad, Victor, Walt, and other workmen, chewing lunch. Narrowed eyes.

Mum ranted on and on. 'How dare you leave Poppy's doors open.'

'What? We closed the doors. It was windy.'

'Closed the doors from the inside or the outside?' The idiotic question came from one of the men.

We struggled to explain.

Mum cut us short. 'Don't both talk at once. Why are you so late?'

'We only rose a short while ago.'

'What? Going to people's places and lying in bed until all hours? Guests have certain responsibilities…'

Engulfed by misery, I turned to the open fire. Sobbing. I didn't care who heard.

Voices tripped over each other. Poppy tried to calm me.

I shuddered at Mum's saccharin sympathy. 'Are you sick or something?'

A torrent of sobs. 'Not until I came here. You're so cranky.'

'Cranky?' She shrieked. 'A person can't even ask where you've been. Stop that nonsense.'

The men made excuses and left.

Poppy handed me hot tea. I struggled to regain control.

Mum put her arms around me. I almost puked. 'All right now?'

My God, what does she think? My worst humiliation ever. Fresh sobs racked my body. To escape the prison of her arms, I pretended to feel better.

Later, Poppy confided, 'Your mum and dad have bickered for days. That's why she's in such a foul mood.'

Even now, decades later, I regard Mum's behaviour as inexcusable.

She should have spoken to us in private. And why didn't Victor reveal our stay with Lizzie Blenkins? I suspect he wanted us to get into trouble.

The Bedford was back in working order.

I asked Walt, 'How come it's repaired so quickly?'

'A lead coupling between the brakes and engine became disconnected.'

To think such a trivial problem almost cost us our lives.

Walt came with us to the farm, helping Dad for a few days. We appreciated his quiet word.

'I couldn't see what all the fuss was about.'

At home, Mum wailed and fumed. Devastated by a discovery in the chook pen. 'All my hens are gone, except the old one which no longer lays – and one scraggy rooster.'

I turned away to hide my smile. There was a God.

24

Dad scowled. 'I'm not taking you girls to the next dance. And that's that.'

A month had passed since the last outing.

Vivi groaned. 'Oh, what will we do?'

'Matt said to ring him if ever we needed a lift.'

She clapped her hands. 'Call him, then.'

'I've never rung a boy.'

'Oh, come on, sis. Just do it!'

I dialled the number.

Dad plonked himself into his favourite armchair. Big ears. Arms crossed. Frown.

Should I put down the phone? Flushing, I hung on. A dozen false connections. Little deaths.

The station-owner's wife, Dora. Her sickly sweet voice. 'You want to speak to one of the Kiwis? Matt? I'll see if he's about.'

The party line might be gone but I guessed Dora would inform the neighbourhood.

I squirmed under Dad's gimlet eyes.

Background of voices. Laughter.

Matt also had an audience, poor bugger. He sounded regretful. 'Sorry. Unable to oblige this time. I'll call by when we begin work at Tomalla Station.'

Burning with embarrassment, I vowed never again to call any boy.

The Kiwis drove by with friendly waves on their way to work. They never visited.

I squirmed. 'Oh, why did I make that silly call?'

Vivi shrugged. 'There may be some other reason why…'

The road contract dragged on. Mum enjoyed days at the site, watching the work. Vivi and I lazed away the hours under a soughing casuarina tree. Or swam in the river. Dreaming of life after the farm.

I emerged from a dip. Greeted by an ageing Lothario. Wisps of grey hair edged a shiny pate.

'I'm Joly's friend. Years since last we met.' He smacked his lips. 'His daughter? I say! You're beautiful.' He praised my smile, my figure… 'If only I were twenty years younger.'

Vivi appeared.

'Your sister?' He gave me a dismissive wave. 'You're all right, Dessie. But your sister. Now, Vivi's a real beauty.' He repeated, word for word, the compliments he'd paid me five minutes earlier.

Mum took it for granted we girls would cook dinner on these visits. We burnt with resentment.

Vivi said, 'Why doesn't she help?'

I giggled. 'Let's give her a turn.'

In darkness we sauntered up to the cabin.

Mum scraped carrots as if she meant to kill them – or us. 'Why haven't you girls made the tea?' She launched into a lecture about laziness and responsibilities.

Later, we laughed until tears came to our eyes. She never guessed it had been a protest.

Completion of road construction approached. After six months, profits had become expenses.

Dad suffered from what he called colds. He handed Walt a brush and can of white paint. 'Do the roadside posts.'

Meticulous as Rembrandt, Walt stood back after each stroke, to admire the effect.

'At the rate he was going,' Dad told me later, 'it would have taken weeks.'

'Let me give you a hand, mate.' Dad took up a second brush. Slosh, slosh slosh – one post was finished. The same with a second, a third…

Walt's eye's bulged. 'Ah! That's how it's done.' He finished the others in record time.

Victor cemented drainage rocks in place. 'I do believe we're done.' They shook on it.

Arriving home, Dad was far from well. 'Alcohol? Never.' He left for town, promising to return for lunch.

About five, we heard a musical toot-toot-toot on the hill. Dad would never use such a greeting.

My heart leapt. 'Yippee. Visitors.'

A car stopped with a flourish. Dogs yelped and leapt. Out stepped Aunt Aileen, Cousin Pat and David. Auntie dubbed him Lover Boy. Overjoyed, we hugged and kissed.

Daddy's Bedford wended down the hill. 'Hello,' he slurred, close to tears. 'Wonderful family. Love you all.' He staggered off to bed.

Drunk and maudlin, I thought, sick to the stomach.

'Poor Joly.' Aileen said. 'He's never violent in drink.'

Mum's voice thickened with fury. 'Poor be damned.' All weakness crushed in herself, she despised it in others.

Aileen changed the subject. We discussed pop music, films, books, boys… Auntie made jokes. Pat or David took a turn. Vivi and I laughed until our sides ached. Victor and Mum didn't raise a smile.

Way past her nine o'clock curfew, Mum kept glancing at the clock. 'It's getting late.'

We exchanged glances. Why didn't she just go to bed?

David chuckled. 'How are you going to cope when the girls have boyfriends? You'll never get any sleep.'

She glared. For once, speechless.

Next morning, Dad staggered from the bedroom, face ashen. We planned to visit the Barrington River.

Mum glowered. 'You're not driving.'

David took the wheel.

I had long heard tell of this magnificent stream. Excited at the thought of seeing it. Vivi and I sat in the back. Dad lay on a blanket, cradling a half-finished bottle of Johnny Walker.

Hour after hour, the Bedford jolted over rocks and holes. We took circuitous routes to avoid fallen trees. I wondered why I'd joined this crazy excursion.

Dad chuckled to himself.

His laughter made me uneasy. 'What's so funny?'

He chortled. 'You don't have to worry about that Matt fellow any more. I told those bloody Kiwis not to come near the place.'

Shock jostled with fury. So that's why – and I'd feared it was my fault. Daddy had sabotaged every relationship in the past two years. Sasha had been unsuitable. But the others? Poppy was right. No boy would ever be good enough for him.

Someone would have the last laugh. And it wasn't him.

The Bedford groaned to a stop. A sere and desolate plain stretched to the horizon. Boulders. Tussocks. A few eucalypts.

Mum pointed out some remarkable feature of this mythic landscape. 'The Barrington River.'

I gaped. Not this miserable stream snaking through that expanse of scrubby timber? Kookaburras echoed my laughter.

Grandfather and Nan arrived for the festive season. Given their beliefs, Celebrate wasn't the word.

Dad gave a cheery wave. 'Won't be long. Off to buy our Christmas pig.'

Vivi and I fanned ourselves. The temperature had reached boiling point. The Kiwi disaster still rankled. Would we ever find boyfriends?

Grandfather scowled. 'Boys, boys, boys. Don't you girls ever think of anything else?'

Giggles. 'What else is there?'

'Humph.' He returned to the Bible.

Clouds of dust billowed along the road. Vivi and I rushed to identify the motor. 'There goes the Hardy ute,' or 'Wonder where the Joneses are off to?'

Grandfather said, 'What would you girls do if you lived near a highway?'

The answer seemed obvious.

Nan fanned herself with the paper. 'I do wish it would cool down.'

Mum glanced at the clock. 'Joly should be here any minute. If you don't mind, I'll hold lunch until one o'clock.'

Nan and Grandfather exchanged anxious glances. Changing a lifetime's habits isn't easy. The hour came and went. Blowflies droned and bashed against the windows. We ate our delayed meal.

Desultory conversation.

Fear flickered in Mum's eyes. Surely he wouldn't – not with her parents there. My stomach churned.

Mid-afternoon. Every motor brought renewed hope.

Nan worried. 'I do hope Joly hasn't had an accident.'

The rumour of another engine. A mixture of dread and anticipation.

Grandfather looked up from the sacred text. 'Is that Joly?'

The vehicle passed. Mum swallowed.

We flung open the windows. A cool evening breeze embraced us. Hours passed.

The heavy groan of a large vehicle. Headlights weaved down the hill.

Mum pursed her lips. Her thoughts were easy to guess. For years she'd hidden Dad's binges from her parents. Humiliated at having them about to learn the truth.

Dad would have fallen had Victor not grabbed him. God alone knew how he had made it around those cuttings. He started to laugh, a hysterical sound that reduced him to the ludicrous.

My grandparents' faces froze. Accusation in their eyes. Their glacial voices bade us goodnight.

I felt a surge of fury. 'You're drunk.'

His eyes tried to focus. 'Whoose drunksh?'

'You.' Mum glared. 'Where's the bloody pig?'

'Pig? Whatcha mean?'

'The Christmas pig. Don't tell me you just went to the pub? Oh, go to bed.'

Victor helped him to the room, took off his boots. Threw a sheet over him.

Dad's head touched the pillow. He snored.

A tremor in Mum's voice. 'Did he even buy the darn thing?'

We took a flashlight to investigate. Victor turned back the tarpaulin. We gagged at the stench. The carcass of a large pig lay beside a case of whisky.

I laughed. 'All that porker needs is a decent burial.'

Mum swallowed. 'It's no joke, Dessie. We'll be eating boiled mutton for Christmas.'

She complained to Dad later. 'You've let me down in front of my parents.'

'But how would they know? Told them I had the flu.'

'You idiot! Do you think they're blind?'

His apologies battered against her silence.

My grandparents unspoken criticism hung heavy over the house. If only they would express outrage, I'd rush to his defence, extol my father's virtues. Protect him from their scorn. Dad's drinking made me mad as hell. But I had the right to criticise him, not them.

The morning of their departure. Words unsaid, emotions stifled. They hugged Mum, pity in their eyes.

One bender merged into the next. Dad blamed everything but alcohol for his problems. He threatened suicide.

Mum glared. 'Time to try AA. Maybe they'll help.'

'Me? Alcoholic? Come off it, Genn. Alcoholics are dirty, unshaven blokes. They swill metho and sleep in pigpens.' He prided himself on the ability to work harder than three men. Could lift a large strainer post, part of a tree trunk, unaided. And often did. Alcoholic? Not him, a respectable fellow with home and family to support.

Mum's eyes blazed. 'The full weight of family responsibilities rest on my shoulders. You never say a word to correct the kids.'

I fancy he thought her criticisms were more than enough.

Mum's ungovernable rages could be sparked by the smallest mis-demeanour. And Dad's binges never helped.

Two weeks staggered into three. The stale odour of alcohol exuded from his pores. I hated the smell. Mum rode back from cattle work.

Dad lurched across the paddock, a bottle clutched to his chest.

Mum towered above her husband on the big black mare. Suddenly, she flayed him with the whip, screaming, 'Why can't you be a man? Won't you ever give it up?'

He bore the blows in silence. As if he deserved every one.

I felt afraid to intervene. Suppose she turned on me?

We heard an anguished shout.

'No, no, Mum. Stop!' Tears streamed down Vivi's face.

Mum's whip-hand halted in mid-flight. Would she hit my sister? Mum flung her weapon to the ground. 'Mind your own bloody busi-ness.' She cantered away.

Ashen-faced, Druce slunk into the house. I felt horrified to think of my little brother witnessing this nightmare.

Afterwards, the incident hid in dark corners. Shameful. Unspoken. Painful.

Grey-faced, Dad searched for a drink. He drained every bottle, even the medicinal sherry. Not enough for a small glass. Our anger jostled with fear.

He turned to Mum. 'Please, luv. Drive me to the pub.'

Mum gave a bitter laugh. 'Certainly not.'

'I must have a drink. To recover.'

'That's what you always say.'

He begged and pleaded. Finally she acquiesced, driving him the twenty-odd miles to Moonan Flat, allowing him one small bottle of brandy.

By morning, not a drop remained. Ashen-faced, Dad shambled around the house. Desperate for another drink. An uncontrollable tremor in his hands.

Mum clucked like an angry hen. 'I knew that brandy was a mistake. Now you're paying for your foolishness.'

The mailman brought bread and other supplies. Rumours had it the driver also supplied illicit booze. Dad lurched up to speak with him.

Mum fumed. 'What's he up to?'

Dad tottered back. He made a great show of putting two bottles of wine on the table. 'Just to tide me over. Then I'll be okay.'

'How long am I expected to tolerate…?'

His voice caught in the throat. 'You pour for me. Just as much as you think.'

Mum grabbed the bottle. With an air of suppressed fury, she gave him a half-glass of claret. The cork squeaked. 'That's it.'

'Please, luv – a little more.'

Mum stood with her arms crossed.

Dad downed it at a gulp. 'I'll go and snooze in the sun. Fresh air will do me good.' He picked up a rug, weaving an uncertain course down the paddock.

Mum paced. 'Fresh air? Who's he kidding?

Sunset faded to twilight.

Mum wrung her hands. 'We should never have let him go. Bet that bloody mailman's hidden more grog.'

Victor said, 'The mail truck stopped near that culvert across the creek.' He found six bottles of wine in the drain, two empty. 'No sign of Dad.'

'Where can he be?' Mum's face creased. 'Let's search. Wait here, Druce. Give us a coo-ee if Dad returns.'

The little boy made to argue. Clearly afraid of being left alone.

'Do as you're told, will you?'

I squelched through swamp, pushing aside reeds. Scrambled between tea trees. 'Daddy! Are you there? Daddyeee…' Cotton dress torn, legs and arms scratched.

Whoosh. A scream of plovers.

Was that a body, half-hidden in the undergrowth? My heart faltered.

Frogs croaked a lonely chorus. I crept closer, weak with relief. Twilight had transformed a twisted stump into the human form. Mist swirled around me. Chilled to the bone, I shouted, 'Daddy! Are you there? Daddy!'

Mum had aged ten years. 'Any sign?'

Victor avoided our eyes. 'Let's spread out. I'll do the top paddock, near the lake. Mum, you and Vivi continue in this area. Dessie, scout along the road.'

Mum whispered, 'But how could he get that far?'

Nobody answered.

Sleet stung my face. I hugged into my old cardigan. We must find Daddy. He'd never survive the night. 'DADDY!'

Victor signalled from the top paddock. Dad lay slumped on a damp rug. Motionless. My heart raced.

Mum's face was ashen. 'My God, Victor – is he dead?'

'Dead drunk. I found him collapsed. Clutching an empty bottle of whisky.'

We half-carried, half-dragged him home.

Druce rushed the door. His face crumpled. I gave him a hug.

All night, Dad raved and shouted. He awoke, confused and sweating.

Our fear was palpable. Later, I learnt it was called delusional melancholia. Delirium tremens. The horrors. It frequently leads to death.

Mum tempted him with broth. 'Have a little.'

Daddy only managed two spoonsful.

Never before had we seen him so ill. Or felt so helpless.

Dad kept getting out of bed. 'Need a walk.' He reached the gate. Stumbled back into the house, wild-eyed. 'Down near that lagoon of wine, there's a mermaid. A gorgeous creature. Dressed in clothes of many hues.' He pointed a tremulous finger. 'She wants me to go down there in the nude. I couldn't do that.'

I put a hand on his shoulder. 'Back to bed, Dad.'

'Don't let her get me, will you? She's trying to outdo your mother.'

'Into bed. You'll be fine.'

His hands shook. 'Go into the room first – see if anyone's there. Shut the windows. So she can't take me.' He trembled, pulling the sheet over his head. 'Stay here, won't you?'

Next morning, his mermaid had vanished. Had the crisis passed?

He only managed broth and fluids for a week. It took a fortnight for his pallor to fade. Slowly, slowly, Dad regained his health.

Even after this brush with mortality, alcohol kept him in its thrall. Daddy left to visit Aunt Aileen.

That evening, we heard a news broadcast: unknown man with red hair rescued from his vehicle after crash near Newcastle. A Bedford truck left the road at Minmi, coming to rest in a grove of small saplings. They undoubtedly saved the driver's life. He had amnesia, so was unable to help police with their inquiries.

Vivi chortled. 'Wouldn't it be funny if that was Dad?'

Mum's eyes bulged. 'Don't be so damned silly.'

The phone jangled. 'It's Aileen. An accident…'

Mum paled. 'Accident? Who? When?'

Auntie said, 'They've just identified Joly.'

'Is he badly hurt? Where is he?'

'Newcastle hospital. Luckily, no injuries. Some sort of blackout. Or he fell asleep.'

'Huh. Suppose he'd been drinking.'

A long silence. 'No, no. I don't believe he'd touched a drop.'

Aileen called back later. 'Joly has memory gaps. He's scared stiff. Promised to attend AA.'

Mum slammed down the receiver. 'And not before time.' She sniffed. 'Trust Aileen to make your father see sense.'

Admitting he had a problem seemed the turning point. AA gave us a sober father.

About then, Dad brought home a couple of antique bottles. 'For you, my dear.'

'Get rid of them, Joly.' Told they were valuable, Mum sought to attend every collectors' meet. She dragged Dad off to distant sites. Dug for old bottles. Amassed a large display. She made swaps and excellent buys. Won silver cups and colourful ribbons.

Given Dad's history, her passion seemed ironic.

25

I'd delayed this moment for two years. 'Mum, I'm going nursing.'

That bleak day in 1958, Mum's crochet hook stopped in mid-twist. 'Nursing?' Her cheeks flamed. 'Don't be so damn silly.' She laughed. 'You can't even stand the sight of blood.'

The fire crackled.

'I'll get used to it.'

'There's more than enough work for you here.'

A cow mooed.

'I hate farm work.'

'Nursing's not the sort of thing one takes up at a whim. It runs in families. You'd never be strong enough.'

After years of calf-wrangling? 'I want to go places, see things.'

'A lot of things you'd be better off not seeing. As for your schooling…'

I grinned. 'I'll sit for the Nurses' Entrance.'

'The wages are a pittance.'

Was she kidding? I recalled hours of menial work, with neither appreciation, nor remuneration. Expected to return the change from handouts. Not even a bank account. 'It's my life, Mum.'

She screeched, 'After my years of hard work. My sacrifices. You're so selfish.'

'I'll train at Newcastle.'

'The city? What a damn silly idea.'

Finally, came her tears.

She thought nursing was a whim. Had she been open to discussion, this conversation would have taken place long ago. I brushed cold lips against her salty cheek. Went to bed.

In the next weeks, she raved, or wept over my plans. Implored me to remain.

Dad said, 'Stay to look after your mother.'

At forty, she could outride anyone.

'Sorry, Dad. I want my own career.'

Vivi grinned later. 'They'd do anything to stop you.'

'Had Mum praised more and criticised less…'

'You'd be trapped.'

Probationer Nurse by Ann Treger became my guide. 'I'll overcome squeamishness.'

Poppy grinned. 'I'm sure you'll make a great nurse.'

Mum said to Victor, 'What do you think of Dessie going nursing?'

He surprised me. 'Seems a good idea.'

Mum vetoed Newcastle Hospital. 'Aunt Aileen would be a bad influence.'

She enlisted Nan's support to scuttle my plans.

'I'm surprised at Dessie's decision to become a nurse. Frankly, I doubt she'll stand it. (If you imagine it's a life of glamour, Dessie, get that idea out of your head.) It's hard work and, I should think, the larger the hospital, the tougher the life. Long hours, night duty, lectures, exams, office work, operating theatre… Suggest a smaller hospital.'

A director of Pitt Son and Badgery, a wool-buying firm, and owner of Tomalla Station, said, 'Enrol at RPAH in Sydney. It's the best.' He gave me an excellent reference, arranging another from GBS Faulkiner of Haddon Rig Stud, at Warren.

Mum suggested Scone hospital.

'Interesting cases go to larger hospitals. It's RPA for me. I've no desire to nurse neighbours.'

I longed to meet people from all levels of society. Not just the narrow spectrum represented by country folk.

August brought the Nurses' Entrance examination at Scone Courthouse.

The supervisor gave a conspiratorial smile. 'You're the sole candidate. Sit here and be comfortable.'

I relaxed in the well-padded green chair of visiting magistrates. Mathematics revision proved its worth. English was my favourite subject. One sentence after another raced me through the set essay. The final question. I checked answers three times. The exam was over.

Outside, suppressed tension exploded into a headache. Other local girls had failed.

The astrology column in the Scone *Advocate* supported my dream. 'You will shortly be starting a new career and will face many frustrations, but will overcome them. Interesting love life until forty.'

Forty? It seemed reasonable at the time.

Our parents paid for a farewell holiday at Newcastle. I read magazine articles to hone up on etiquette and behaviour.

We swapped the Northern Tablelands Express for a bus to Warner's Bay. Brakes screeched, music to me. 'The sound of civilisation.'

I reminded Viv of my visit as a seven-year-old. 'A blonde goddess took my eye. Mum declared her hair colour came from a bottle.'

Vivi laughed. 'Mum always thinks others are deaf.'

My cousins said, 'Delighted you've chosen RPA Hospital, Dessie. Soon it'll be you leaving, Vivi.'

She groaned. 'Not soon enough.'

Pat gave us the house key. 'Treat our home as yours.'

Our friend Detta lived at Hamilton. From our bus, I glimpsed a tall young man about my age. Missing a leg, he hopped along on a crutch, laughing with friends. I admired his *joie de vivre*.

We sipped Cokes in Detta's sun-dappled lounge room. She recalled her Hunters Springs visit. Flushing over Mum's rudeness. 'Has Victor a girlfriend?'

'One or two.'

'My, he is coming out.'

I winked. 'Shall we go out?'

She glanced at her elder brother. 'Great guys hang out at a local –'

He glared. 'Don't go near that Greek's.'

'Do you think I'm stupid, Tom?'

'Just checking.'

Her brother left. Detta tossed her red hair.

The Greek milk bar owner welcomed us with a wide smile.

Vivi glanced around. His sole customers. 'Where's the local talent?'

Detta shrugged.

Fluorescent lights matched our pink and green socks. Thrilled by Detta's forbidden world, we played Johnny O'Keefe's 'Wild One' on the jukebox, his latest record.

Detta's bravado vanished. 'Best go. Don't want Tom telling Mum I was here.'

Our adventures delayed a visit to Aunt Aileen.

In the second week, Pat confided, 'Mum's very offended you haven't called, or rung.'

I shared a horrified glance with Vivi. How could we have been so dense? I wouldn't have hurt my beloved aunt for anything. And hadn't she encouraged us to have fun?

A hasty change of plans. Profuse apologies. At the very least, we should have brought flowers.

Auntie seemed unable to share enthusiasm over our exploits. We left, at a loss how to remedy the situation. Her wisdom had meant so much to us over the years.

On parting, she hugged me. 'I'm overjoyed you're going nursing.'

Vivi and I floated on a cloud of exuberance. Clad in brilliant white jeans and bright sweaters, we raced past unroofed areas at Newcastle stadium. An hour remained before Johnny O'Keefe began his 1958 concert. He was Australia's answer to Elvis Presley.

We dodged puddles. Guys gave us the eye, whistling approval. We returned their bold glances.

Suppressed sexuality sizzled on the twilight air. One oldie laughed. Others frowned. Criticism was part of the narrow world I longed to escape.

Under the narrow awning, drizzle gusted against clothes and faces. A bodgie with slicked-back dark hair offered to share his black leather coat. I enjoyed being warm and dry – until his hand slid onto my boob. I pushed it away.

The doors opened. Catcalls and whistles. A surge of jostling teenagers. We pushed and shoved into a cavern of multicoloured lights and muted shadows. The first fifty patrons received a free record. We clutched ours.

The Wild One bounded onto stage. He glittered in white, a Prince of Youth. Screams of ecstasy. The crowd were mesmerised by his gyrations. The throb of rock 'n' roll reverberated throughout the stadium.

Who cared – or heard – if he faltered over high notes?

Johnny O'Keefe was one with every teenager. A symbol of rebellion. Fuelled by the same confusions and desires that drove us all. He planned to conquer the world. Who didn't?

Vivi and I assumed and discarded personalities and acquaintances as easily as we changed fluorescent socks. A heady mix of flirtation and laughter.

Romances blossomed and vanished, rainbows of soap bubbles.

Boys with made-up faces posed for friends. Their clothes emphasised slim figures. Widgies with cropped hair and leather gear, female cult figures of the era, shrilled bastard, or Christ with every second word, competing with male counterparts, the Bodgies, in sleazy jokes. I didn't like that.

Two youths claimed to be from Sydney University.

Vivi's eyes glittered. 'Next to RPA? Why, that's where Dessie's going.'

One gave me a stern glance. 'Don't go near the place. It's a bloodbath.'

The other grinned. 'Actually, I'm in the medical field myself. Make contact lenses from the bottom of gin bottles.'

After such fabrications, they had the gall to ask us out.

I winked at Vivi. 'Sorry. My husband's the jealous type.'

We giggled over their astonished faces.

Two ocker boys tried to chat us up. We assumed thick accents.

'Ya, ya. My sister and me. We Australians.'

One waxed indignant. 'Pull the other one. You're Germans pretending to be Aussies.'

We lost them in the crowd.

Full skirts and roped petticoats. Black suede flatties pirouetted to a ritual we'd seen in the movie *Six o'clock Rock*. A boy with brilliantined hair and pegged trousers grabbed my hand. He spun me around his back and through his legs in a series of contortions, leaving me in no doubt as to his gender.

Cheeks hot, I said to Vivi, 'No wonder ministers of religion rail against this dance.'

In this Alice-in-Wonderland world, teenagers appeared, and were quaffed by darkness.

One handsome young man said, 'Gee, you're pretty. One day you'll look in a mirror and say, "Wow-what a doll."'

I blinked.

Vivi gaped. 'Who was that?'

'Wish I knew.'

Cinderella noticed the time. 'Gosh. Let's hurry. Don't want to miss the last bus.'

Rivulets of moisture ran down the deserted bus shelter. We shivered. Waited. Fumed.

I glanced at my watch. 'That darned bus should have arrived long ago.'

Vivi shot me an anxious glance. 'It's gone – oh, what are we going to do?

I clutched my suede purse. A cab would cost more than our budget allowed.

Along cruised a big, black Ford. A couple of boys from the concert waved out the window.

One said, 'A lift, girls?'

All parents warn their daughters about lifts from strangers. A moment's hesitation. I wasn't a risk-taker but... We hopped in. An exchange of names. They seemed friendly and fun. I began to relax.

Almost immediately, the driver, Guy, said, 'We need petrol.'

He accepted my offer to pay. I thought, cheaper than a taxi.

We laughed and joked all the way to Warner's Bay. Johnny O'Keefe music blared on the radio.

Outside Cousin Pat's place, Guy put his arm around my shoulders. I thought he wanted a kiss. Something about his smile, and that odd look in his eyes made me uneasy.

'How's country hospitality?'

An expression new to me. The meaning was plain enough. I froze. 'No good.'

Guy's charm vanished in a string of expletives. We made a speedy exit. The Ford roared off, leaving half their tyres in the gravel.

A packed dance floor. Bathed in a rainbows of light from a mirrored lamp, I waltzed with a boy called Max.

'My sister and I are in Newcastle on holiday.'

He laughed. 'You wouldn't be the two girls who plan to paint the town red?'

He'd read my paragraph in *Weekend*, a paper filled with jokes and fun. My par had appeared along with gems like 'Nobody knows, nobody cares, what kind of pyjamas a bachelor wears. The reply? Nobody laughs, nobody grins, at the kind of spinning a spinster spins.'

Max shook his head. 'Wow. I wondered if I'd meet that girl at the palais tonight.'

'And here I am.'

We made a date for soccer the following afternoon.

He shared tips about the game. A red coin blazed its path towards the horizon. We took a car ferry across the Hunter River. A faint breeze caressed me. Nat King Cole's bitter-sweet 'Too Young' sped me into nostalgia.

Darkness drew a quilt over the landscape. We shared a delicious Chinese meal, a first for me. Afterwards, I marvelled at the city glitter from King Edward Park. Couples parked all along the promenade. We held hands. An intoxication of kisses.

I feared loss of control. 'We'd better go.'

Max sighed. 'Must we?' He drove away, one arm around my shoulders. Having difficulty on bends.

'Do the corners worry you?'

He laughed. 'Not the corners. The curves.'

Vivi and I crushed excitement into battered suitcases. We farewelled our cousins.

A young man on the train carried one of the new transistor radios.

'Wow – isn't it neat?'

He grinned. 'Sure is.'

Vivi's eyes sparkled. 'With one of those, we could hear the Top Forty anywhere.'

The express slowed to a stop at Scone station. I glimpsed Mum on the platform. My spirits hit the tarmac.

'Did you see that?'

Vivi nodded, speechless.

That was Mum's latest hat. Gaudy pink, yellow and blue foam flowers nestled among lurid green plastic fern leaves.

Vivi said, 'I could kill handicraft experts.'

'The *Women's Weekly* has a lot to answer for.'

We greeted our parents, and slipped away. Drooling over the shops.

The hat bore down on us. 'I've run all over town to track you girls down. We're about to leave.'

'Sorry, Mum.' I wasn't.

Powdery dust seeped into the four-wheel drive. It covered clothes, faces… Dilapidated houses. Farms weighed down with rusting equipment and hulks of vehicles. A kelpie leapt and barked on its chain. Women with red, lined faces, ambled through the paddocks of their days. Offspring owned like cattle. Nettles shivered.

I daren't fail that nurses' exam. Dogs gave us a stocking-ripping welcome.

We recalled the sexy faces of boys we'd kissed. A devilish laugh. Wet pavements, blinking neon lights. Music throb. Roar of surf, wind in our hair. And now? Trapped by the stygian blackness.

An application form arrived from RPA. It failed to lift my mood.

Mum glowed. 'Did you like my new hat?'

Bloody awful probably wasn't the thing to say. 'Well, maybe a bit tall.'

'Tall? Rubbish.'

'The flowers are so – bright.'

'Victor told me it looked very nice.'

'There's just – something about it.' Translate that to everything. 'Men don't always know these things.'

She didn't wear it again.

An aquatic carnival celebrated the opening of Glenbawn Dam.

Certain folk looked askance at our white jeans and bright tops. 'Sailing or fishing?'

I laughed. 'Both.'

We kept bumping into the same four boys.

Bob took our photos. 'Tell me your names and I'll send you copies.'

The afternoon chuckled along on a string of jokes.

One girl stared our way. 'They have two each. Two each.'

We roared with laughter.

Colourful craft whizzed past, zooming towards the finish line. We perched on a steep knoll, the perfect view.

I sighed. 'I'd do anything for a ride in a speedboat.'

'Anything?' Bob said, with crude emphasis.

The boys offered to drive us home.

'But we live in the mountains.'

Bob persisted. 'Well, part of the way?'

We invented a previous meeting at Newcastle, hoping to give our friendship validity. 'The boys will drive us to Moonan Flat. Okay?'

Mum and Dad hesitated. 'I suppose so,'

We drove off before they could change their minds. Our Ford roared along the highway. Wind rushed through open windows. Johnny O'Keefe's 'Wild One' and Elvis Presley's 'Heartbreak Hotel' blared from the radio. We sang at the top of our lungs. Other vehicles gaped disapproval. We giggled. The world was ours. The sooner oldies accepted it, the better.

Bob and I kissed. I let my tongue explore his mouth in a sensual way.

He gasped. 'I've never met anyone who kisses like that. Where did you learn?'

'Oh, I just learnt.'

'My, you're experienced.'

'I wouldn't say that.'

'I would.' His teeth teased my tongue.

Puzzled why he wanted to change places, until he tried to undo my side zipper. French kissing was one thing. I drew the line at other forms of petting.

'Where I come from, it means something if a boy bites your tongue.

I chuckled. 'Luckily, we aren't where you come from.'

The others roared with laughter.

'Wow. I'd really like to get you on your own.'

'No chance of that.'

We drove at well over fifty miles an hour, the limit.

The Ford had barely parked when Dad's old army Land Rover panted up beside us. We farewelled our friends.

Daddy drove off, grim-faced. 'Where did you meet those boys?' The Newcastle ploy failed to satisfy him. 'It's a great risk, getting into cars with strange boys.' And so on.

The windscreen wipers clunked away drizzle.

I said, 'The boys were fine. Honestly. We just sang and that.' Slightly guilty about the way I'd kissed. But Bob did stop when I drew the line. I'd be more prudent in Sydney.

Slushy road. Snow drifting over the bonnet. I couldn't wait to leave.

A letter arrived from the Nurses Registration Board. I held it my hand, as if its weight might reveal the verdict.

Vivi said, 'Aren't you going to open it?'

I tore the flap. Squealed. 'Hurrah! I've passed the Nurses' Entrance.'

Poppy hugged me. 'Congratulations. Well done, girl.'

The look on Mum's face told me her worst fears had been confirmed.

Auntie's warm letter in response to mine brought joy. 'Congratulations! It's a wonderful profession. I know you'll make a splendid nurse.'

Mum took me to Sydney for a RPAH medical, and interviews. I tagged along behind her like a six-year-old. Without one penny of my own, accepting her bad mood with equanimity, sensing her loss and grief.

A taxi drove us to the hotel, a sleazy old building in Newtown. I couldn't have been more excited had it been a palace in Paris or London. Close to the hospital, too. Perfect for my first interview at nine a.m.

I gazed at the cosmopolitan crowd in King Street. Soon I'd be part of that parade. I'd make friends, attend theatres and concerts. Things other teenagers took for granted.

We found a small bistro for dinner.

I spooned up the froth and spice on top of a cappuccino, new to Australia. 'It's the most marvellous drink I've ever tasted.'

'That may be going a bit too far.'

Noise from the public bar kept Mum awake. I fell into a dreamless sleep.

Reality slammed into my solar plexus. I barely touched my breakfast. How could I leave everything and everyone I'd known?

'Eat something. You'll be hungry later.' Maybe Mum saw the look on my face. For once she fell silent, handing over a few coins for lunch. Perhaps she told me to have a good day. 'Druce and I are off to Taronga Park.'

I longed to join them.

At RPA in Missenden Road, I admired mellow buildings of the old hospital, impressed by the stained-glass windows. A tremor in my hands. What am I doing here?

Matron's office.

A secretary smiled. 'Usually, there are several applicants.'

The sole candidate. I'd hoped to make a friend.

A deputy matron interviewed me. 'Take things quietly, until you find your way around.' She asked me to write an essay about my expectations of hospital life. Once again, Ann Treger's *Probationer Nurse* set ideas flowing.

I fronted for the medical examination. A second-year Cockney nurse gave me a specimen bottle. Handing over the urine sample, I couldn't meet her eyes.

'Get undressed. Then put the Nightingale around your neck. Wait in this cubicle.'

Did she mean for me to take everything off? And what would the flannel Nightingale keep warm?

Draped under a sheet, I padded, barefoot, to the next room.

Nurse caught a glimpse of bare flesh. 'Do you have your pants on?'

I felt my face burn. 'No.'

'I'll fetch them.'

The doctor peered down my throat. He listened to my chest. Palpated my abdomen. Took blood pressure. Asked about my general health. Checked the results of my urine test. 'You're a very fit young woman.'

'Now for your uniform fitting.' Nurse whizzed up and down corridors. I could scarcely keep up.

A frowning seamstress greeted me. She took my measurements with astonishing speed. The mystery would be solved the day I slipped into those loose-fitting checked uniforms, optimistically called tailor-made.

In Grose Street, the nurse pointed to an eleven-storey building. 'That's Queen Mary Nurses Home. You'll be on the first floor.'

It amazed me she knew the location of my room. Shyly, I asked, 'Do you like nursing?'

Her eyes glowed. 'Love it.'

I teetered on the edge of my seat for my interview with Matron. Willing myself to relax.

'What is your goal in going nursing? How do you propose to approach this new life? What are your interests?'

I found my voice.

'Excellent. Tread carefully while you adjust to city life.' She beamed, offering her hand. 'All that remains is approval from the hospital board. Good luck.'

I returned home, unable to settle. Suppose the hospital board rejected my application?

Mail day.

I rushed to unlock the postbag. A letter from RPA.

You are to commence on 29 October. There is already a Wright. You must choose an additional title.

I couldn't bear to start a new life as Stephens-Wright. Not with my maternal grandparents' gift for negativity. Seberg, the surname of an actress, glowed with possibilities.

I offended Nan. 'Our name isn't good enough for her.'

Should I explain? It could make things worse.

My final day at home. A hundred times I checked my suitcase. Exhilaration jangled with anxiety. I scorched the fabric of my white shorts.

Poppy chuckled at my tragic face. 'Give them to me. It's nothing a second wash and iron won't fix.'

Dad pressed a cheque for sixty pounds into my hands, a lot of money in those days. 'Until you get paid.'

I gave him a big hug. 'Thanks, Dad.'

Poppy and Walt's jokes and laughter eased the pain of impending loss.

She said, 'Get a good night's sleep, girl. It's a big day tomorrow.'

I kissed my parents goodnight. A warm embrace. Moisture in their eyes and mine.

Life shimmered within my grasp.

Epilogue

Mum's obsession with Victor left little room for her girls. She had no insight into the effect of her rages. Or how to become our confidante and friend.

Years afterwards, I visited her in hospital, bringing flowers.

Her eyes glowed. 'I knew you'd come.'

Mum's letters arrived every week. For over thirty years, she wrote to us. Telling of life on the farm, and current activities of 'the men'.

Having completed sixth grade, Mum regarded herself as the educated one. She helped Dad with the spelling and typing of his bush stories. Dad's alcoholic lapses were her greatest disappointment. The fuss over her errant husband must have been annoying.

Philip Adams admired Dad, a true bush man. People warmed to his friendly style and humorous tales. Photographers took his picture for magazines and newspapers. An imposing figure with a ready smile, he slipped into the required pose. Hat tipped back, to show his smile. An upraised arm indicated the vista of our dam.

Mum's eyes bulged at the photo. 'Fancy posing like that. It's plain flash.'

He grinned. 'I only did as I was told.'

Mum considered her bush doggerel to be of superior quality to his work. She castigated the ABC over free verse. 'Poems must have rhyme. Encouraged to read good poets, she raged, 'I can't bear modern stuff.'

Mum pedalled away on Dad's wedding gift, a Singer sewing machine, for more than sixty years. She patched, mended and made. After her death, it found a home in a grand Georgian house owned by her grand-daughter, in Bath, England. Mum would have been astonished. She developed motor neurone disease in 1991, passing away, aged seventy-five.

Dad followed his ancestors in fossicking for gold. In the late 1950s, he discovered a sizeable gold deposit near Tomalla. 'It saved me from abandoning the property.'

It enabled the purchase of a slow-combustion stove, hot-water service, and electricity. Two Oliver D6 bulldozers allowed Victor to build dams and clear scrub. They bought two Land Rovers. Victor chose a Holden ute for his family.

A lesser man might have kept all the proceeds. Dad gave his brothers, Sid and Bill, third shares.

Sid's portion bought a caravan park, then country acres.

Bill's windfall allowed him several tours of Europe, a lifetime dream. Poor eyesight never limited his enjoyment of life. English tourists huddled in their Parisian hotel, afraid to venture out. Bill showed them around, truly a case of the blind leading... He died at eighty-three. His wife called him 'The kindest man I ever knew. My sister and I are forever grateful for Uncle's support.'

Dad endured the freckled skin of many red-haired people. As a boy, one woman said, 'Yuk. What horrible hands.' The slur haunted him into old age. A hospital nurse said, 'My, what wonderful hands.' His massive hands impressed doctors at RNH Hospital. And a sculptor preserved one of them in bronze.

In the 1980s, Daddy needed two hip replacements. The surgeon warned, 'Keep to level ground.'

Undeterred, Daddy resumed bush activities. Young geologists from Sydney asked him to show them gold-bearing outcrops.

He grinned. 'You blokes will have to bear with me. I may be a bit slow. Two hip replacements. And a dicky ticker.'

Fit from a lifetime of labour, Dad's mountain legs tackled the steepest incline. The younger men were left far behind. They caught up, breathless and sweaty.

One said, 'Artificial hips? Bad heart? I'd give a thousand quid for your doctor to see you now.'

Daddy and his brothers helped their father build a netting fence at Kurricabark. Packhorses carried swags, tents, camp ovens and food. At twelve, he took turns to cook. They carried water from the valleys far below. The fence took eighteen months to complete, snaking for miles across the spine of a stony mountain.

Aged eighty-three, he fronted up for a fourth hip replacement. His orthopaedic surgeon owned the property where Dad had laboured. A framed aerial photograph showed the very fence Daddy had built. Bushies still regarded it as a remarkable achievement.

He died at eighty-seven. After a lifetime of low doorways and short beds, the inadequate length of his coffin almost reduced me to tears. Even in death, his poor old knees were bent, his body squeezed into the standard-size casket. At least, he didn't suffer.

What would Vivi and I have done without Poppy's support in our teenage years? Her help enabled us to enjoy a social life. Her generosity was legendary.

Aunt Aileen held a special place in our hearts. Her wicked sense of humour brightened the darkest situation. Her support and understanding enriched our lives. She encouraged us to seize opportunities, not to be put off by imagined duty to others.

We loved Uncle Bill for his warmth, understanding and advice.

Victor's destiny was decided from birth. Dad needed his labour. Did he feel trapped in the fulfilment of his parents' dreams? I hope Victor came to embrace them.

In later life, our interactions were constrained. Once, I laughed at one of his assertions. After a lifetime of adulation, he seemed perplexed. Why did I feel guilty?

I recall one happy evening of fun and laughter with my brother at a dance. We arrived home in the early hours. Mum and Dad were in a panic. The police had combed the highway for us.

He scorned expert advice. Hole in the ozone layer? It didn't exist. Colon cancer? It had no genetic link. Rushed to hospital after a large rectal haemorrhage, the doctor did no examination, nor run tests. By the time Victor sought advice, his condition was terminal. Around his bed we battled grief and shock.

He seemed oddly cheerful despite the prognosis. 'I don't fear dying. I've time to smell the flowers. Watch the glory of stars. See each miraculous dawn.' Morphine kept Victor comfortable.

It delighted me to talk without undercurrents of hostility. We shared nostalgic recollections. Childhood games shimmered before us.

He told of embarrassment over Mum's sewing efforts. 'At a sports carnival, my shorts almost fell off.'

I shouldn't have been surprised to hear Dad and Mum had vetoed his girlfriends, long after he was old enough to decide for himself. It didn't surprise me that his city bride endured a difficult relationship with Mum. 'Cath begged me to take her away from that woman.' An expert at hurtful, public remarks, Mum couldn't tolerate the mildest criticism.

A decade earlier, following a tumour resection, Dad had been given only six months to live. He used meditation and visualisation. Victor needed to identify the right type of meditation before he began.

Victor predicted the night he would die. Numb over the news, Druce and I followed a fan-shaped, pink cloud. It drew us on and on, through the Hunter Valley. Victor's spirit seemed everywhere. A skeletal tree, silhouetted in the golden glow, his metaphor for mortality.

I arranged his funeral service. Family and friends read poems and tributes. Glimpsed through other eyes, I saw a different brother. People paid tribute to his intellect, his wit, his ability to converse on any subject. 'Victor's creation of dams with a bulldozer was a sort of poetry. He shaped the earth into curves, expanses of water for all to enjoy.' Saying farewell, I glimpsed a brother who had eluded me.

Vivi escaped four years after me. She worked as a telephonist in Sydney. Married to her first husband, she finished secondary studies at TAFE. Medicine at the University of NSW included a stint as junior resident in NZ. On the break-up of her marriage, she travelled overseas, receiving a psychiatry degree in Canada. At the time of writing, she's with her third husband.

And my first love? Decades ago, our paths crossed one last time.

303

Sasha returned my greeting with a vacant stare. His memory had been destroyed by years of alcohol abuse. His journey included multiple admissions to psychiatric hospitals.

Bibliography

All the Rivers Run, Nancy Cato.

Maxwell's Ghost, Rick Frere. Page 120 (New Year 1940): 'I saw it happen on a mountain top in a flurry of snow and an unholy darkness that was punctuated with flashes of St Elmo's Fire. It had been the first day of 1940 and not inappropriate.'

Your Life as Story, Tristine Rainer.

Tales of the Old Woodlander, Valerie Porter.

Over the Mountain, Gail Goodwin. 'If you...love your life, it seems ungrateful to belabour old injustices... Especially those in childhood...isn't it possible that the very betrayal that...constricts your heart, led to a development in character that enabled you to forge your present life?' (from *New American Short Stories*, page 351).

True North, Jill Ker Conway, Vintage UK

Women Alone, Kim Knox. Page 182: 'Some blamed a poor environment for their failures while others triumphed over it. Others, born to virtually everything, failed.'

Acknowledgements

Many thanks to Siobhan Colman, our former convenor, Colleen Keating, Lyn McCready and many more in the Women Writers' Network critique group at Writing NSW, aka the NSW Writers' Centre. Their encouragement and advice has been invaluable.

I must also pay tribute Nathalie Apouchtine for her initial editing. And also to my readers, John Wright and Colleen Keating, for their time and efforts on my behalf.

Thank you to my brother, Laurence, whose anecdotes have enriched this story.

I'll always be indebted to Aunt Aileen, Uncle Bill, Polly and Charlie Stephens for their support during my formative years. Their advice and encouragement helped my decision to undertake probationer nurse training at Royal Prince Alfred Hospital, Sydney. Friendships from that era have endured to this day.